D1610027

CULTURE, LANDSCAPE, AND
THE ENVIRONMENT

Culture, Landscape, and the Environment

The Linacre Lectures 1997

Edited by
KATE FLINT
and
HOWARD MORPHY

OXFORD
UNIVERSITY PRESS

*This book has been printed digitally and produced in a standard specification
in order to ensure its continuing availability*

OXFORD
UNIVERSITY PRESS

Great Clarendon Street, Oxford OX2 6DP

Oxford University Press is a department of the University of Oxford.
It furthers the University's objective of excellence in research, scholarship,
and education by publishing worldwide in

Oxford New York

Auckland Cape Town Dar es Salaam Hong Kong Karachi
Kuala Lumpur Madrid Melbourne Mexico City Nairobi
New Delhi Shanghai Taipei Toronto
With offices in
Argentina Austria Brazil Chile Czech Republic France Greece
Guatemala Hungary Italy Japan South Korea Poland Portugal
Singapore Switzerland Thailand Turkey Ukraine Vietnam

378-7

. Engraving from *De Paris
napus (1858 edition).

ACKNOWLEDGEMENTS

The seventh series of Linacre Lectures was possible through the generous sponsorship of Riche Monde (Bangkok) Limited. The editors wish to thank the staff and Fellows of Linacre College for their support and interest and in particular Jane Edwards, the College Secretary, for her invaluable advice and assistance. Frances Morphy has helped prepare the manuscript for submission to Oxford University Press.

K. F and H. M.
Oxford and Canberra

CONTENTS

CONTRIBUTORS

Isobel Armstrong, Professor of English at Birkbeck College, University of London, has interests in Romantic and Victorian literature, feminist criticism and literary theory. Her publications include *Victorian Scrutinies* (1972), *Language as Living Form in Nineteenth-Century Poetry* (1982), and *Victorian Poetry: Poetry, Poetics and Politics* (1993), and with Joseph Bristow edited *Nineteenth-Century Women Poets* (1996). She is currently working on a study of glass, text, and culture in the nineteenth century.

Barry Cunliffe is Professor of European Archaeology at the University of Oxford. His professional research interests focus on European communities in the First Millennium BC and their interaction with Mediterranean societies. He is currently working on the Atlantic Seaways as one of the major axis of communication.

Kate Flint is Reader in Victorian and Modern English Literature at the University of Oxford, and Fellow of Linacre College. She is author of *The Victorians and the Visual Imagination* (2000), *The Woman Reader, 1837–1914* (1993), and *Dickens* (1986), as well as numerous articles on Victorian and twentieth-century literature, painting, and cultural history. Her current research is on the place of the Americas in the Victorian cultural imagination.

John House is Professor of the History of Art at the Courtauld Institute of Art, London. He is the author of *Monet: Nature into Art* (1986), and many articles and essays on French nineteenth-century painting, and has curated a number of exhibitions, among them *Landscapes of France: Impressionism and its Rivals* at the Hayward Gallery, London and the Museum of Fine Arts, Boston, in 1995–6.

David Lowenthal is Emeritus Professor of Geography at University College London, and Visiting Professor of Heritage Studies at St Mary's University College, Strawberry Hill, Twickenham. Among his books are *George Perkins Marsh, Prophet of Conservation* (2000), *The Heritage Crusade and the Spoils of History* (1996), *The Past Is a Foreign Country* (1985), and *West Indian Societies* (1972).

Howard Morphy was Professor of Anthropology at University College London, and is now Director of the Centre for Cross-Cultural Research at the Australian National University. He is a Fellow of Linacre College, Oxford. He has written widely on Aboriginal art and religion and collaborated with Ian Dunlop on a number of films on Arnhem Land Society. His current research is on biography and landscape. His most recent books include *Ancestral Connections* (1991) and *Aboriginal Art* (1998).

Fred R. Myers is Professor and Chair of Anthropology at New York University. He is the author of *Pintupi Country, Pintupi Self: Sentiment, Place and Politics among Western Desert Aborigines* (1991), co-editor of *The Traffic in Culture: Refiguring Art and Anthropology* (1995), and numerous articles on the development and significance of Western Desert Aboriginal acrylic painting.

Roy Porter is Professor in the Social History of Medicine at the Wellcome Institute for the History of Medicine. Recent books include *Doctor of Society: Thomas Beddoes and the Sick Trade in Late Enlightenment England* (1991), *London: A Social History* (1994), and *'The Greatest Benefit to Mankind': A Medical History of Humanity* (1997). He is a co-author of *The History of Bethlem* (1997), and has recently written a history of the Enlightenment in Britain. He is interested in eighteenth century medicine, the history of psychiatry and the history of quackery.

Harriet Ritvo is the Arthur J. Conner Professor of History at the Massachusetts Institute of Technology. She is the author of *The Animal Estate: The English and Other Creatures in the Victorian Age* (1987) and *The Platypus and the Mermaid, and Other Figments of the Classifying Imagination* (1997), and is currently at work on a book about Victorians and the environment.

Marilyn Strathern is Professor of Social Anthropology at the University of Cambridge. Her interests are divided between Melanesian and British ethnography. *The Gender of the Gift* (1988) is a critique of anthropological theories of society and gender relations as applied to Melanesia, while *After Nature* (1992) comments on a cultural revolution at home. A collection of recent essays, *Property, Substance and Effect*, appeared in 1999.

LIST OF FIGURES

Introduction

Howard Morphy and Kate Flint

THE ENVIRONMENT we inhabit is inseparable from human culture. Our landscape, our cities, our seas are shaped, traversed, harvested in accordance with the needs, practices, and desires of particular societies. More than this, our awareness of the world, and our representation of its beauties, its potential, its exploitation, and its significance to us is mediated through written, oral, and visual forms which take their expression and values from countless different social formations and traditions. The environment, as well as being made up of innumerable interdependent and sometimes precariously fragile ecosystems; as well as requiring care in its management and protection—in other words, in addition to being considered in holistic terms—becomes a site for the display and expression of cultures. Culture is that which enables people to survive in a particular environment, to express themselves in relation to it—although there is no guarantee that they will operate in harmony *with* it. Indeed, the environment, and our changing conceptions of it, at both macro and micro levels, forms the ideal ground for the interrogation of that notoriously vexed word 'culture' itself.

In this volume we are able to move through time and space to compare the ways in which environment is differently constructed across cultures. The contributions by Porter, Armstrong, Ritvo, House, and Lowenthal cover the transformations in Western European conceptions of the environment following the age of the Enlightenment that provides the background to current intellectual debates. Roy Porter's and David Lowenthal's essays together provide an overview of the changes in attitudes to the environment that occurred from the sixteenth century to the late twentieth century. Isobel Armstrong, Harriet Ritvo, and John House overlap in time, focusing on that crucial period of the nineteenth century when Europe was on the edge of modernity. The other three chapters provide conceptual perspectives from outside contemporary Europe. Barry Cunliffe moves us through 4,000 years of Wessex history to the time of the Roman invasion of Britain. He provides evidence of environmental transformations and changes in the built environment ('the writing on the landscape') that imply cultural correlates, while posing the question as to how it is possible to access the cultural ideas that influenced the form of the archaeological record. Fred Myers and Marilyn Strathern are both concerned with non-European societies, the Pintubi of Central Australia and the people of the Papua New Guinea Highlands. These societies are themselves caught up in global processes and it is possible to see the way in which their ideational systems both influence the trajectory along which they are travelling and in turn respond to global pressures to change.

Culture is a word with multiple definitions, used in many different senses by different disciplines, but there are two broad senses which can be abstracted. On the one hand, culture refers to the bodies of knowledge that human beings live by, and on the other, it refers to qualitative dimensions of human life and production, reflecting the values that people have and the bases on which they make judgements. However, these two senses of the word are interrelated: values reflect and affect ways of doing things as well as providing the goals of action. Culture concerns our consciousness of the world, how we understand it and how we act in relation to it. Particular forms of consciousness are associated with particular conceptions of the environment and ways of conceptualizing the relationship between people and nature. The very existence of a concept of environment or nature as a separate dimension of reality is something that varies in space and time. The Pintubi of Central Australia (Myers), the Highlanders of Papua New Guinea (Strathern); nineteenth-century European glassmakers (Armstrong), and twentieth-century British environmentalists (Lowenthal), all have very different concepts of the environment, and the degree to which it is conceived of as separate from the phenomenology of human life varies from case to case.

In recent discussions of culture and the environment, these two prevalent meanings of culture may be seen to break down, or at least to interact in new and profitable ways. In part, this has resulted from the increasing politicization of the environmental movement, which operates both within formal political spheres and as a more popular movement: the gentle and logical transition of the cultural historian Raymond Williams from Marxist to green politics may be taken as symptomatic in this respect. We have witnessed a number of historical studies which have concentrated on the interrelations of humans, the planet they inhabit, and the other creatures which live there also, from Keith Thomas's *Man and the Natural World* (1983) and Simon Schama's *Landscape and Memory*

(1995) through Clive Ponting's *A Green History of the World* (1991), Donald Worster's *The Wealth of Nature: Environmental History and the Ecological Imagination* (1993) to Richard Grove's *Green Imperialism* (1995). Whilst such analyses come out of, and are helping to reshape, historiographic traditions, ecologists are themselves writing histories that look at the processes of evolution and change in the natural world both before and subsequent to human intervention—processes which in turn have considerable bearing on how we think about future resource management. Tim Flannery's *The Future Eaters* (1994), taking a long and somewhat contentious view of Australasia's ecological development, provides an interesting case study. Recent anthropological studies have provided a comparative perspective on the relationships between conceptions of the environment and cultural process. Two edited volumes in particular—Barbara Bender's *Landscape: Politics and Perspectives* (1993) and Eric Hirsch and Michael O'Hanlon's (1995) *The Anthropology of Landscape*—have added greatly to an understanding of the cultural constructions of landscape. And recent literary criticism has begun to engage with environmental issues. Gillian Beer, in *Darwin's Plots* (1983) showed how culture and theories concerning the environment in the nineteenth century could not be separated from one another: the very patterns of constructing narratives in science and fiction were interdependent. More recent work, including Jonathan Bate's *Romantic Ecology: Wordsworth and the Environmental Tradition* (1991), Tim Morton's study of Shelley's vegetarianism, *Shelley and the Revolution in Taste: The Body and the Natural World* (1994) and Michael Wheeler's collection of essays on that early environmental activist and polymath, John Ruskin, *Ruskin and the Environment* (1995) have helped inaugurate what has come to be known as ecocriticism—as witnessed by Cheryll Glotfelty and Harold Fromm's *The Eco-criticism Reader: Landmarks in Literary Ecology* (1996). What all this scholarship bears witness to, in its turn, is how effectively the topic of culture and the environment breaks down conventional disciplinary boundaries: this interdisciplinarity is very strongly evident in the essays that make up this volume.

How one considers the relationships between culture and the environment involves, inevitably, a consideration of our own positionality: as observers, as participants, as shapers, both materially and linguistically, of our world. The environment, as many of our contributors remind us, is not just a protean concept in historical terms, but changes according to where we place ourselves. Unsurprisingly, therefore, a number of the essays which follow focus on acts of perception.

Lowenthal and Porter both show how the currently dominant concept of environment as something that exists external and separate to the person is a relatively recent development in European thought. For much of European history environment was conceived of as surroundings, which included equally the cultural and natural worlds. Environment was an integral part of the process of life and there was no self-conscious separation of people from nature. Porter argues that this view resulted partly from an encompassing religious schema in which the invisible and visible mingled together as part of a process that created a world ordered by God: 'a sacred amphitheatre with designated roles'. From the Enlightenment onwards we see an increasing separation of people from nature. Lowenthal maintains that rather than nature and Man being seen as the product of cosmogony, Man for a while was the product of his environment. Theories that the environment determines the way of life of small-scale societies or influences national character continued to be applied until well into the twentieth century. However, the continuities between pre-Enlightenment and post-Enlightenment theories should not be overlooked. Although nature was now outside God's order it was still subject to human needs. In the one case nature had its God-given role, in the other it was seen as subject to human control. Finally Lowenthal argues that the situation is now being reversed. Nature is perceived to be threatened by human action and environmentalism has arisen as an ideology to protect nature: 'Previously nature's passive pawns, we now see ourselves as its historic destruction and, we hope, its future regeneration'. But again he is able to see continuities across time. A belief that human action can result in catastrophe is equally part of the pre-Enlightenment and post-Enlightenment positions, though in the former it is moral behaviour that results in flood and plague whereas in the latter case it is bad land-management and overproduction. He makes the important point that how the environment is perceived and what it is thought to comprise varies over time and according to the values held. Nature moves from being wild, dangerous, untamed, ungodly to being vulnerable, fragile, and sacred. At times it is subordinate to humans, at other times it excludes them. Likewise, the view of other cultures depends on the observer's cultural lens: hunters and gatherers can be at one with nature or antithetical to it, alien animals in a balanced universe of other creatures. Yet the views of hunters and gatherers or subsistence agriculturalists themselves are unlikely to coincide with either of these.

The essay by Roy Porter which opens this collection comprehensively surveys the sweep of ideas about the environment in England which led into the industrial era: the era which produced the particular human-created forms which do most to threaten the global environment. He shows that anxiety about the environment is nothing new; that at the end of the seventeenth century, the notion of the *mundus senescens*, the ageing, tiring, deteriorating earth was invoked, an apparent punishment for original sin. But this was replaced by a Georgian celebration of the long-term stability of the earth, in which apparent decay was explained away as part of a longer-term divinely ordained strategy for enhancing the globe's fertility. Such political and religious concepts fuelled the move to 'improve' the land, in a spirit of cooperation between humans and nature: a form of environmental ethics, which aimed at avoiding waste. Thus the capitalist farm, and the common fields, 'became parables of industry and idleness respectively'. Malthus' *Essay on Population* (1798) shattered the idea that good environmental management of this kind guaranteed human progress, however, and enthusiasm for enclosure turned, in some cases, to a recognition that environmental degradation, as well as human impoverishment, had been its result. This awareness, and a growing respect for the perceived integrity of nature, went hand in hand with the post-Enlightenment emergence of 'natural supernatur- alism', the aesthetic celebration of the wild—whether in the form of an inaccessible mountain peak or a rampant garden—and, of course, the intrusion of industry into the countryside, and the threat it posed to the natural environment. Whilst such a threat could be turned into a form of beauty in those paintings which tried to integrate—literally, to natural- ize—the iron furnace or mining operation into the rural sublime, this art amply reinforces Roy Porter's major point: that 'Environments . . . are imagined landscapes; ecology lies in the eye of the beholder'.

Cunliffe opposes the concept of landscape as a construct, 'enmeshed in a network of beliefs and values' to environment as a global process that exists outside the particularities of any one culture. Seen in this way, environment signifies processes of change in the physical and natural resources of a region—climate, soil fertility, flora and fauna—viewed independently of the way it is conceived of by the human inhabitants at any particular point of time. Such a view of the environment does not see it as independent of those human agents or unaffected by human culture, but nor does it view it in the same terms as the actors themselves. The view is one that enables questions to be posed about the relationship between human cultures and the environment over time as part of more general questions to do with environmental change. How has human use of the environment modified it? To what extent can the forms of human occupation be explained by features of the environment? As we have seen this view of the environment as a relatively independent level of reality is itself a viewpoint that has a history. It too is a cultural construction, albeit a cultural construction that should be able to take into account other ways in which human beings have constructed the environment.

Marilyn Strathern analyses changes consequent on European colonization, in the economic and social environment of Mount Hagen society of the New Guinea Highlands following and, in particular, the consequences of the inflation of shell valuables. These changes, in turn, have an impact on the natural environment since the system of prestige with which the value creation processes are linked encourages an increase in the production of agricultural products for trade and exchange. She shows the intricate and complex connections between different dimensions of social process. One dimension is scale-insensitive, comprising analogies that establish the value of actions and transactions—for example, external wealth as a sign of internal strength. Another dimension is scale-sensitive: factors of scale, such as the measure of wealth, can enter into the process of decision making and sometimes have transformational consequences. These two dimensions relate to the different senses of the word 'culture' that we have identified and Strathern shows how they articulate with the world in different ways. One is associated with internal determinations and value structures, the other is on a trajectory directly influenced by resources, connections with the outside world, colonialism, and so on. The view which sees culture as a process of production with measurable effects brings into existence a view of the environment that is external and separable from human society. The environment in this sense is something that is acted upon, something that affords opportunities and possibilities, through the interaction of the forces of nature and the forces of production. However, such a perspective is only relatively separate from the non-scale-sensitive domain of value creation in which measurements of scale are seen to depend on analogic propositions, by which the productivity of the land is seen as being causally related to the fertility in the land. Increases in production are analogically produced by increases in fertility of which they are an outer sign. The insider view in the case of many New Guinea societies is centred on social relationships: on flows and exchanges rather than on production. There is no separate environment out there; an external environment is not part of what is imagined.

The reality is that ongoing cultural process exists not in any one dimension or the other but in the complex relationships between them. It is 'a double process' that can be conceived of as a dimension in between internal–agentive–conceptual process and the wider socio–historical–environmental context in which people act. Many concepts used in analysis can benefit from being viewed in relation to this schema. Scale, for example, is associated more with the outsider view: it concerns the measurement of production and consumption, the impact of widening trade networks, the introduction of goods by colonizers and missionaries. In the case of the New Guinea Highlands the factors in the outside world that resulted in the great increase in shell valuables had little to do with the internal operation of the system though they were to have a great effect on how it operated. The motivations from within that produced inflation in shell valuables had little to do with the motivations of those who imported them in vast numbers from outside. The trajectory that results is the product of that dimension which exists between the inside and the outside, and as the process continues the meaning of things, the workings of the imagination from the inside also undergoes transformation. Inflation, the escalation of demands, of needs, of resources, of connections which resulted in the internal transformation of ceremonial exchange systems is a sign of the greater resources the societies need to extract from the world outside if they are not to diminish in scale. The internal motor in the Highlands was that resource accumulation was seen as a reflection of the underlying power of the person or group extracting it. Hence the move to an economy of extraction in which value is scaled up 'according to the developer's ability to pay' was in harmony with existing 'world views' and value structures. In the Highlands, compensation developed out of a local trajectory in the context of inflation. Yet as a concept for the present it was relevant elsewhere and has rapidly spread across Papua New Guinea, where in turn it is incorporated within local cultural contexts. The dialogue results both in the spread of new concepts appropriate for changes in the external environment and their reincorporation within local differences. Thus, transformations which occur in response to global changes also reinstitute local differences.

Fred Myers, likewise, is concerned to emphasize that the cultural construction of landscape is a process that results through people interacting with the world rather than the stamping of order on to the world through the imposition of a pre-existing cultural template. Extreme forms of cultural constructivism imply that the form and content of people's actions are predetermined by the structured world into which they are born. In the popular literature on Aboriginal Australia the Dreamtime order of the universe is sometimes presented as an invariant foundation in which the sacred mythology of place never alters and in which people are attached to place by rigid rules of group membership; where the future is a mere reproduction of the past. Such a position certainly accords with aspects of Aboriginal ideology, in which continuity with the past is emphasized and spiritual beings are given agency in determining the parameters of human life. But it is human beings who reproduce the form of the Dreamtime and they do so through the process of changing human lives and in the context of changing conditions of existence. The changed circumstances of post-colonial Australia have certainly increased the need for Aboriginal people to respond to change. Culture is a prescription for action but it also contains sets of values. Aboriginal relations with land in Central Australia have changed over time, and also as a result of European invasion and the disruption to their way of life. But the trajectory of change has been influenced both by Aboriginal ways of doing things and by the values associated with those ways of doing things that differentiate Aboriginal from European Australian society. That does not mean that there is an absolute boundary between the two, nor that the one does not influence the other, merely that the processes of reproduction result in a continuing reproduction of difference.

Myers takes a moderate position in the cultural constructionist debate, arguing that the value that places have in the Dreaming is in reality an objectification of values gained through the engagement of place in social processes. The value of places are not absolutely fixed and indeed vary according to a person's relationship to them. In the Central Desert region people are continually establishing new relationships to places as groups reform over time and as circumstances change. People die without descendants, or lose touch with a place as they move away on marriage, or as a result of a breakdown in social relations. To Myers, 'place enters into Aboriginal social life in a fashion similar to other material forms, mediated by social action, as a potential formulation of similarity and difference as a token of identity and exchange'. But he also shows that place or country is not a mere token but a token with content: holding a country and all that goes with that is also a primary objective, holding a country entails performing ceremonies associated with it, holding rights in sacred objects associated with it, being named after it, being consulted over it. Thus, country to the Pintubi has particular characteristics as an object that differentiate it from the way the same area of land would be seen by non-Pintubi, or perhaps non-Aboriginal Australians. Its value not only includes the ongoing set of social relations that cohere around it but also the spiritual values that are attributed to it and which have the power to transform people. Colonization has changed the conditions of life for the Pintubi and other Aborigines, disrupting their previous relationships with land, changing the demographic structure, and changing the land itself through the building of roads, townships, and mining or pastoral exploitation. However, the process of Aboriginal attachment to land and the cultural construction of place through ongoing social process has enabled groups to reform and reattach themselves to the transformed places of the post-colonial landscape, sometimes shifting locations, sometimes altering meanings, but continually re-establishing linkages.

Reviewing 4,000 years of Wessex prehistory, Barry Cunliffe identifies two long trajectories in which society seems to be reworking similar themes in reproducing its relationship with the environment. These are divided by a major discontinuity, almost a paradigm change, in which both the form of society and the fundamental concerns of the people changed. The earlier period, stretching from 4000 BC to around 1300 BC, saw the progressive development of a landscape marked with monuments to the dead in which succeeding generations added to the significance of the same set of places and the pattern of territorial division of the landscape existed in continuity with what went before. Towards the end of the second millennium BC it seems that a new order was imposed on the landscape, often literally cutting across the old as new boundary features cross-cut the previously established pattern of field systems. At the same time there seems to be a change in religious iconography with a greater emphasis on fertility. The occurrence of such dramatic shifts simultaneously in the economic management of land and in the symbolic sphere suggest that change may have been stimulated by a dramatic change in circumstances. Cunliffe posits that the stimulus may have been either a general deterioration in climate conditions over a period of a few centuries or more controversially a major environmental catastrophe resulting in famine and a loss of confidence in the previous order of things. The transformations occurring in Pintubi and Highland New Guinea society may provide an analogue for the catastrophe theory, although in neither case was environmental disaster the direct cause. In both cases it is a change in the social environment as a consequence of colonialism which has stimulated a change in the scale of their relationships to the world. While the Pintubi and Highlanders appear to be maintaining control of the trajectory of their societies by utilizing internal processes to adjust to changes in scale and power relations, the timescale is too short to be visible archaeologically. Short-term coping may be a step in the journey towards long-term transformation, and yet at the same time it may be that the long lens of prehistory overdramatizes the discontinuity between the two systems and has failed so far to reveal evidence of the way in which the one may have transformed into the other without creating a sense of turbulence at the time.

Most of the essays considered so far take culture in a very broad sense; as the practices by which certain societies live—and, by extension, the interpretative practices which both they and we invoke and employ to make sense of them. By contrast, three of the contributions to this volume focus on 'high' culture in its much more traditional sense, in that they engage with the intersection of painting, literature, garden design, and the environment, more specifically, that highly cultivated Western European landscape which has, over the last few centuries, increasingly become a site for the pursuit of leisure activities as well as the source of produce. This is true of the examples in Roy Porter's contribution, even though it simultaneously raises some very broad questions about the conceptualization of the idea of one's environment. John House's piece, on the treatment of French rural scenery by both mainstream painters and by the Impressionists, quite explicitly links in shifts in viewing and representing the scenery around Paris, and further afield, with such an expansion. He shows how the language of guidebooks, the directing of the uninformed gaze, is directly related to the particular framings of a scene which different groups of artists explored. Such an expansion was necessarily linked to industrialization: to urban growth and the concomitant distancing of the rural, an estrangement of what had been taken for granted by generations of country-dwellers, which enabled subsequent aestheticization. Yet, he also makes the important point that we should not fall into the trap of looking at paintings as though they reflect, or directly express attitudes towards, the physical environment. For they, like other forms of culture, are inevitably mediated through conventions: in this case, the conventions of fine art painting in the late nineteenth century.

In the paintings of the industrial sublime to which Porter draws our attention—by Wright of Derby, or Francis Danby—aesthetic conventions play such a dominant role that one could easily fall into the error of forgetting about the workers whose place of labour is shown in these grandiose scenes. That the labour which went into producing the objects consumed by the growing middle classes was often overlooked is one of the underlying themes of Isobel Armstrong's essay, on 'glass consciousness', where she also is centrally concerned with the beholder's perceiving eye. Glass, she maintains, transformed consciousness by creating new physical traditions. Revolutionary modes of industrial production led to a culture of mass transparency, which transformed the optical imagination. For glass—the glass in a window, in particular—was both a barrier and a medium, and for us to focus on its presence within nineteenth-century culture is also to look at how the mediums through which we view the world are themselves both filters, and taken for granted by those who use them. The environment, she tacitly demonstrates, is continually being remade according to the tools of perception that we use to examine it. But she raises a number of other crucial points. Like John House, she is concerned with framing: not the frame provided by the edges of a picture, but the lines of a window, that intersection of individual and socially organized space at the point of their dissolve; a collapse of inside and outside which raises a whole set of questions about the ways in which one may be said to possess a landscape. For possession is not just about enclosure or land rights, but about the ability and authority to comment on what lies before one. The issue of whether painting vast scenes is itself an attempt to master and understand through appropriation on to canvas is one which is pertinently raised by the huge canvases on display in the 1998 show (seen in Canberra, Melbourne, Hartford, CT, and Washington, DC) of nineteenth-century Australian and American landscape art, *New Worlds from Old*. Is, Armstrong asks, the wide expanse which meets the eye through a long Le Corbusierian expanse of glass not potentially *more* about the possession and consumption of a scene than that gaze directed outwards through a vertical window from a bourgeois interior?

In posing such questions about power and positionality, Armstrong suggests, as Marilyn Strathern does, that issues of inside/outside are going to be of crucial importance in analysing where any individual stands in relation to both their immediate environment, and to the wider global context of which that environment forms a part. Armstrong's examples, however, are taken from literature; from Charlotte Brontë and from Charles Dickens, writers who display uneasy relationships in their work with both the imminent industrial world of mid-Victorian Britain, and its larger colonial ambit. Glass is intimately bound in with these issues, as she shows. The hothouse made it possible for rural experience and controlled environments to be transported anywhere. The colonial could be naturalized in a temperate context, allowing the repression of difference, or at the very least a confusion of taxonomies such as one saw, on a scale which mingled the industrial with the natural, within the glassy structures of the Great Exhibition. Glass could also have been used to reinforce taxonomies, had plans gone ahead with placing central London under massive glass arcades, keeping in the protected, and keeping out the polluting—whether the mephitic vapours of the graveyards, the stinking Thames, or the poor themselves. Within the glass used in all these localized environments—whether Paxman's spaces, or the domestic conservatory, or even the leaded window through which the terminally bored Lady Dedlock gazes, or which Lockwood so savagely severs—there is, however, something that distinguishes it from all other building forms. It is more than the product of someone's physical labour: it contains their breath itself. This intimate connection between body and manufacture explains, Armstrong argues, some of the passion associated with its production. It also serves as a pointed reminder of how any human-created environment carries the traces of the effort of its production within it.

The pieces so far discussed put the human at the centre of the environment, whether as perceiver, consumer, or creator. But Harriet Ritvo's piece on 'Our Animal Environment' reminds one of the importance of the non-human in creating the landscapes we see. Open plains or pastures, for example, are as much sites for a form of industrial production as are smoke-blackened mill environs, since the animals grazing on them are the source of meat and milk and leather and wool, not just picturesque ornamentation to add scale to a painter's composition. Moreover, the dividing line between human and animal has never been a clear one, and she explores some of the implications of this for our understanding of the world we inhabit—not least that animals fall under the unquestioned control of the classifier, an abstract vulnerability which mirrors the physical vulnerability that most of them endure. Like Isobel Armstrong, Ritvo explores taxonomies, and the effect that ordering our environment in certain ways has on our perception of where certain borderlines are drawn, whether these lines serve to demarcate the beginnings and endings of humanitarianism (where did the Victorians place the Irish? freed West Indian slaves? dogs? apes?), or species. She investigates how establishing taxonomies according to anatomical affinity, or moral affinity, can both lead to these lines being set down in very different ways, and throw up some inconsistent patterns of relationship. Nor is this pattern confined to the Victorian period. By calling on recent debates about rabies, and about BSE (mad cow disease), she shows how taxonomic differences continue to be disturbed, not least because those animals who have come to be thought of as close to humans (whether in terms of intelligence, or as affectionate companions, or as the bearer of symbolic worth) emerge as the vectors of terrible diseases. Moral and anatomical affinities may, she concludes, be closer than we think: moreover, the shock caused by such circumstances has the effect of throwing into relief how people tend to be constrained by the environments they have defined for themselves, unable to see beyond their limits.

Adopting the viewpoint on the environment of the Pintubi, or the Hageners, or the Enlightenment thinker, focusing on the history of a particular technology in relation to the environment or the attitudes towards other animals in the environment provides salutary lessons. The very act of switching creates a concept of environment that is outside any particular cultural construction yet paradoxically demonstrates the deep entanglement of environment with human life, an entanglement that is motivated by cultural understandings and evaluations. The environment, these essays all show, lies outside us—but it also lies within. The very idea that the environment is culturally constructed and that by implication conceptions of a good environment are relative to the culture of the person concerned, is an anathema both to certain philosophical and scientific positions and to certain environmentalists. The idea is threatening since it removes the certainty that the environment exists in a universal form external to the processes of history. Lowenthal shows that universalists often hold a normative view of nature maintained at a particular point of time and/or one that rejects humanly created environments, putting human beings outside nature. A relativistic view however need not imply that environmental problems, such as deforestation and global warming, cannot be seen to exist independent of particular cultural understandings of them. Rather, the solution involves engaging particular local conceptions so that political commitment can be directed towards addressing the problem. What is required is an intermediate position between the one in which human action is predetermined by the concepts that are inherited from the past, and the one that sees life as being the result of pragmatic or practical action directed towards making a living out of a world that can to all intents and purposes be considered to exist outside the person. Most of the contributors adopt the position that culture is part of a dialogic process which involves human action in a world that is subject both to local trajectories and external forces, whether those be environmental change, colonialism, or other forms of globalization.

REFERENCES

Bate, Jonathan (1991). *Romantic Ecology: Wordsworth and the Environmental Tradition*. London: Routledge.

Bender, Barbara (1993). *Landscape: Politics and Perspectives*. Oxford: Berg.

Beer, Gillian (1983). *Darwin's Plots*. London: Routledge & Kegan Paul.

Glotfelty, Cheryll and Fromm, Harold (1996). *The Eco-criticism Reader: Landmarks in Literary Ecology*. Athens, GA: University of Georgia Press.

Flannery, Tim (1994). *The Future Eaters*. Chatswood, NSW: Reed Books.

Grove, Richard (1995). *Green Imperialism*. Cambridge: Cambridge University Press.

Hirsch, Eric and O'Hanlon, Michael (1995). *The Anthropology of Landscape*. Oxford: Oxford University Press.

Morton, Tim (1994). *Shelley and the Revolution in Taste: The Body and the Natural World*. Cambridge: Cambridge University Press.

Ponting, Clive (1991). *A Green History of the World*. London: Sinclair-Stevenson.

Schama, Simon (1995). *Landscape and Memory*. London: HarperCollins.
Thomas, Keith (1983). *Man and the Natural World*. London: Allen Lane.
Wheeler, Michael (1995). *Ruskin and the Environment*. Manchester: Manchester University Press.
Worster, Donald (1993). *The Wealth of Nature: Environmental History and the Ecological Imagination*. New York: Oxford University Press.

1

'In England's Green and Pleasant Land': The English Enlightenment and the Environment

Roy Porter

'ENVIRONMENT' is a term we owe to Thomas Carlyle, but environmental anxieties are nothing new. My aim here is to explore attitudes in eighteenth-century Britain, concentrating on the mainstream but glancing at cross-currents.

'It is with much regret', bemoaned the *Bath Chronicle* on 30 May 1799,

that for some years past we have remarked considerable injury to have been suffered by the woods and young timber around this city in consequence of wearing oaken sprigs in the hat, and the decorating of shop-windows and apartments of houses with oaken branches, on the 29 of May [i.e., the anniversary of the Restoration of Charles II]. If the practice alluded to be meant as an expression of *Loyalty*, we would just suggest that this is a very improper display of it: since it would never sanction that injury to individuals and loss to the publick, which are produced by these annual depredations on private property.[1]

As this editorial hints, then as now Nature as public patrimony or even patriotism, and Nature as private property, could easily be at odds.

Of course, the word these days from cultural studies and the history of science is that Nature is a social category. 'For although we are accustomed', writes Simon Schama, 'to separate nature and human perception into two realms, they are, in fact, indivisible. Before it can ever be a repose for the senses, landscape is the work of the mind. Its scenery is built up as much from strata of memory as from layers of rock'.[2] What passes today in England for 'Nature'—the chequerboard fields, hawthorn hedgerows and tidy coppices which conservationists defend against

---

[1] Trevor Fawcett (ed.), *Voices of Eighteenth-century Bath. An Anthology of Contemporary Texts Illustrating Events, Daily Life and Attitudes at Britain's leading Georgian Spa* (Bath: Ruton, 1995), 191.

[2] Simon Schama, *Landscape and Memory* (London: Harper Collins, 1995), 6–7.

developers—such is the product of Georgian agribusiness, landscape gardening, and peasant-cleansing. In declaring 'All Nature is but Art unknown to Thee', Alexander Pope meant to be pious, but he was also providing the code-breaker to environmental history.[3]

What framed the Georgian mental landscape? Vistas of Nature were widening: the Ptolemaic closed world had yielded to the infinite Newtonian Universe, while circumnavigators like Captain Cook encouraged poets and philosophers alike to portray the Earth as an organic whole, pointing to Alexander von Humboldt's lofty vision of Cosmos and perhaps, in due course, towards James Lovelock's Gaia. This terraqueous globe was Nature's backdrop to Enlightenment cosmopolitanism.[4]

Yet horizons, we must not forget, were also spectacularly shrinking. When visualizing the Universe, our eighteenth-century Fellow of the Royal Society, unlike his Restoration precursors, had probably excluded from his sights Heaven, Hell, and all the Satanic squadrons of daemons and witches that suffused eschatologies from Calvin to Milton.[5] 'The truth is', reflected Thomas Carlyle in 1829:

men have lost their belief in the Invisible, and believe and hope and work only in the Visible . . . Only the material, the immediate practical, not the divine and spiritual, is important to us.[6]

But though we here catch anticipations of the Weberian disenchantment of the world, the planet had not yet been reduced to the meaning-

[3] Alexander Pope, 'Essay on Man', in J. Butt (ed.), *The Poems of Alexander Pope* (London: Methuen, 1965), 515. For 'thinking the environment', see Denis Cosgrove and Stephen Daniels (eds), *The Iconography of Landscape: Essays on the Symbolic Representation, Design and Use of Past Environments* (Cambridge University Press, 1988, 1989); Y.-F. Tuan, *Topophilia: A Study of Environmental Perception, Attitudes and Values* (Englewood Cliffs: Prentice-Hall, 1974); Derek Wall, *A Reader in Environmental Literature, Philosophy and Politics* (London: Routledge, 1994); David Pepper, *The Roots of Modern Environmentalism* (London: Croom Helm, 1984); Clive Ponting, *A Green History of the World* (London: Sinclair-Stevenson, 1991). The finest historian of the environment is Donald Worster; see his *The Wealth of Nature. Environmental History and the Ecological Imagination* (New York: Oxford University Press, 1993); *idem*, *Nature's Economy: A History of Ecological Ideas* (rev. edn) (Cambridge University Press, 1985).

[4] Alexander von Humboldt, *Cosmos*, 4 vols (London: Longman, Brown, Green & Longmans, 1846); James Lovelock, *Gaia: A New Look at Life on Earth* (Oxford University Press, 1979); Roy Porter, 'The Terraqueous Globe', in G. S. Rousseau and R. S. Porter (eds), *The Ferment of Knowledge* (Cambridge University Press, 1980), 285–324; B. Smith, *European Vision and the South Pacific, 1768–1850: A Study in the History of Art and Ideas* (Oxford: Clarendon Press, 1960); Barbara Maria Stafford, *Voyage Into Substance: Art, Science, Nature, and the Illustrated Travel Account 1760–1840* (Cambridge, MA, MIT Press, 1984); Neil Rennie, *Far-fetched Facts: The Literature of Travel and the Idea of the South Seas* (Oxford: Clarendon Press, 1995).

[5] See Marijke Gijswijt-Hofstra, Brian P. Levack, and Roy Porter, *Witchcraft and Magic in Europe*, vol. 5: *The Eighteenth and Nineteenth Centuries* (London: Athlone, 1998).

[6] [T. Carlyle], 'Signs of the Times', *Edinburgh Review*, lix (1829), 439–59, 452–3.

less mass of congealing magma that filled Tennyson and other Victorian honest doubters with dread; with Pope as their spokesman, the Georgians unfailingly read Nature as a masterwork of Divine artistry—one looked 'from Nature up to Nature's God'. Filing out of church of a Sunday, the devout gazed up in awe:

> The Spacious Firmament on high
> With all the blue Etherial sky
> And spangled Heav'ns, a Shining Frame
> Their great Original proclaim.[7]
>
> (Psalm 111 rhymed and regularized
> by Joseph Addison)

In that confident Christian worldview, there could be no such thing as mere Nature; there was Creation, and that remained, as ever, a sacred amphitheatre with designated roles, costumes, and scripts for all creatures great and small, from stones, herbs, and beasts, up through the Chain of Being, to Addison's great Original. The perception of the terrestrial economy as a drama or, equally, as an estate, matched the daily material realities of the interlocking of the human with the natural world, so superbly delineated by Keith Thomas.[8] Most people still lived on the land—in 1700 only 13 per cent of England's population resided in towns of over 5000; sheep outnumbered people. There was an overwhelming proximity, physical, mental, and emotional—sometimes friendly, sometimes frightening—between humans, flocks, and fields. The sense that everything had its rank and station in Creation was enrolled in a popular mentality whose folk-tales mingled children, wolves, giants, and monsters; in an elite culture exemplified by Gilbert White's *Natural History of Selborne*, where swallows and hedgehogs were humanized into honorary parishioners;[9] and not least in a faith that was breathtakingly anthropocentric. Unlike many other world religions, Christian theology affirmed that all had been divinely adapted for mankind, because humans alone had immortal souls and so could be saved. Genesis had granted man 'dominion over the fish of the sea, and over the fowl of the air, and over the cattle, and over all the earth and over every creeping thing that creepeth upon the earth'. And even after the Fall and Flood, had not the

---

[7] The Pope quotation is in *ibid.* (note 3), 546; for Addison see Basil Willey, *The Eighteenth Century Background: Studies on the Idea of Nature in the Thought of the Period* (London: Penguin, 1962), 51.

[8] Keith Thomas, *Man and the Natural World* (London: Allen Lane, 1983).

[9] Marina Warner, *From the Beast to the Blonde: On Fairy Tales and Their Tellers* (London: Chatto & Windus, 1994); Gilbert White, *The Natural History and Antiquities of Selborne*, Richard Mabey (ed.) (Penguin: Harmondsworth, 1977; first published 1789).

Lord reissued His mandate: 'Be fruitful and multiply and replenish the earth and subdue it'?[10]

Nature, in other words, was not some disputed territory occupied by Satan; nor was it intrinsically holy—the Churches had always battled to quash stubborn paganism or budding pantheism. Rather, Nature was a resource, 'principally designed', asserted Richard Bentley, Anglican divine and Newtonian popularizer, 'for the being and service and contemplation of man'.[11] 'We can, if need be, ransack the whole globe', maintained his fellow physico-theologian, the Revd William Derham, 'penetrate into the bowels of the earth, descend to the bottom of the deep, travel to the farthest regions of this world, to acquire wealth, to increase our knowledge, or even only to please our eye and fancy'. And so providently benevolent was the Creator that, no matter how acquisitive man might be, 'still the Creation would not be exhausted, still nothing would be wanting for food, nothing for physic, nothing for building and habitation, nothing for cleanliness and refreshment, yea even for re-creation and pleasure'.[12] Even at the dawn of the nineteenth century, the geologist William Phillips could reassure his readers that '*everything* [was] *intended for the advantage of Man*', the 'Lord of Creation', a sentiment mirrored in Paley's *Natural Theology* and in the *Bridgewater Treatises*.[13]

Scripture-religion sustained an ingrained sense of a milieu adapted to the needs of the rich man in his castle and the poor man at his gate in pursuit of their daily business.[14] There were sermons in stones and the writing was on the trees. The trunk was a tree of life, carrying echoes of Calvary; but timber had social morals to point too:

[10] See C. Glacken, *Traces on the Rhodian Shore: Nature and Culture in Western Thought from Ancient Times to the End of the Eighteenth Century* (Berkeley: University of California Press, 1967); John Passmore, *The Perfectibility of Man* (London: Duckworth, 1968, 1972); idem, *Man's Responsibility for Nature* (London: Duckworth, 1980).

[11] Richard Bentley, 'Eight Sermons Preached at the Hon. Robert Boyle's Lecture in the Year MDCXCII', in A. Dyce (ed.), *The Works of Richard Bentley* (London: Francis Macpherson, 1838) vol. iii, 175.

[12] William Derham, *Physico-Theology: or a Demonstration of the Being and Attributes of God, from His works of Creation* (London: Innys, 1713), 112, 54–5.

[13] William Phillips, *An Outline of Mineralogy and Geology* (London: Printed and sold by William Phillips, 1815) 193, 191; William Paley, *Natural Theology* (London: Printed for R. Faulder, 1802). The *Bridgewater Treatises* formed a series of natural theological works produced during the 1830s, in according with the will of the Earl of Bridgewater, the aim being to illustrate the argument of Divine Design.

[14] See Charles C. Gillispie, *Genesis and Geology: A Study in the Relations of Scientific Thought, Natural Theology, and Social Opinion in Great Britain, 1790–1850* (Cambridge, MA.: Harvard University Press, 1951); John Hedley Brooke, *Science and Religion: Some Historical Perspectives* (Cambridge University Press, 1991).

Hail, old *Patrician* Trees, so great and good!
Hail, ye *Plebeian* underwood!

sang Abraham Cowley in 1668, anticipating Burke's paean to the 'great oaks which shade a country'.[15] Just as in the body politic, everything had its place and purpose in Nature, its meanings and morals. Where diseases were endemic, God had surely planted natural remedies. The Revd Edmund Stone's discovery in the 1760s of the therapeutic properties of another tree, willow bark—the first stage on the road to aspirin—arose in part because he was piously confident that wetlands would yield cures for, as well as causing, rheumatism; a vindication of all-is-for-the-best Optimism of which Dr Pangloss might have been proud.[16]

All the environment was thus a stage—in his popular natural history Oliver Goldsmith extolled the 'great theatre of His glory'—and, if God was the Celestial Artist, Nature was properly to be appreciated through painterly eyes, as a backdrop designed to elicit seemly responses.[17] 'After tea we rambled about for an hour, seeing several views', recorded the blue-stocking Elizabeth Montagu in 1753, 'some wild as Salvator Rosa'. Where did this tea party experience their Rosian *terribilità*? Just outside Tunbridge Wells.[18]

This representation of Nature as an ideal habitat arose in part because Addison's generation, that class of '88 which gloried in the Glorious Revolution, had inherited a profound environmental crisis which it zealously combatted. 'The opinion of the World's Decay is so generally received', George Hakewill had observed in 1630, 'not onely among the Vulgar, but of the Learned, both Divines and others'.[19] Reformation commentators had affirmed the old Classical tropes and Biblical prophecies: this vale of tears was a wreck, old and decrepit; the end of the environment was nigh.[20]

---

[15] Edmund Burke, *Reflections on the Revolution in France* (London: J. Dodsley), 76; Abraham Cowley, 'Of Solitude' (1668), in John Sparrow (ed.), *The Mistress with Other Select Poems of Abraham Cowley* (London: Nonesuch Press, 1926), 178. The metaphor of the 'great oaks' occurs in Edmund Burke, *Reflections*.

[16] Miles Weatherall, *In Search of a Cure: A History of the Pharmaceutical Industry* (Oxford University Press, 1990), 10.

[17] Oliver Goldsmith, *A History of the Earth and Animated Nature* (London: Printed for J. Nourse, 1774) i, 401.

[18] Charlotte Klonk, *Science and the Perception of Nature: British Landscape Art in the Late Eighteenth and Early Nineteenth Centuries* (New Haven/London: Yale University Press, 1996), 9.

[19] George Hakewill, *An Apologie* (2nd edn) (Oxford: printed by William Turner, 1630; first published 1627), Preface.

[20] Gordon Davies, *The Earth in Decay* (London: MacDonald, 1969); Y.-F. Tuan, *The Hydrologic Cycle and the Wisdom of God: A Theme in Geoteleology* (University of Toronto Press, 1968).

Everywhere, champions of *mundus senescens* had declared, the climate was deteriorating, the soil was growing exhausted, and pestilences were multiplying. Originally, insisted Thomas Burnet in his *Sacred Theory of the Earth* (1684), the face of the Earth had been as smooth as an eggshell; but the very existence of mountains, and, furthermore, their perpetual denudation, showed that all was cracking up, becoming reduced to a pile of 'Ruines and Rubbish'; nowadays what man inhabited was a *'little dirty Planet'*, a superannuated sphere, punishment for original sin.[21] (figure 1.1)

If Burnet's prose resonated with Baroque oratory, rhetorically trilling on the motif of mutability, others could point to environmental decay of a wholly tangible kind: collapsing cliffs, landslips, earthquakes, volcanic eruptions, silting estuaries and the like. At home John Evelyn deplored smoke pollution and deforestation, while abroad, as Richard Grove has brilliantly shown in his *Green Imperialism*, observers on Barbados and other new colonies were alarmed at how rapidly slash-and-burn defor-estation and plantation monocultures like sugar-cane brought on droughts, flash-floods, and devastating soil erosion, turning once fertile terrains arid.[22] Original sin and modern greed together explained what many diagnosed as the symptoms of a planet terminally sick.

But such theological eco-pessimism came under challenge. The Glori-ous Revolution enthroned a new regime which professed to stand for freedom, order, prosperity, and progress; and its apologists, for instance the Boyle Lecturers, provided environmental visions that vindicated the new governmental order by naturalizing it. Like the political settlement of 1688, and all the more so the Hanoverian succession of 1714, the natural order now became praised for its stability: the 'grand design of Providence', deemed the Newtonian geologist and physician, John Woodward, was thus the 'Conservation of the Globe' in a 'just aequilibrium'.[23]

In his *An Essay Towards a Natural History of the Earth* (1695), Wood-ward frankly admitted that events like the Deluge *prima facie* suggested 'nothing but tumult and disorder':

---

[21] Thomas Burnet, *Sacred Theory of the Earth*, translated from the 1681 Latin original (London: Printed by R. Norton, 1684–90), quoted in Glacken, *Traces on the Rhodian Shore* (Berkeley: University of California Press, 1967), 411.

[22] John Evelyn, *Silva: or A Discourse of Forest Trees* (York: Printed for J. Dodsley, 1776. first published 1662); see also Richard Grove, *Green Imperialism. Colonial Expansion, Tropical Island Edens and the Origins of Environmentalism 1600–1800* (Cambridge University Press, 1995).

[23] John Woodward, *An Essay Towards a Natural History of the Earth* (London: Printed for R. Wilkin, 1695), 30, 32. See the discussion in M. C. Jacob, *The Newtonians and the English Revolution, 1689–1720* (Ithaca, NY: Cornell University Press, 1976).

FIGURE 1.1   The title-page of Thomas Burnet's *The Sacred Theory of the Earth*, 1697. (Reproduced by kind permission of The Wellcome Institute Library, London.)

yet if we draw somewhat nearer, and take a closer prospect of it . . . we may there
trace out a steady hand producing . . . the most consummate order and beauty
out of confusion and deformity . . . and directing all the several steps and periods
to an end, and that a most noble and excellent one, no less than the happiness of
the whole race of mankind.[24]

As with England, the Earth's turbulent revolutionary career was over;
all was now equilibrium, the body terrestrial was healthily balanced; and
the final global revolution—the Deluge—had been constructive not puni-
tive, a 'Reformation' introducing a new 'constitution' 'into the Government of the Natural World'. Through that revolution the Lord had
transformed mankind 'from the most deplorable Misery and Slavery, to
a Capacity of being Happy', by rendering the post-diluvial Earth nig-
gardly, thereby forcing man to labour by the sweat of his brow, and
compelling industry.[25]

Eighteenth-century geological theorists further insisted that the laws
of Nature governing the globe were 'immutable' and 'progressive', and
familiar phenomena were reinterpreted in the light of design.[26] Decom-
posing mountains had formerly been taken as dysfunctional, betokening
environmental catastrophe; now their positive uses were stressed—'the
plains become richer, in proportion as the mountains decay', explained
Goldsmith.[27] No mountains, no rainfall, no fertility, argued a new generation of physical geographers, dishing the ecological doomsters. The
Scottish physician and geologist, James Hutton (figure 1.2), showed in
his *Theory of the Earth* (1795) how decomposition of mountains produced the detritus which, flowing down the rivers to form the seabed,
would, millions of years hence, become the basis of new strata, whose
ultimate decay would once again form rich soil, and so on, in endless
cycles. Likewise with volcanoes and earthquakes, a sore topic after the
calamitous Lisbon earthquake of 1755: all such apparently destructive
processes were actually integral to the operation of Nature. Hutton
insisted that the globe was self-sustaining and self-repairing, forming an
enduring habitat, perfect for man.[28] (figure 1.3.) Praising him, a reviewer
observed the switch from eco-gloom to eco-glory: 'the dreary and dismal

[24] John Woodward, *An Essay Towards a Natural History of the Earth* (London: Printed
for R. Wilkin, 1695), 35.

[25] Ibid. 61, 94.

[26] Roy Porter, 'Creation and Credence: the Career of Theories of the Earth in Britain,
1660–1820', in B. Barnes and S. Shapin (eds), *Natural Order* (Beverly Hills: Sage, 1979),
97–123.

[27] Oliver Goldsmith, *A History of the Earth and Animated Nature* (London: Printed
for J. Nourse, 1774), i, 163.

[28] See James Hutton, *Theory of the Earth*, 2 vols (Edinburgh: Cadell, Davies & Creech,
1795). T. D. Kendrick, *The Lisbon Earthquake* (Methuen: London, 1956).

FIGURE 1.2   An etching of James Hutton by J. Kay, 1787. (Reproduced by kind permission of The Wellcome Institute Library, London.)

view of waste and universal ruin is removed, and the mind is presented with the pleasing prospect of a wise and lasting provision for the economy of nature'.[29]

The Enlightenment's new environmental vision married Newton and Locke. Along with this law-governed Earth-machine went a Lockean

[29] Jean Jones, 'James Hutton's Agricultural Research and his Life as a Farmer', *Annals of Science*, xlii (1985), 573–601.

FIGURE 1.3   An illustration from James Hutton's *Theory of the Earth*, 1795.
(Reproduced by kind permission of the British Library, London.)

possessive individualism that rationalized the Divine donation of dominion through a labour theory of property and value: man had the right,
divine and natural, to appropriate the Earth and its fruits.[30] The Biblical
mandate to man to master the Earth and multiply was thereby given
rational sanction. The age of Donne had seen mutability—'tis all in
pieces'—and the Puritan Saints had anticipated the apocalyptic over-
throw of Anti-Christ in fire and floods; but from the 1690s the environment was philosophically stabilized.[31] Both pious Christians like John
Ray and later Deists like Hutton portrayed a steady-state terrestrial
economy, rather as Adam Smith would deem the free-market economy
optimal. Illustrating these views, Goldsmith depicted the Earth as a
godsent 'habitation', a mansion for the Lord's tenant to enjoy—on condition he toiled to improve his estate, for:

    [30] C. B. Macpherson, *The Political Theory of Possessive Individualism: Hobbes to Locke*
(Oxford University Press, 1964, 1983); Anthony Pagden, *Lords of all the World: Ideolo-
gies of Empire in Spain, Britain and France c. 1500–c. 1800* (New Haven: Yale University
Press, 1995).
    [31] G. Williamson, 'Mutability, Decay and Seventeenth Century Melancholy', in *idem,
Seventeenth Century Contexts* (London: Faber & Faber, 1961), 73–101; V. I. Harris, *All
Coherence Gone* (London: Frank Cass, 1966); Christopher Hill, *Antichrist in Seventeenth
Century England* (Oxford University Press, 1971).

while many of his wants are thus kindly furnished, on the one hand, there are numberless inconveniences to excite his industry on the other. This habitation, though provided with all the conveniences of air, pasturage, and water, is but a desert place, without human cultivation.

A world thus furnished with advantages on the one side and inconveniences on the other, is the proper abode of reason, is the fittest to exercise the industry of a free and a thinking creature.[32]

So: the Earth was not in crisis, it was a self-adjusting system, governed by universal laws and made for man. Latitudinarian Anglicanism backed such thinking: God was Benevolent, the Devil was *de facto* discredited (there might be a *ghost*, but there certainly were no *gremlins*, in the machine). And this environmental philosophy propped the politics of the Hanoverians: God was the architect of natural order rather as Walpole was the manager of political stability.[33]

And more than stability, *improvement*. As was long ago maintained by Weber and Tawney, Protestant theology highlighted the individual's duty of self-realization; cultivating Nature promised spiritual improvement no less than daily bread. Authors had few qualms about man's right—his duty even—to harness Nature, 'bringing all the headlong tribes of nature into subjection to his will', according to Goldsmith, 'and producing . . . order and uniformity upon earth'.[34] Had not the noble Lord Verulam proclaimed 'Knowledge itself is power' and that 'the end of our foundation is . . . the enlarging of the bounds of human empire, to the effecting of all things possible'. Through natural philosophy, maintained Joseph Glanvill, reiterating Bacon, 'nature being known . . . may be mastered, managed, and used in the services of humane life'.[35]

Such views, of course, underwrote what Europeans had anyway been doing to the environment for centuries, clearing the forest, embanking, ploughing, planting, mining. Draining and deforestation were praised for freeing the land from dankness and disease, and so turning wasteland into wealth. But radical and feminist historians have recently reproved the aggressive, macho element in Baconian thinking, for replacing notions of

---

[32] Oliver Goldsmith, *A History of the Earth and Animated Nature* (London: Printed for J. Nourse, 1774), i, 400.

[33] See W. M. Spellman, *The Latitudinarians and the Church of England* (Athens, GA: University of Georgia Press, 1993).

[34] Oliver Goldsmith, *A History of the Earth and Animated Nature* (London: Printed for J. Nourse, 1774), i, 401; Max Weber, *The Protestant Ethic and the Spirit of Capitalism* (London: Allen & Unwin, 1930); Richard Tawney, *Religion and the Rise of Capitalism* (New York: Harcourt Brace, 1926).

[35] Francis Bacon, 'Of Heresies', in J. Spedding, R. L. Ellis, and D. D. Heath (eds), *The Works of Francis Bacon*, 14 vols (London: Longman, 1857–74) vii, 253; *idem*, *New Atlantis*, in ibid. iii, 156. Joseph Glanvill, *Plus Ultra* (London: Printed for James Collins 1668), 87.

Mother Earth with a new vision of Nature exploited, raped, and forced to yield up her fruits. Human Dominion must not be hindered by sentimentality: 'Know that by nature', Descartes wrote, 'I do not understand some goddess or some sort of imaginary power. I employ this word to signify matter itself'. 'The veneration wherewith men are imbued for what they call nature', grumbled Robert Boyle in a similar anti-superstitious vein, 'has been a discouraging impediment to the empire of man over the inferior creatures of God: for many have not only looked upon it, as an impossible thing to compass, but as something of impious to attempt'. An end to such scruples![36]

It is right to note these strains of environmental violence, but they must be kept in perspective. For the key paradigm of man's relation to the environment in the Georgian age was not conflictual but cooperative, indeed georgic. 'I have now placed thee in a spacious and well-furnish'd World', the botanist John Ray imagined God informing mankind:

I have provided thee with Materials whereon to exercise and employ thy Art and Strength . . . I have distinguished the Earth into Hills and Vallies, and Plains, and Meadows, and Woods; all these Parts, capable of Culture and Improvement by Plowing, and Carrying, and Drawing, and Travel, the laborious Ox, the patient Ass, and the strong and serviceable Horse . . .[37]

Once the Deity had explained to man his place in the divine scheme of things, Ray reflected upon God's assessment of what might be called the Divine Assessment Exercise:

I persuade myself that the bountiful and gracious Author of Man's Being . . . is well pleased with the Industry of Man, in adorning the Earth with beautiful Cities and Castles; with pleasant Villages and Country-Houses; with regular Gardens and Orchards, and Plantations of all Sorts of Shrubs and Herbs, and Fruits, for Meat, Medicine, or Moderate Delight . . . and whatever differencth a civil and well-cultivated Region, from a barren and desolate Wilderness.[38]

---

[36] René Descartes, *Le Monde* in F. Alquié (ed.) *Oeuvres Philosophique de Descartes* (Paris: Garnier, 1973, 1, 349, quoted in Brian Easlea, *Science and Sexual Oppression: Patriarchy's Confrontation with Woman and Nature* (London: Weidenfeld & Nicolson, 1981), 72; Robert Boyle, 'A Free Inquiry into the Vulgarly Received Notion of Nature', in *The Works of the Honourable Robert Boyle* (London: A. Millar, 1744), iv, 363; for the critique see, e.g. C. Merchant, *The Death of Nature: Women, Ecology and the Scientific Revolution* (San Francisco: Harper & Row, 1980; London: Wildwood House, 1980); A. Kolodny, *The Lay of the Land: Metaphor as Experience and History in American Life and Letters* (Chapel Hill: University of North Carolina, 1975); Brian Easlea, *Science and Sexual Oppression: Patriarchy's Confrontation with Woman and Nature* (London: Weidenfeld & Nicolson, 1981).
[37] John Ray, *The Wisdom Of God Manifested in the Works of the Creation* (London: Printed for Samuel Smith, 1691), 113–14.   [38] Ibid. 484.

The model typically defining the proper relations between man and Nature was thus the farm. According to Ray's contemporary, Sir Matthew Hale, God was the great freeholder, the world his estate, and man his tenant. 'The end of man's creation', the Chief Justice explained in legal terminology, 'was to be God's steward, *villicus*, bailiff or farmer of this goodly farm of the lower world'. For this reason was man:

invested with power, authority, right, dominion, trust and care, to correct and abridge the excesses and cruelties of the fiercer animals, to give protection and defence to the mansuete and useful

—in short, 'to preserve the face of the earth in beauty, usefulness and fruitfulness'.[39] Everyone would have understood Hale's paternalistic metaphor of the good steward, be he in the Bible or in Bedfordshire. Nature would yield and yield well, but only if the principles of good husbandry were upheld: matching stock and crops to soils, adopting sound rotations, planning for long-term sustainability—quite literally, to use the Weberian metaphor, ploughing back the profits.[40]

Such images of stewardship—paternal rather than plundering—sanctioned action and ordained environmental ethics and aesthetics. Pioneering in this respect was the work of John Evelyn, whose *Silva: or A Discourse of Forest Trees and the Propagation of Timber in His Majesty's Dominions* (1662), condemned wasteful land practices, exposing how, so as to provide charcoal and pasture, 'prodigious havoc' had been wreaked through the tendency 'to extirpate, demolish, and raze . . . all those many goodly woods and forests, which our more prudent ancestors left standing'.[41] Evelyn's belief that economic growth depended on sound conservation practices set the tone for the new managerial approach to Nature widely advocated in the eighteenth century.

In such promotion no one was more tireless than Arthur Young (figure 1.4), farmer, traveller, author, editor of the *Annals of Agriculture* and finally Secretary of the new Board of Agriculture.[42] 'Agriculture', he proclaimed, 'is beyond all doubt the foundation of every other art, business, or profession', and he outlined the great commandment of agricultural improvement: 'Make two blades of grass grow where one grew before'. The formula? '*To cultivate* THAT *crop, whatever it be, which*

[39] Matthew Hale, *The Primitive Origination of Mankind* (London: printed by William Godbid, 1677), Sect. 4, ch. 8, 370.
[40] For an account of eighteenth-century agriculture see G. E. Mingay, *A Social History of the English Countryside* (London: Routledge, 1990).
[41] John Evelyn, *Silva: or A Discourse of Forest Trees* (York: Printed for J. Dodsley, 1776, first published 1662), 1.
[42] J. G. Gazley, *The Life of Arthur Young* (Philadelphia: American Philosophical Society, 1973); G. E. Mingay (ed.) *Arthur Young and his Times* (London: Macmillan, 1975).

FIGURE 1.4   A portrait of Arthur Young. (Reproduced by kind permission of
The Wellcome Institute Library, London.)

produces the greatest profit VALUED IN MONEY'. The obstacle? The vicious circle of agricultural poverty with all its dire consequences: put little in and you would get little out.[43]

For Young and his supporters, the new agriculture promised a more efficient environmentalism than old farming. Common fields spelt waste—they were, he argued, a waste of Nature and hence of God's largesse, they were wasteful to individuals and the nation alike. Was it not revealing that the baulks and margins on the open fields were actually known as the 'waste'?[44] So the shift from what E. P. Thompson has called 'moral economy' to political economy, from partial usufruct to complete privatization, would end the waste of Nature and ensure the gain of all: 'The universal benefit resulting from enclosures, I consider as fully proved'.[45] The capitalist farm and the common fields thereby became parables of industry and idleness respectively. Young rode the nation, raising hymns to environmental betterment:

All the country from Holkham to Houghton was a wild sheepwalk before the spirit of improvement seized the inhabitants, and this glorious spirit has wrought amazing effects: for instead of boundless wilds and uncultivated wastes inhabited by scarce anything but sheep, the country is all cut into enclosures, cultivated in a most husbandlike manner, richly manured, well peopled, and yielding a hundred times the produce that it did in its former state.[46]

Wherever enclosure went, it did not merely improve the land. Though 'the Goths and Vandals of open fields' still touched 'the civilization of enclosures', enclosing had 'changed the men as much as it has improved the country':

When I passed from the conversation of the farmers I was recommended to call on to that of men whom chance threw in my way, I seemed to have lost a century in time, or to have moved 1,000 miles in a day.[47]

In this national drive, the captains of agriculture should rightly be the nobility, though they too must abandon notorious aristocratic waste:

[43] For the quotations see Arthur Young, *The Farmer's Letters to the People of England* (London: Printed for W. Nicoll, 1767), 84, 3.

[44] J. M. Neeson, *Commoners: Common Right, Enclosure and Social Change in England, 1700–1820* (Cambridge University Press, 1993).

[45] Arthur Young, *The Farmer's Letters to the People of England* (London: Printed for W. Nicoll, 1767), 91. For 'moral economy', see E. P. Thompson, *Customs in Common* (London: Merlin, 1991). For the history of enclosure, see M. Turner, *English Parliamentary Enclosure: Its Historical Geography and Economic History* (Folkestone: Dawson, 1980); *idem*, *Enclosures in Britain, 1750–1830* (London: Macmillan, 1984).

[46] Arthur Young, *A Six Weeks' Tour Through the Southern Counties of England and Wales* (London: Printed for W. Nicoll, 1768), 21.

[47] Arthur Young, *View of the Agriculture of Oxfordshire* (London: Printed for R. Phillips, 1809), 36.

'never forget that there is fifty times more lustre in the waving ears of corn, which cover a formerly waste acre, than in the most glittering star that shines at *Almack's*'.[48] Yet the basic message was simplicity itself: 'He, who is the BEST FARMER, is with me the GREATEST MAN': presumably Farmer George was meant to read that.[49]

Many echoed Young's sentiments. James Hutton was concerned not just with geology but with agriculture too: indeed he saw these twin disciplines as land economy in its natural and human dimensions respectively. Likening a well-run farm to the cycles of Nature, Hutton saluted agriculture as the paragon of the relationship between humanity and nature, and science as the key to its perfection: for through agronomy man becomes 'like a God on earth . . . and commands this species of animal to live, and that to die, this species of plant to grow, and that to perish'.[50]

With over two thousand enclosure Acts and more than six million acres of land affected, enclosure and progressive agriculture in general presented a model of proper environmental superintendence, wedding profit to paternalism, yet also incorporating cherished values. Traditional arcadian, pastoral myths could be accommodated—Nature as spontaneous bounty and harmony:

> O the Pleasure of the Plains,
> Happy Nymphs and happy Swains,
> Harmless, Merry, Free, and Gay,
> Dance and sport the Hours away.
> For us the Zephyr blows,
>   For us distils the Dew,
> For us unfolds the Rose,
>   And Flowers display their Hue,
> For us the Winters rain,
>   For us the Summers shine,
> Spring swells for us the Grain,
>   And Autumn bleeds the Vine.[51]

---

[48] Arthur Young, *The Farmer's Letters to the People of England* (London: Printed for W. Nicoll, 1767), 306. For the involvement of the nobility in progressive agriculture, see G. E. Mingay, *English Landed Society in the Eighteenth Century* (London: Routledge & Kegan Paul, 1963).

[49] Arthur Young, *A Six Months' Tour Through the North of England*, 4 vols, 2nd edn (London: Printed for W. Strahan, 1771), i, 1, xiv.

[50] James Hutton, *An Investigation of the Principles of Knowledge, and of the Progress of Reason, from Sense to Science and Philosophy*, 3 vols (Edinburgh: Printed for A. Strahan and T. Cadell, 1794), ii, 483.

[51] For the poetics of the bucolic, see Raymond Williams, *The Country and the City* (London: Chatto & Windus, 1973); for pastoral painting see Ann Bermingham, *Landscape and Ideology: The English Rustic Tradition 1740–1860* (Berkeley: University of

Thus the chorus in Handel's *Acis and Galatea*. A quasi-physiocratic doc-
trine could also be grafted on—Nature as the root of all value, or, in
Adam Smith's dictum, 'the land constitutes by far the greatest, the most
important, and the most durable part of the wealth of every extensive
country'.[52] And finally the Protestant ethic would serve as fertilizer:
labour consecrated private gain into a public and ecological good. Hence
it became the received wisdom under Farmer George that what was good
for farming was good for the nation; a friend of England was a friend of
the Earth. Robert Andrews, Esquire, and his new bride, Frances, surely
agreed: ownership, affluence, and aesthetics clearly coalesced in their
politics of landscape, as famously painted by Gainsborough. Lords of
all they surveyed, no waste ground, no wretched paupers and poachers,
and not even any happy Nymphs encroached upon their power and
privacy.[53]

Yet this vision of environmental bounty, if primarily Whig and patrician, was not exclusive to the privileged. It could equally serve the pro-
grammes of progressives who saw the economy of Nature supporting the
march of mankind. 'Three-fourths of the habitable globe, are now uncultivated', commented the scandalized William Godwin, rationalizing the
Biblical 'go forth and multiply' into a political programme for radical
advance. Properly managed, Nature would sustain boundless human
improvement: 'Myriads of centuries of still increasing population may
pass away, and the earth be yet found sufficient for the support of its
inhabitants'.[54] Not just that, but for Godwin and many others whose
thinking had been touched by Montesquieu's environmentalism, the
domestication of Nature furthered the civilizing process—for wild environments bred uncouth people. While Addison and Steele's *Spectator*
was polishing the urban bourgeoisie, agriculture was sowing civility in
the shires.[55] This formed a cosy consensus that remained in place until

California Press, 1986); Christiana Payne, *Toil and Plenty. Images of the Agricultural
Landscape in England 1780–1890* (London: Yale, 1993); Nigel Everett, *The Tory View of
Landscape* (New Haven: Yale University Press, 1994).

[52] Adam Smith, *An Inquiry into the Nature and Causes of the Wealth of Nations*
(London: Printed for W. Strahan and T. Cadell, 1776), i, 304; Stephen Copley and Kathryn
Sutherland (eds), *Adam Smith: 'The Wealth of Nations'* (Manchester University Press,
1995).

[53] For discussion of Gainsborough's painting, see Denis Cosgrove and Stephen Daniels
(eds), *The Iconography of Landscape: Essays on the Symbolic Representation, Design and
Use of Past Environments* (Cambridge University Press, 1988, 1989); John Berger *et al.
Ways of Seeing* (London: British Broadcasting Corporation, 1972); Andrew Graham-
Dixon, *A History of British Art* (London: BBC, 1996).

[54] William Godwin, *An Enquiry Concerning Political Justice* (London: Printed for
G. G. J. and J. Robinson, 1793), quoted in Clive Ponting, *A Green History of the
World* (London: Sinclair-Stevenson, 1991), 150.

[55] Roy Porter, 'Medical Science and Human Science in the Enlightenment', in C. Fox,
R. Porter, and R. Wokler (eds), *Inventing Human Science: Eighteenth Century Domains*

dynamited by Malthus' *Essay on Population* (1798). Parson Malthus'
version of the eco-system as a zero-sum game did not only deflate revolutionary utopians; it amounted to an abandonment of entrenched
broad-church assumptions about how environmental management guaranteed human progress.[56]

I have been arguing that the Georgian apologists represented the environment as a farm, promoting policies for the responsible management of
natural resources for private profit and long-term public benefit. The
mastering of the wild was a source of pride:

> I sing Floods muzled, and the Ocean tam'd,
> Luxurious Rivers govern'd, and reclam'd
> Waters with Banks confin'd, as in Gaol,
> Till Kinder Sluces let them go on Bail;
> Streams curb'd with Dammes like Bridles, taught t'obey,
> And run as strait, as if they saw their way.[57]

—a verse celebration of the draining of the Fens, penned by Sir Jonas
Moore, Charles II's Surveyor-General of the Ordnance: and one need not
be a devout Foucauldian to catch the tenor of this fantasy of the great
confinement of Nature.[58] Taming the wilderness remained a favourite
theme. 'When we behold rich improvements of a wild and uncultivated
soil', enthused the Cumbrian chauvinist John Dalton:

we are struck with wonder and astonishment, to see the face of Nature totally
changed. It carries an air of enchantment and romance: and the fabulous and
luxuriant description, given us by the Poet, of yellow harvest rising up instant-
aneously under the wheels of the chariot of Ceres, as it passed over the barren
deserts, hardly seems . . . too extravagant an image to represent the greatness and
seeming suddenness of such a change.[59]

(Berkeley: University of California Press, 1995), 53–87; Norbert Elias, *The Civilizing
Process*, 1, *The History of Manners* (New York: Pantheon, 1978); 2, *Power and Civility*
(New York: Pantheon, 1982); 3, *The Court Society* (New York: Pantheon, 1983); James
Dunbar, *Essays on the History of Mankind in Rude and Cultivated Ages* (London: Printed
for R. Strahan, 1780).

   [56] Thomas Robert Malthus, *An Essay on the Principle of Population as it Affects
the Future Improvement of Society, With Remarks on the Speculations of Mr Godwin, M.
Condorcet, And Other Writers* (London: J. Johnson, 1798); M. Turner (ed.), *Malthus and
his Times* (Basingstoke: Macmillan, 1986).

   [57] Jonas Moore, *The History of Narrative of the Great level of the Fens, called Bedford
Level* (London: Printed for Moses Pitt, 1685), 72.

   [58] Colin Jones and Roy Porter (eds), *Reassessing Foucault: Power, Medicine and the
Body* (London: Routledge, 1994).

   [59] John Dalton, *A Descriptive Poem Addressed to Two Ladies at Their Return From
Viewing the Mines at Whitehaven* (London: J. & J. Rivington, 1755), iii.

But as the wild was being rendered both profitable and pleasing, a question mark arose against another aspect of the environment: the garden, traditionally a rather formal and often walled appendage to the country seat.[60] Growing affluence and ambition promised to change that: why think small in an age of aristocratic aggrandizement marked by ever statelier homes? 'May not a whole Estate', sugggested Addison, 'be thrown into a kind of garden by frequent Plantations ... A man might make a pretty Landskip of his own Possessions', that is, create the impression that one's property stretched boundlessly throughout Nature, an illusion enhanced by William Kent's invention of the ha-ha.[61] But that modest proposal merely compounded the problem of the garden, since it seemed to muddle or destabilize the distinctive elements of the estate.

So long as Nature had worn a wild air, its antonym, the garden, was bound to be orderly, hence the classical formal gardens of the Renaissance with their Euclidean plans, mazes, hedges, alleys, and statuary, seemingly echoing model cities, and serving as citadels, protecting civilization against the horrid wilderness. But as Nature itself became regularized into a farm, geometrized by the parliamentary surveyors' charts and chains, the artificial garden inevitably lost its compelling rationale. Yet with Nature tamed, wildness itself could at last become aesthetically prized, rather as, once Enlightened elites had divested themselves of belief in witchcraft and diabolical possession, the supernatural was ripe for repackaging in Gothic novels and ghost stories.

Repudiating what were increasingly denounced as the claustrophobic regimentation of the Italian garden or the barren symmetries of La Notre's Versailles, the English garden was refashioned to follow Nature, abandoning its overt artifice and manicured paraphernalia. The great house would abandon the formal garden and would hide the home farm and kitchen garden out of sight. Inspired by Capability Brown, a generation of gardeners fostered a new Arcadian escapism by turning the great house into an island lapped by a sea of parkland, whose austere simplicity—mere turf, tree clumps and sheets of water—could pass for Nature thanks to the art that conceals art.[62] The cultural psychology underlying

---

[60] On English gardening and landscaping, see Christopher Hussey, *English Gardens and Landscapes, 1700–1750* (London: Country Life, 1967); C. Thacker, *The Wildness Pleases: The Origins of Romanticism* (London: Croom Helm, 1983); Tom Williamson, *Polite Landscapes: Gardens and Society in Eighteenth-Century England* (Stroud: Sutton, 1996).

[61] Joseph Addison, *The Spectator* 414, in D. F. Bond (ed.) *The Spectator* 5 vols (Oxford: Clarendon Press, 1965) iii, 551–2; for the ha-ha, see C. Thacker, *The Wildness Pleases: The Origins of Romanticism* (London: Croom Helm, 1983), 32–3.

[62] For Capability Brown, see Tom Williamson, *Polite Landscapes: Gardens and Society in Eighteenth-Century England* (Stroud: Sutton, 1996), 77–99.

this new departure was perfectly understood by that great Victorian gardener, John Claudius Loudon:

As the lands devoted to agriculture in England were, sooner than in any other country in Europe, generally enclosed with hedges and hedgerow trees, so the face of the country in England . . . produced an appearance which bore a closer resemblance to country seats laid out in the geometrical style; and, for this reason, an attempt to imitate the irregularity of nature in laying out pleasure grounds was made in England . . . sooner than in any other part of the world.[63]

Tastes never stand still; Brown was soon being mocked in his turn as one obsessed with shaving, trimming, and cropping, and his successors, notably Humphry Repton and Richard Payne Knight, while upholding his touchstone of artless nature, took it to its logical conclusion; paying court to fancy, they unashamedly brought wildness right up to the house itself by waving 'the wand of enchantment' over the estate, as is urged by Marmaduke Milestone, the Reptonian landscaper in Peacock's *Headlong Hall*, who promised to impart 'a new outline to the physiognomy of the universe'.[64] Some predictably found this new proximity of naked Nature threatening. 'Knight's system appears to me the jacobinism of taste', muttered Anna Seward, deploring the 'uncurbed and wild luxuriance, which must soon render our landscape-island as rank, weedy, damp and unwholesome as the incultivate savannas of America'.[65]

Yet this new noble savagery in landscaping was hard to resist completely, since it was sanctioned by a sea change in taste. 'The wildness pleases', Lord Shaftesbury had declared at the beginning of the century, 'We . . . contemplate her with more delight in these original wilds than in the artificial labyrinths and feigned wildernesses of the palace'.[66] And such judgements, with their plausible, Whiggish, liberty-loving credentials, wrought great change in the aesthetics of the environment.

Take mountains. The *mundus senescens* trope had regarded them as pathological, Nature's pimples. Joshua Poole's poet's handbook, *English Parnassus* (1657), commended some sixty epithets for mountains, many expressing distaste—'insolent, surly, ambitious, barren, . . . unfre-

    [63] J. C. Loudon, *The Suburban Gardener and Villa Companion* (London: Printed for the author, 1838), 162.

    [64] For Payne Knight see Marilyn Butler, *Peacock Displayed* (London: Routledge & Kegan Paul, 1979), 30f. 6; see also Richard Payne Knight, *The Progress of Civil Society: In Six Books* (London: printed by W. Bulmer & G. Nicol, 1796); David Garnett (ed.), *The Novels of Thomas Love Peacock* (London: Rupert Hart-Davis, 1948), 'Headlong Hall', 22.

    [65] A. Constable (ed.), *The Letters of Anna Seward, 1784–1807*, 6 vols (Edinburgh: A. Constable, 1811), iv, 10.

    [66] Shaftesbury, *The Moralists* (1709), quoted in C. Thacker, *The Wildness Pleases: The Origins of Romanticism* (London: Croom Helm, 1983), 12.

quented, forsaken, melancholy, pathless', and so forth. What Marjorie Hope Nicolson has dubbed 'mountain gloom' lingered long: as late as 1747 the *Gentleman's Magazine* judged Wales 'a dismal region, generally ten months buried in snow and eleven in clouds'.[67]

The aesthetic elevation of mountains owed something to the much mocked critic John Dennis, who championed Longinus. While describing the Alps as 'Ruins upon Ruins', he could relish their 'tremendous' and 'dreadful' qualities.[68] Within a generation, responses had turned to awestruck admiration. 'Not a precipice, not a torrent, not a cliff but is pregnant with religion and poetry', fluttered Thomas Gray, crossing the Alps in 1739.[69] Such an ennoblement was possible because mountains could be validated through the lenses of art, perceived rather as paintings than as mere natural objects: thus Horace Walpole: 'Precipices, mountains, torrents, wolves, rumblings, Salvator Rosa'.[70] Indeed, the very essence of the Picturesque creed, theorized in the 1780s by William Gilpin, was that the test of a scene lay in how well it actualized the qualities constituting a fine painting.[71] The true challenge, however, to the entrenched aesthetics of civilized order came with Edmund Burke's *Philosophical Enquiry into our Ideas of the Sublime and the Beautiful* (1757), which extolled the stupendous, rugged and bleak and all else productive of 'ideas elevating, awful and of a magnificent kind'. Crags, precipices and torrents, windswept ridges, unploughed uplands—all now became the acme of taste, precisely because they had not been ruled and refined by human hand.[72] 'Compared to this

---

[67] See Joshua Poole, *English Parnassus* (London: Printed for Tho. Johnson, 1657), 137–8; *The Gentleman's Magazine* (1747), quoted in David Pepper, *The Roots of Modern Environmentalism* (London: Croom Helm, 1984), 80; Marjorie Hope Nicolson, *Mountain Gloom and Mountain Glory: The Development of the Aesthetics of the Infinite* (Ithaca, NY: Cornell University Press, 1959).

[68] John Dennis, cited in C. Hussey, *The Picturesque* (London: F. Cass & Co., 1967), 87.

[69] Paget Toynbee and L. Whibley (eds), *The Corespondence of Thomas Gray*, 3 vols (The Clarendon Press, 1935), i, 128.

[70] Horace Walpole (letter to Richard West, 28 September 1739), in W. S. Lewis (ed.), *The Yale Edition of Horace Walpole's Correspondence* (New Haven: Yale University Press, 1948), xiii, 181.

[71] For William Gilpin, see Malcolm Andrews, *The Search for the Picturesque: Landscape Aesthetics and Tourism in Britain, 1760–1800* (Stanford, CA.: Stanford University Press, 1989); Stephen Copley (ed.), *The Politics of the Picturesque: Literature, Landscape and Aesthetics since 1770* (Cambridge University Press, 1994); Walter John Hipple, *The Beautiful, the Sublime, and the Picturesque in Eighteenth-century Aesthetic Theory* (Carbondale: Southern Illinois University Press, 1957).

[72] Edmund Burke, *Philosophical Enquiry into the Sublime and the Beautiful* (sl: sn, 1757), 52. For Burke see Tom Furniss, *Edmund Burke's Aesthetic Ideology: Language, Gender and Political Economy in Revolution* (Cambridge University Press, 1993); Samuel H. Monk, *The Sublime: A Study of Critical Theories in Eighteenth Century England* (Ann Arbor: University of Michigan Press, 1960).

what are the cathedrals or palaces built by men!', rhapsodized Sir Joseph Banks on seeing Fingal's Cave; and he supplied the answer to his own question:

mere models or playthings, imitations as diminutive as his works will always be when compared with those of nature. What is now the boast of the architect! regularity the only part in which he fancied himself to exceed his mistress, Nature, is here found in her possession, and here it has been for ages undescribed.[73]

Through suchlike sentiments there emerged what has been called natural supernaturalism, the Romantic and neo-pagan notion that Nature is sacred and 'measureless to man', feelings perhaps mirrored in Goethe's use of the term 'a friend of the earth', and the new respect for living beings evident, say, in the vegetarianism of Shelley's *Vindication of Natural Diet* (1813).[74]

The cult of the sublime threatened aesthetic disorientation; and what constituted choice scenery was being called into question at precisely the moment when the countryside itself was experiencing a disturbing intrusion: heavy industry. If caves, crags, and chasms could be sublime and hence objects of taste, what about furnaces and factories? Two sites in particular became laboratories for this aesthetic experiment: Shropshire and Derbyshire. 'Coalbrookdale itself is a very romantic spot', commented Arthur Young, still on his travels, in 1785:

it is a winding glen between two immense hills . . . all thickly covered with wood, forming the most beautiful sheets of hanging wood. Indeed too beautiful to be much in unison with that variety of horrors art has spread at the bottom: the noise of the forges, mills, &c. with all their vast machinery, the flames bursting from the furnaces with the burning of the coal and the smoak of the lime kilns, are altogether sublime.[75]

---

[73] Joseph Banks in T. Pennant, *A Tour in Scotland, and Voyages to the Hebrides*, 2 vols (vol.1, Chester: Printed for J. Monk; 2, London: B. White, 1774–6), ii, 262. For Banks, see John Gascoigne, *Joseph Banks and the English Enlightenment: Useful Knowledge and Polite Culture* (Cambridge/New York: Cambridge University Press, 1994).

[74] Percy Bysshe Shelley, *Vindication of Natural Diet* (London: Printed for J. Callow by Smith & Davy, 1813).

[75] For Young see *Annals of Agriculture and Other Useful Arts*, 46 vols (London: Arthur Young, 1784–1815) iv, (1785), 166–8; Barry Trinder, *The Industrial Revolution in Shropshire* (Chichester: Phillimore, 1973); Francis D. Klingender, *Art and the Industrial Revolution*, ed. A. Elton (London: Paladin, 1975; 1st edn, 1947); Ann Bermingham, *Landscape and Ideology: The English Rustic Tradition 1740–1860* (Berkeley: University of California Press, 1986), 79; Humphrey Jennings, *Pandaemonium: the Coming of the Machine as Seen by Contemporary Observers 1660–1886*, eds Mary-Lou Jennings and Charles Madge (New York: The Free Press; London: Andre Deutsch, 1985).

The agronomist's aesthetic bafflement is what we might expect. Anna Seward, being a poet, had more definite ideas. She was no enemy to industry, enthusing about Birmingham, where 'Hedges, thickets, trees, upturn'd, disrooted' had been improved into 'mortar'd piles, the streets elongated, and the statelier square'—that is, urbanization and industry created civilization. But the right place for industry was in town, and her tone changed when she turned to once-lovely Shropshire:

> O, violated COLEBROOK! . . .
> —Now we view
> Their fresh, their fragrant, and their silent reign
> Usurpt by Cyclops;—hear, in mingled tones,
> Shout their throng'd barge, their pondr'ous engines clang
> Through thy coy dales; while red the countless fires,
> With umber'd flames, bicker on all thy hills,
> Dark'ning the Summer's sun with columns large
> Of thick, sulphureous smoke.[76]

John Sell Cotman's 1802 watercolour, *Bedlam Furnace, near Madeley*, suggests a similarly disapproving judgement on a nearby industrial site. Here industry clearly ravaged nature—indeed forged Bedlam. The Romantic conviction was gaining ground that industry wrecked the environment, both in actuality and in its aesthetic capabilities.[77]

Industrial Derbyshire too became a spot of aesthetic controversy. Its economy and beauties found many champions, notably Joseph Wright, who painted vocal worthies like the cotton spinner Richard Arkwright, and also renowned locations: Dovedale, Matlock High Tor, and the Derwent valley with its caves, castles, mines, mineral springs, and factories (figures 1.5 and 1.6). Praising Wright's 'sweet and magic pencil', James Pilkington's *View of the Present State of Derbyshire* (1789) declared: 'Perhaps no country . . . can boast of finer scenes'. Wright's *Arkwright's Mill. View of Cromford, near Matlock*, shows nature and industry as twin sources of delight, complementing each other. The painter and theatre designer, Philip James de Loutherberg, in his sets for *The Wonders of Derbyshire*, staged in 1779 at Drury Lane, likewise sought to show how industry and dramatic scenery both partook of the sublime.[78]

[76] Sir Walter Scott (ed.), *The Poetical Works of Anna Seward* (Edinburgh: J. Ballantyne, 1810), ii, 314–15.

[77] Ann Bermingham, *Landscape and Ideology*, 80; see also Stephen Daniels, *Fields of Vision: Landscape Imagery and National Identity in England and the United States* (Cambridge: Polity Press, 1993).

[78] James Pilkington, *View of the Present State of Derbyshire* (Derby: Printed by J. Drewry, 1789), 49. For a major discussion of the above see Stephen Daniels, *Fields of*

FIGURE 1.5   Joseph Wright of Derby's watercolour of Dovedale, Derbyshire. (Reproduced by kind permission of Derby Museums and Art Gallery.)

FIGURE 1.6   Joseph Wright of Derby's oil painting of Matlock Tor, Derbyshire. (Reproduced by kind permission of the Fitzwilliam Museum, University of Cambridge.)

Not everyone was convinced. 'Speaking as a tourist', remarked the crusty traveller John Byng in 1790:

these vales have lost their beauty; the rural cot has given way to the lofty red mill . . . the simple peasant . . . is changed to an impudent mechanic . . . the stream perverted from its course by sluices and aqueducts.[79]

His indignation was equally great when he lighted upon 'a great flaring mill' in the 'pastoral vale' of Aysgarth:

All the vale is disturb'd; treason and levelling systems are the discourse; the rebellion may be near at hand . . . Sir Rd. Arkwright may have introduced much wealth into his family and into the country, but as a tourist I execrate his schemes.[80]

As is evident, for Byng, as for Anna Seward in her comments on picturesque landscaping, the creation of natural disorder was bound to be a licence for social disorder.

Byng's condemnations were endorsed by experts in the aesthetic. The landscape theorist, Uvedale Price, loved the 'striking natural beauties' of the River Derwent, and so deplored the factories erected on its banks near Matlock: 'nothing can equal them for the purpose of disbeautifying an enchanting piece of scenery'; 'if a prize were given for ugliness', he quipped, 'those factories would win'.[81]

More tellingly still, it even came to be argued that what had long been championed as agricultural improvement actually spelt environmental degradation and aesthetic impoverishment. Capitalist agriculture had always, of course, had its critics. Oliver Goldsmith's *The Deserted Village* damned the depopulating effects of enclosure; William Cowper censured the rural asset-stripping that enclosure unleashed: 'Estates are landscapes . . . gaz'd upon awhile and auctioneer'd away'; and John Clare later took up the charge.[82] But what is remarkable is that former enthusiasts also

Vision: Landscape Imagery and National Identity in England and the United States (Cambridge: Polity Press, 1993), 60f; Charlotte Klonk, *Science and the Perception of Nature: British Landscape Art in the Late Eighteenth and Early Nineteenth Centuries* (New Haven/London: Yale University Press, 1996).

[79] John Byng, *The Torrington Diaries*, ed. C. Bruyn Andrews, 4 vols (London: Eyre and Spottiswoode, 1934–8), ii, 194.

[80] Ibid. iii, 81.

[81] Uvedale Price, *Essays on the Picturesque*, 3 vols (London: printed for J. Mawman), i, 198.

[82] Oliver Goldsmith, *The Deserted Village* (London: W. Griffin, 1770); William Cowper, *The Task* (1785), Book III, Lines 755–6, in James Sambrook (ed.). *W. Cowper, The Task and Selected Other Poems* (London: Longman, 1994), 136; Roger Sales, *English Literature in History, 1780–1830: Pastoral and Politics* (London: Hutchinson, 1983); John Barrell, *The Idea of Landscape and the Sense of Place, 1730–1840: An Approach to the Poetry of John Clare* (Cambridge University Press, 1972); *idem, The Dark Side of the*

grew disgruntled. Even Arthur Young came to question his sacred cow, recognizing how improvement had made things worse for rural labourers: 'I had rather that all the commons of England were sunk in the sea, than that the poor should in future be treated on enclosing as they have been hitherto'.[83]

It is a crisis reflected in the career of Humphry Repton, after Capability Brown's death the leading designer of landscape parks. By 1800 embittered by difficulties and debts, his last work includes a homily on the irresponsibility of the landed interest. 'I have frequently been asked', he reflected:

whether the Improvement of the Country in beauty has not kept pace with the increase of its wealth ... I now may speak the truth ... The taste of the country has bowed to the shrine which all worship; and the riches of individuals have changed the face of the country.[84]

Repton illustrated these distasteful changes by coming up with a parody of his own technique. He had won fame through his 'Red Book', presenting clients and the public with 'Before' and 'After' scenes that showed the merits of landscaping. But now he contrasted the horrors of a recently 'improved' estate with the original, before it had been sold by its 'ancient proprietor' to one of the *nouveaux riches*.

The unimproved view was handsome. In the foreground an 'aged beech' shading the road, its branches pointing to a family reposing on a bench. A stile marks a public footpath through a park full of 'venerable trees'; on the right there is a wooded common. The impression is one of landed benevolence (figure 1.7).

All has been wrecked by the new owner, for whom 'money supersedes every other consideration':

By cutting down the timber and getting an act to enclose the common, [he] had doubled all the rents. The old mossy and ivy-covered pale was replaced by a new and lofty close paling; not to confine the deer, but to exclude mankind, and to protect a miserable narrow belt of firs and Lombardy poplars: the bench was gone, the ladder-stile was changed to a caution about man-traps and

Landscape: The Rural Poor in English Painting, 1730–1840 (Cambridge University Press, 1983).

[83] Arthur Young, *Annals of Agriculture and Other Useful Arts* 46 vols (London: Arthur Young, 1784–1815), xxvi, 214.

[84] Humphry Repton, *Fragments on the Theory and Practice of Landscape Gardening* (London: T. Bensley & Sons, 1816), 191.

There is a delightful spoof on Repton in Tom Stoppard's play *Arcadia*, in which the landscape gardener, Noakes, insists that 'irregularity' is 'one of the chiefest principles of the Picturesque style': *Arcadia* (London: Samuel French, 1993), 11.

IMPROVEMENTS

FIGURE 1.7   Illustrations from Humphry Repton's *Fragments on the Theory and Practice of Landscape Gardening*, c. 1816. The lower view shows the landscape before 'improvements'. (Reproduced by kind permission of the British Library, London.)

spring-guns, and a notice that the footpath was stopped by order of the commissioners.[85]

This *nouveau riche* was perhaps the model for Sir Simon Steeltrap in Peacock's *Crotchet Castle*, who, as 'a great preserver of game and public morals' had

enclosed commons and woodlands; abolished cottage-gardens; taken the village cricket-ground into his own park, out of pure regard to the sanctity of Sunday; shut up footpaths and alehouses.[86]

The environment has thus been ruined, both for the villagers and also for the spectator. Small wonder perhaps that John Constable was to declare, 'a gentleman's park is my aversion. It is not beauty because it is not nature'.[87]

William Blake too hated commercial capitalism, its metaphysical foundations (the evil trinity of Bacon, Locke, Newton) and its artistic toadies (Reynolds), its inhumanity and its ugliness. The poem popularly known as his 'Jerusalem'—actually the prefatory verses to his epic, *Milton*—looks back to England's green and pleasant land, contrasting it with the modern 'dark satanic mills'. But if that makes him sound like one of the aesthetic tourists I've just been mentioning, scouting round Coalbrookdale or Derwentdale, nothing could be further from the truth. Blake was a Londoner through and through, born in Soho, resident in Lambeth; indeed, as Peter Ackroyd has suggested, those dark satanic mills may well have been not Arkwrightian cotton factories but the steam-powered Albion flour mills, on the south bank opposite Blackfriars. And when Blake writes about the New Jerusalem, where in the green and pleasant land does he imagine it?

> The fields from Islington to Marybone,
> To Primrose Hill and Saint John's Wood,
> Were builded over with pillars of gold;
> And there Jerusalem's pillars stood.

Environments, as this Blakean coda shows, are imagined landscapes; ecology lies in the eye of the beholder. Eighteenth-century elite culture, I have tried to suggest, created environments of the mind and the soil that fantasized the harmony of human production and natural sus-

---

[85] Humphry Repton, *Fragments on the Theory and Practice of Landscape Gardening* (London: T. Bensley & Sons, 1816), 193.

[86] David Garnett (ed.), *The Novels of Thomas Love Peacock* (London: Rupert Hart-Davis, 1948), 'Crotchet Castle', 85.

[87] C. R. Leslie, *Memoirs of the Life of John Constable* (London: John Lehmann, 1949), 111.

tainability. Contradictions appeared, yet such a quest is one from which we cannot shirk. With Blake's call for 'Mental Fight' in mind, however, we must always remember that green issues—past, present, and future—may have more to do with crises of consciousness than with the countryside.[88]

[88] Peter Ackroyd, *Blake* (New York: Knopf, 1995); Jon Mee, *Dangerous Enthusiasm: William Blake and the Culture of Radicalism in the 1790s* (Oxford: Clarendon Press, 1992); William Blake, *Blake's Complete Writings*, ed. G. Keynes (Oxford University Press, 1966), 649, 480–1.

2

Environments Within:
An Ethnographic Commentary on Scale

Marilyn Strathern

SOCIAL ANTHROPOLOGY bases its practice on what we might call the unpredictability of initial conditions, unpredictable, that is, from the viewpoint of the observer. Ethnography, the kind of comprehensive account which gathers everything in, encourages the thought that one cannot predict at the outset of an enquiry where it will lead or what will turn out to be relevant to exposition. It also encourages the observer not to specify completely in advance where to look for the correlates and conditions of the outcomes he or she observes, and thus to confront unpredictabilities in social life.

In the past, social anthropologists have produced all kinds of justifications for ethnographic comprehensiveness, such as the idea of holistic societies which had to be described in the round. But while the justifications nowadays appear theoretically flimsy, the practice is as important as it ever was. And it is particularly important in the study of environmental issues. The unfolding of complex interchanges 'between' culture and environment makes the observer repeatedly aware of 'the unpredictability of initial conditions': factors that may have momentous impact can, until the impact is known, seem small or obscure. Recent developments in Papua New Guinea afford an interesting illustration. In the spirit of the exercise, I begin at a point that might seem at the outset to have little bearing on environmental issues as such.

Acknowledgements. This paper is for Alfred Gell, who has illuminated many landscapes. My particular thanks to Kupi Kundil (Mrs Oiee) for letting me use a photograph of her as a young girl (figure 2.3). I am grateful for the comments of the Cambridge Department of History and Philosophy of Science on an earlier version, and in particular Simon Schaffer's observations with regard to measurement. Mark Mosko's elucidation of Bush Mekeo remains a source of inspiration. My thanks to Eric Hirsch for his comments. I should also add that this account presents several arguments made familiar, and in places controversial, by a substantial Melanesian anthropology that is not separately acknowledged here.

THE IMPORTANCE OF SCALE

The man in figure 2.1, who is from Mount Hagen in the Highlands of Papua New Guinea, was photographed more than thirty years ago.[1] He is gazing at inflation. Inflation has been the anthropologist's term for what was brought about by a massive influx of shells into the local economy following Australian pacification of the region. Pearlshells stream down the ceremonial ground from the men's house at its head.

Gold prospectors, administrative officers, and then missionaries of diverse persuasion flew in planeloads of shells of all kinds, with which they were able to obtain food in the form of root crops and pigs.[2] The goldlip pearlshell that had formerly circulated in often broken but highly prized pieces now became available as whole specimens and in great number. They were absorbed into people's transactions with one another. The effects were political as well as economic, there being a corresponding increase of occasions such as that illustrated in figure 2.1, clan displays of wealth in the context of a war compensation payment, given as recompense for help to allies and to both allies and enemies as recompense for loss.[3] Such payments acquired a momentum of their own, developing into reciprocal exchanges between groups who vied to outdo one another. Donors challenged recipients to make as good a return of wealth. If this served the pacification policy of the Australian administration in the 1950s and 1960s, it also served continuing clan assertiveness, expressed through the commemoration of losses suffered and injuries inflicted during battles now of course in the past. *The increase* of such occasions is well documented.

I doubt, however, if inflation is in this man's mind. He might, though, be reflecting on group strength, here evinced in the capacity to draw shells together and disperse them again, which mobilizes numerous connections among people. If he were a recipient, he might be counting them; but anyone may inspect their visible quality, their 'skin'.[4] Such shells are also worn on the donor's skin, and he himself has on his chest a bamboo

[1] The same photograph is described from a rather different perspective in M. Strathern (1993); both this (fig. 2.1) and fig. 2.3 appear in ch. 10 in M. Strathern (1999). This essay overlaps with, and is a companion paper to, chs 9 and 10 in that book.

[2] The goldlip pearlshell, particularly prized in Hagen, figured in bridewealth and mortuary payments, as well as homicide compensation, contexts in which pigs were also transacted; initially it was the only valuable which the expatriates could use to 'purchase' meat (live pigs). Cowrie and other types of shell were accepted for vegetable food and labour.

[3] The authority on such compensation payments, which he has documented over a 30-year period, is Andrew Strathern (e.g. 1971; and recently 1993, 1994).

[4] Küchler (1993: 94) explores a New Ireland conceptualization of 'skin' (in the context of landscape) not as surface but as something which has surfaced 'and is constructed in terms of a hidden, interiorised pattern'.

FIGURE 2.1 Spectators at a death compensation payment; Mount Hagen, Western Highlands Province, Papua New Guinea, 1964. (Photograph by the author.)

tally that records his own prowess in transactions—every slat indicating an occasion on which a set of eight (or ten) shells were given. Pigs would come in return for shells, and later return gifts of shells. In the 1960s, people took a keen interest in what we might call the exchange rates, and looked back to the days when one shell was equivalent to one pig. But rather than bemoaning the drop in value of individual items, they tended to regard themselves as more fortunate than their ancestors. Their sense of importance was in no way diminished. Instead, men became more demanding over the quality and quantity of specimens, their critical judgement keeping pace with the new opportunities. The shells *retained* their signification of wealth and strength. This was so until the late 1960s, when their value was overtaken by a second influx of wealth tokens, money.

Note the double process. The scale of wealth that poured into the New Guinea Highlands in those early years—at one point Highlanders were extracting from the tiny expatriate population shells of all kinds at the rate of half a million a month[5]—had repercussions on many aspects of political and economic life, and no historical account of the region can ignore the scale of the changes. At the same time, shells had an impact precisely because of what was kept constant: the value put on wealth as a sign of strength and the capacity that wealth revealed. For ambitious men in Hagen, this was above all the capacity to dispense or distribute wealth resources through ceremonial exchange, for that in turn was a sign of a commensurate ability to elicit or extract resources from others. Individual care and attention continued to be paid to each item; it was just that more shells circulated faster among more people.[6] Without this constancy, then, we cannot complete the description of the effects of increase. From any one person's perspective their power seemed expanded, for they brought more people into their orbit; yet the prominence which that power had in the past given to one or two persons who took the lead in such exchanges was now gained at costlier price. Keeping in place the ratios between wealth and prominence or wealth and strength took more resources. That meant both finding the extra wealth to do so, thereby

---

[5] Described in Hughes (1978: 315).

[6] Inflation in a 'commodity economy', based on productive consumption, implies a readjustment in the ratio of good and money to one another. What would inflation in a 'gift economy' (cf. Gregory 1982: 31), based on consumptive production, look like? Presumably, it would entail changes in the rates by which relationships are reproduced. Inflation in a gift economy might be defined as an increase in the quantity of items, goods or money, against the capacity of relations to absorb them (i.e., reproduce themselves by them). In short, relationships expand to meet the increased circulation of items. The result is not necessarily 'more relationships'—but the underlying premise of reciprocity or obligation in relationships evoked more frequently and at higher level of internal demand. So what is subject to increase are the occasions on which relations are activated.

increasing the scale of diverse enterprises, and keeping unchanged the value placed on wealth extraction as a sign of influence, and thus conserving the equation between the two.[7]

This no doubt sounds familiar enough. It introduces a query however. When does scale matter in our accounts of social life and when does it not? Or rather, is there any mileage to be gained from thinking about the relationship between the systemic effects of scale change on the one hand and on the other the capacity of systems to retain their features across different orders of scale? There is a reason for asking this question.

My little vignette from the 1960s presents a state of affairs long superseded by other events. Inflation has had its final effect; there are no shells in circulation these days. Yet that period ought to remain interesting as one of the pasts from which the present has come. The conditions for the present are there; the question is how to identify them. Can one actually seek and identify conjunctures which might make for unpredictability? We may have a case in point here. When parts of a system have been drawn into one vortex (scale changes introduced through the influx of shells have their own repercussions), while an essential part of the same overall system is behaving quite differently, drawing other elements towards it in its own vortex (sustaining a constancy of values that disregards scale), do we not start describing a particular kind of bifurcation? If so, then how the system develops will depend neither on the autonomy of the two separate trajectories, nor on a dialectical relation between them, but on a dimension somewhere between—on the conditions which make each the starting point for the form which the other takes. This is how I have been describing inflation. If inflation points to processes that are both scale-sensitive and scale-insensitive, it is entirely unpredictable how this combination will develop. Let me treat that period of inflation in the Highlands of the 1960s as a set of initial conditions for a present-day outcome. We shall see what that outcome is in due course.

Meanwhile, my question is: when does scale matter and when does it not?[8] Some of the variation between Papua New Guinean societies is

[7] Big men initially accomplished this by attempting to control the flow of wealth, drawing it to themselves and then making sure it went out of circulation (in truck purchases and the like).

[8] In this example, the question is addressed to the influx of shells and the constancy of their signification; it may of course be addressed to models of analysis. Consider, for example, Arizpe's plea that anthropologists focus 'on the dynamics of interculturality at different levels of magnitude: local, national, regional and global' (1996: 97), an appeal to scale. When she considers connotations of the global, however, she proffers a scale-effacing suggestion: 'the new "globality" is, in fact, a new "*locality*"' (1996: 89–90). She would find many anthropologists agreeing with both these observations.

germane to my argument, although this is not the place for detailed comparisons and I make no more than a gesture to the ethnographic record. In general, these are societies typically referred to as 'small-scale', without centralized polities, whose technologies are based on root crop horticulture, with greater or lesser emphasis on fishing, hunting, and sago-processing. People's perspectives are often heavily gendered; when I pointed out that it was a man who was gazing at the shells, I meant that to carry a gender inflection.

CULTURAL LANDSCAPES

Let me put some landscapes in your mind's eye.[9] Leaving aside the coast-line and island Papua New Guinea, there is great diversity on the main-land itself. Indeed, in some places the pictorial concept of landscape itself seems inappropriate. Forest and bush may press in on human settlement to the extent that it is impossible to get an overview at all—there is simply no overall vantage point. Elsewhere, by contrast, cleared land gives vistas over miles of empty man-made grassland or shows up dense settlement and cultivation.[10] Local variations also mean that a place like Mount Hagen in the central Highlands may contain within itself some of the differences encountered on larger scale, as is to be expected from a techno-logical regime of intensive cultivation that continuously cuts gardens from wooded areas also encouraged to regenerate.

Not all Papua New Guinean societies have that internal difference available to them. Alfred Gell comments on the unrelenting effect of living in a place where one could never get a view; one was always sur-rounded by 'the tactile, scented gloom of the forest'.[11] The difference between cleared and uncleared areas was restricted to village and garden, rarely affording a visual landscape more than a few metres. He remarks on similar conditions elsewhere in Papua New Guinea for the effect they have on iconicity in language; where auditory stimulation takes over from

[9] There has been a recent burgeoning of anthropological interest in the subject of land-scapes (e.g. Bender 1993; Tilley 1994; Hirsch & O'Hanlon 1995; Feld and Basso 1996). The phrase, 'cultural landscape', comes from the American geographer Sauer, quoted by Hirsch and O'Hanlon (1995: 9).

[10] Hirsch (1995c: 9–10) draws a contrast between two strikingly different attitudes towards the visibility of the landscape. Zafimanary in Madagascar (Bloch 1995) yearn for the panoramic view of the village set out clearly before them; when shamans from the Amazonian Piro (Gow 1995) gain a view of the landscape through dreams or other altered states they conceptualize trees and rivers as houses full of people.

[11] Gell (1995; and see 1975), writing of the Umeda of Sandaun Province, Papua New Guinea.

the visual, the sounds people make echo a landscape full of sound.[12] There
are other consequences. Dances are often at night, or inside a house, and
display is canopied as though it were taking place in a sounding chamber.
The dancers themselves may be half concealed or you may only half-see
them in firelight or torchlight.[13] The audience in turn is drawn into the
light shed by the fire or must crowd into the house where the performance is put on. There could not be a more dramatic contrast to the staged
visual displays of those Highlanders who expose themselves to the
midday sun on open air ceremonial grounds cleared for the purpose.
The congregation is limited only by the size of the dance ground. There
may be pockets of darkness, as in the decorations that conceal the
dancer's identity and the forest leaves that make him 'dark', but the
overall effect is of a vista, and dancers often form a straight line precisely
so that their number and extent is visible.

In these details we see how landscapes comprise environments of
human activity. Their features are drawn into the orbit of people's practices, and not least by regimes of economic exploitation. Social anthropologists working in Papua New Guinea have long been interested in the
relative 'development' of some landscapes by contrast with others. This
was particularly stimulated by the opening up of the Highlands in the
1930s, and the discovery of its high density populations, and indeed in
the 1960s and 1970s led to a Highlands-centric ethnographic view of the
island about which colleagues have been complaining ever since. As we
shall see, however, that centrism is not restricted to anthropologists.

We are dealing with obvious differences between regions in the scale
of human activity when it is measured in terms of land use, impact on
vegetation regimes, and so forth. Within regions we find micro gradients
of those same differences in the mix between hunting/gathering and sago-
processing and the cultivation of root crops, often registered in the size
of settlements.[14] One such scale is population density.[15] Many sago-
processing regimes support in the order of five to six persons—sometimes down to one or fewer—per km². Elsewhere, mixed taro and sweet
potato regimes may support populations ranging from eight to sixteen

---

[12] Notably Kaluli (Schieffelin 1976; Feld 1982); Foi (Weiner 1991). These all happen to
be 'low production' regimes (see later) in which sago-processing has an important
economic role, but I do not want to make too much of such dimensions.

[13] See Gell's drawing of the Umeda dancer (1975: 181), and Feld's photograph of the
half-seen Kaluli dancer (1982: pl. 7).

[14] These distinctions can be repeated at other scales; thus among the groups on the
Bosavi–Strickland area, there are observable micro differences between regimes based on
greater or lesser dependence on sago, hunting, and so forth.

[15] For examples of comparative work on population densities, see Modjeska (1982: 53),
Hyndman and Morren (1990: 17), Kelly (1993: 33).

persons per km². In the central Highlands, intensive sweet potato cultivation leads to densities in places well beyond 100 persons per km².
Roughly along this scale, domestic pigs increase in number and
importance.[16] One can construct gradients here in degrees of resource
exploitation and transformation.

This is one anthropological understanding of the concept of culture:
the workings of human activity as such. Whether one talks of economic
effort or ritual relations or horticultural techniques, culture is a register
of human enterprise. The effects of that enterprise vary. If we say the consequences are measurable 'on' the environment, we mean that what we
call 'environment' becomes the measure—provides a scale of sorts—for
the extent of activity. In these Papua New Guinea examples, scale is
evident to the observer in the contrasts between high and low production regimes and in changes in the area of land brought under cultivation
or the population it can support, features that become observable from
an overview of the whole country. In addition to that: in extended as
opposed to restricted landscapes, 'scale' may become locally or 'culturally' visible. In this sense, land exists as a culturally salient environment
for Hagen people, that is, as one in terms of which they construct scales
themselves. As we shall see, through its products land gives a measure of
its own extent and fertility. These in turn measure the scale of an individual's enterprise, as when people line up the pigs they have reared
(Figure 2.1 shows pig stakes in readiness). But this has introduced a
second sense which anthropologists give to the concept of culture.

Here culture lies in the value which people give to things and the concepts through which they express it. It involves the facility for imagining one's own conditions of life. Scales, whoever constructs them, are
thus cultural artefacts. At the same time, the observer would not give any
scale to the facility itself: culture lies in the repetition or replication of
ideas, and what gives a culture its internal richness are the different
junctures at which specific values are repeated and thus recognized
or encountered over and over again. This is the sense in which cultures
behave as self-referential systems.

Across Papua New Guinea, for example, ideas about energy and vitality are frequently linked to alternations in body states over time or in the
pattern of events. The body indicates the relative expansion and contraction of activity. This expansion and contraction itself occurs in all
kinds of contexts, themselves neither large nor small. There may, for
example, be periodic renewal of the vitality or fertility of plants and
animal life through rituals which gather together people otherwise

---

[16] The causal relationships are not, however, straightforward, see Lemonnier (1993).

scattered over the landscape.[17] Or people display their ability to concentrate energy within themselves and then disperse it again, as a clan may
celebrate the nubility of its daughters before sending them off in marriage. In order to effect the display, the preceding period of growth and
accumulation will be marked by behind-the-scenes activity; the shut
house or encircling garden fence are much repeated images of enclosure.
Only what is kept hidden will grow. The 'initiation' process which in
many societies (not Hagen) marks the passage to maturity invariably
involves seclusion and secrecy of a kind. This leads to a (culturally) salient
inference: what you see in public or on the surface of the skin is the effect
of growth that has occurred elsewhere.[18] 'Display' is the revelatory
moment at which that is communicated or imparted to others.

In Hagen this moment is captured in women's routine act of digging
tubers out of the ground in order to feed people—they are around her
in her mind so to speak—or the unpacking of an earth oven. The success
of those occasions where people gather depends both on a local appre-
hension of a scale effect, in that the more people the more vitality is displayed by the hosts, and on a sustained analogy, between concealment
and revelation and between growth and flow, that does not depend on
scale at all. And that analogy can be replicated over and again. Thus, the
men's house which draws people to the ceremonial ground is also the
conceptual source of the wealth that will stream from it, in the same way
as the man's own head is regarded as the fount of his inner, secret
prowess. The head may become the focus of enlargement, an object of
adornment centred by the plumage above as well as the aprons below, a
position which is sometimes repeated within the adornments themselves
which have their own centrepiece.[19] The relationship between revelation
and display was also in the past repeated between the sexes, it being men
who 'displayed' and women who, bar special occasions, were excluded.
When a woman in an enclosed garden is engaged in domestic production, this is a private and secluded domain of affairs kept from the public
eye, in the same way as shells are hidden in the men's house for private
deployment after a display.

In a series of associations of this kind, we might say that the analogies
have a self-similar quality to them. While across Papua New Guinea
the relationship between growth and flow, concealment and display,
concentration and dispersal, centre and periphery, is played out in

[17] See especially Hirsch (1995b) on the Fuyuge of the Papuan highlands. His argument
about the alternative modes of description which Fuyuge draw upon in recounting ritual
activity (at once specific and event-filled *and* generalized and timeless) gives a temporal
cast to the contrast between scale-sensitivity and scale-insensitivity.

[18] Biersack's original formulation (1982) has been substantiated in many other contexts
since (e.g. O'Hanlon 1989).

[19] See the photograph of the feathered plaque being inspected (Strathern 1997).

different transformations, there are also striking continuities (cf. Hirsch 1995a: 65). Many Papua New Guineans would recognize the image of vitality and growth in the Hagen simile of people thronging a ceremonial ground being likened to birds flocking to a fruit tree or, for that matter, to feathers fringing a headdress. The analogies on which such imagery is based flow across contexts. But where has the environment gone?

I have suggested two ways in which social anthropologists consider the concept of culture. One refers to human activity, to the organization of life and livelihood, whose consequences have a scale effect. It is scale-sensitive. Here we may imagine the environment just as landscapes have been imagined, as showing the impact of or limits to human enterprise, and as offering enablement to and constraints on it in turn.[20] The environment in this sense is definitely 'outside' or 'in interaction with' human activity; or rather, it is everything that registers the effect, and thus the extent or degree of that activity.[21] From a second understanding of culture, which anthropologists have in the past glossed with terms such as world view, ethos, or webs of significance, I take the extensibility of the imagination, and have focused on one characteristic, the fact that people's imaginings observe no scales. They are scale-insensitive. Analogies and values retain their relationships—equations or ratios between diverse elements—and thus their significance, across different domains of life regardless of the dimensions of an event; here the sense of an outside environment may disappear altogether.

I have hinted that Hagen people would share both understandings, at least to a degree. But in order to give full cultural weight to these Hagen understandings, and thus deal with them in their own terms, we need to approach them through other materials, and I choose materials from elsewhere in Papua New Guinea.

ENVIRONMENTS INSIDE AND OUT

It is almost tautologous to say that culture in the first sense, as the workings of human activity, requires exchange with the environment, a cycling of resources through the human community and back again.[22] This is a condition of survival.

The Mekeo, who live along the reaches of the Biaru River in lowlands

---

[20] A view which Tilley (1994) and the contributors to Bender (1993) and Hirsch and O'Hanlon (1995) take to task in diverse ways.
[21] Including the registration of 'no effect', as in the view of unchangeable natural constraints.
[22] For an excellent review, see Ellen (1982).

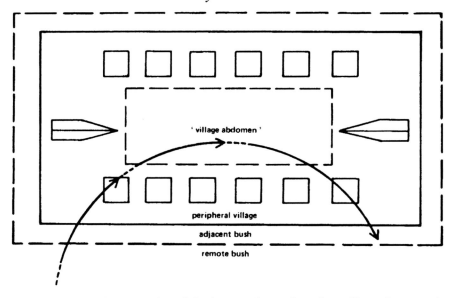

F I G U R E 2.2   Schematic plan of the layout of a Bush Mekeo village (from Mark Mosko *Quadripartite Structures*, 1985: 26, fig. 2.1). (Reproduced by kind permission of the author and Cambridge University Press.)

Papua New Guinea, have a wonderful diagram of this process in their village layout (see figure 2.2).[23] Clubhouses of the resident clan chiefs are built at each end, while domestic dwellings and other structures have been erected in parallel rows. In the centre is an area cleared of permanent features. The village is separated from the bush beyond. Indeed 'village' and 'bush' are conceptualized as distinct domains of activities and powers, and a well-defined croton hedge bounds the periphery of the village. The bush yields an array of resources, including garden food and hunting products. What is beyond the village is thus brought into the village for consumption, and wastes are thrown back into the bush. But Mekeo do not just draw a difference between village and bush: each is further divided, creating a series of zones that determine everyday activities. Food is brought from the remote bush to the village, not to the centre but to the peripheral dwelling houses where it is eaten in the evening, while the rules of waste disposal mean that in the early morning each villager makes his or her way to the bush, not the remote bush but the peripheral bush just over the fence, to empty their abdomens. When

---

[23] The so-called 'Bush Mekeo' of Central Province; I draw principally on Mark Mosko's (1985) original ethnography referring to the 1970s.

they return, they clean up the village, sweeping refuse into the centre plaza. The rubbish is piled up in the centre, before being carried to the edge of the village and dumped where human beings have also evacuated. It is as though the abdomen of the village were cleaned out too. Indeed, the central plaza is called just this: 'village abdomen'. What we might call the activity of extracting materials from the environment and then consuming them is thus visualized by Mekeo as a perpetual passage between bush and village, in which the village both consumes food and gets rid of waste, just as the human body does. The bush in turn yields produce and receives waste. The village models, we might say (Mekeo have already said it in other terms), 'culture' as the workings of human activity, and divides the world beyond the fence in the same way as the human habitation is divided.

But what might Mekeo imagine as the environment here? There is no measure of human activity beyond the activity itself. That is because these people have, as it were, focused on the exchange rather than the products. It would seem to be *the flow* of resources that interests them, imagined by them as a perpetual travelling back and forth.[24] The result is that whatever the observer might want to call the environment folds back on itself. And that in turn releases countless possibilities for imaginative extrapolation. The further result is a flow of analogies.

Consider the village plan again. We saw that waste is separated from produce within the village, even as the source of produce in the remote bush is separated from the adjacent bush where waste is deposited: the relationship between immediate and surrounding bush is repeated in the relationship between village periphery and village plaza. On the surface, it looks as though these indicate scale, degrees of distance from a centre that calibrates human activities. Certainly, the central plaza is used for feasting and other occasions when guests are brought into the village. However, Mekeo do not conceive of this as the centre of a centre or as the inmost part of the inside. On the contrary these zones fold in on themselves in interesting ways.

The relationship between bush and village is not quite as 'Euro-American'[25] observers might imagine: it is the bush that is categorically 'inside' and the village that is categorically 'outside'. It is as though the environment were within. To make this image intelligible, we have to think in terms of persons and their social identities.

---

[24] An observation Hirsch (1995a: 65) emphasizes apropos their distant neighbours, the Fuyuge, and see the discussion in Feld and Basso (1996).

[25] My term for a discourse derived largely from twentieth-century North American and Northern European cultures to which the language of analysis (such as the one in which this essay is written) belongs.

Imagine the bush as the closed territory of the tribe, an endogamous unit composed of people who are all related to one another; internal divisions within the tribe (into clans) means that people are also by virtue of clan affiliation rendered different from one another. Members of at least two clans live in each village, which is in this sense socially heterogeneous. Moreover, each village full of people is open to people from elsewhere with whom they have dealings and traffic of various kinds. As a place where people meet with, entertain, and visit others, then, the village is in social terms a microcosm of a heterogeneous 'outside' world. Think now of the alimentary tract through the body as taking in food from the outside, as Euro-Americans would say, and returning it there, as though those inner chambers were exposed to the outside.[26] Turn this imagery inside out, and think instead of food coming from the tribal territory as coming from a socially homogeneous, inside, place, and being brought outside into the socially heterogeneous village before being returned as waste to the inside bush. When Mekeo refer to the central plaza as the village's abdomen, they are envisaging this plaza as an 'inside' place homologous to the territory beyond the village. A qualification is that since the village as a whole is an 'outside' place, the centre (the 'abdomen') has to be the outside's inside (Mosko uses the phrase 'inverted outside', 1985: 27). And if the village abdomen is an inversion of (village) 'outside' space, the area over the fence is correspondingly an eversion of (bush) 'inside' space.[27] So the bush immediately adjacent to the village is distinguished from the more remote as a kind of everted region ('everted inside'). The relationship between inside and outside presents each as a version of the other.

This Mekeo attention to the flow of resources across different zones does not indicate an ecological model of human–environment exchange. The interchange is between 'places' endowed with distinct social identities.[28] Rather than imagining an 'environment' which registers human activity, Mekeo invite us to imagine a landscape of different zones ('places') which elicit different actions from people. Indeed, the bisected

[26] Mekeo also imagine degrees of openness, which they monitor through changes in body shape: both men and women undergo regimens of body fattening and fasting, going from less open to more open states. According to Mosko (1983) the way in which they perceive the body as open or closed to the outside world replicates the way in which persons are open or closed to influence from others. Bodies thus become registers of their interactions with persons from other clans and villages.

[27] 'By virtue of the daily transfers of objects between village and bush', writes Mosko (1985: 25), 'outside and inside domains are bisected by a reversal or inversion of each, such that the outside village has its own inside place (i.e. an inverted outside) and the inside bush has its own outside (i.e. an everted inside)'. I draw on this example in a further discussion of inside and outside places (M. Strathern 1998).

[28] I use 'place' here with the connotations Casey (1996) bestows on the term.

dualities are the spatial beginnings of a complex series of conceptual operations by which Mekeo visualize the interfolding nature of social relations.[29] The zones do not in themselves point to a scale based on distance, as a Euro-American might extrapolate from the notions of inside and outside. On the contrary, they are the basis of a series of analogies that disregard scale. It will come as no surprise to learn that the Mekeo body is bisected twice, divided into four regions, so that its own ingestion and egestion follows a pattern similar to that of the village, as does the whole Mekeo tribe. The clans to which I have referred compose four specific segments of the tribe between whom there are specific rules for flows of cross-generational transfers and intra-generational marriages.

CALIBRATIONS

In commenting on the bifurcation in the anthropologist's two senses of culture, the one scale-sensitive and the other scale-insensitive, I have imagined analogy as a kind of counterpart to scale itself. Both constructs offer possibilities of measurement: scale offers dimension and analogy offers comparison.[30] One might be forgiven for imagining them as belonging to separate traditions of knowledge. A Euro-American perspective includes interest in recording the extent of human achievement— what seems quintessentially an outsider's view—whereas Mekeo and other peoples construct what to outsiders seems like a symbolic universe replete with insides and outsides and flows of persons and things. Yet in the same way as Euro-Americans use many analogic devices in their quantifications, such as the dial or thermometer, so does dimension enter into the way Melanesians draw comparisons.[31] There are peoples who make most discriminating calculations of the number and size of items at their disposal, measurements evident in the exchange of things against one another and based on finely attuned notions of *equivalence*. There is also the reckoning of *compensatory values*, the idea for instance that one item (person) grows at the expense of another.[32]

[29] They concern kinship and affinal relationships, reproduction and marriage, supernatural powers, chiefship, and so forth. The fourfold spatial layout of bisected dualities evident in the relationship between village and bush is replicated over and over again in the involutions of social relationships.

[30] See, e.g. Donald (1991: 335f) on 'analog models' of time and space; analogies measure one dimension of reality in terms of another, as temperature may be recorded (measured) by a column of mercury. One may also think of relationships between values held stable in the form of an equation or ratio.

[31] I use 'Melanesian' rather than (in this case) Papua New Guinean as the counterpart to 'Euro-American' discourse.

[32] Argued with elegance by Biersack (1995).

In some areas of Papua New Guinea,[33] demonstrations of vitality may appear as a male ideology of virtue which rates men's activities in production and exchange a sacrifice, a matter of spending their energy on others, so a man can expect a gradual depletion of a life-force as it is imparted to the next generation, one body growing large as the other shrinks. There is a measurement of a kind here. As men grow old their life-force flows into others, so that the diminishing vitality of seniors is measured in the increasing vitality of juniors. The more vigorous the younger men, the more the older men have given evidence of their virtue in passing their vitality on. This is an analogic calculation between states imagined as the inverse of each other. A one-way flow across generations means that seniors are becoming empty, so to speak, as juniors are filled up. We can see a similar analogic calibration in the reciprocal exchanges of Mount Hagen, although instead of the process taking place over a lifetime, it takes place at much shorter intervals, in which men alternately put themselves into the position of being now donor and now recipient.[34] While from one point of view each is an alternative version of the other but at different temporal moments, at the same time each is also the measure of the other. The more the recipient receives the more he is challenged to give next time, and that occasion then becomes the retrospective measure of his first success. The obverse is the ability to deplete through injury.

Now whereas one body may afford a visible measure of another body, in the Hagen case measurement also lies in the visible wealth that passes between persons. Here the receiving body, so to speak, is rendered as large as the size of the gift. It is under these latter conditions that local conceptions of scale become significant. In social terms, the prominence of a man is measurable by the extent of his network, and networks extend with the gifts. People start making more of their calculations of size and number. For they are not just measuring the growth of persons through quantity of resources; they also measure certain resources by other resources—how many pearlshells for how many pigs. If land contains so many pigs and so much garden, the two quantities reflect each other. The size of the garden is planned in relation to the future demands on the pig herd. This is one of the ways in which scale becomes visible: land gives a measure of its own extent and fertility in its products (see figure 2.3).

---

[33] I base the following description largely on Etoro (Kelly 1993).

[34] What Kelly (1993: 146, my italics) says of life cycle processes in Etoro could also be said of Hagen exchange: 'The life-cycle processes of conception, growth, maturation, senescence, and death are attributed to the acquisition, augmentation, depletion, and loss of life force in these transactions [such as sexual intercourse]. In each instance, *a recipient's growth entails a donor's depletion*, such that one individual flourishes while another declines'.

However, these scaler measurements depend on analogic ones similar to those I have just described. Let me elaborate. Ethnographers of the central areas of the Papua New Guinea Highlands tend not to talk of life-force; they do talk of 'fertility' embedded in persons and pigs, and in land. It is as though it were not just through the rotted bodies and body fluids of their buried ancestors (Harrison 1988 quoted by Tilley 1994: 58) that land is made fertile, but as though life-force were now in the soil. In any event, land becomes conceived as a source of fertility. Evidence lies in turn in what the land grows, and it is regarded as growing people as well as pigs and plants. They all become carriers of land, portable manifestations of it, so that when you see a pig you see the food that the land has grown. These are analogic measurements. And there are others. One can assess soil quality by the growth of trees, tall trees also being analogues of male potency and ancestral support, while high crop yields and fat pigs are themselves indicative of ancestral favour. Fertility is thus given a measure of sorts. It leads to action; people estimating what gardens they must plant, given the expectations of a changing pig population, become conscious of what the land can support. That feeds back in turn into measurement of people. The amount of wealth a man attracts becomes an element in his very capacity to exchange, and thus his assessment by others; clans measure themselves, competitively, by the size of the war reparations they can muster and the amount of resources these indicate. We are back to scalar measurements.

In the 1990s, Hagen residents talked of (recent) population increase. They experienced their landscape—what they look out over—as over-crowded; complained that there were too many houses too visible all at once. Conversely, I heard it said that the wild spirits that once inhabited desolate places are now frustrated at having nowhere to hide. But land is also short because it is a measure of resources; through cash-cropping and vegetable marketing, land has become a source of money. One place, near Hagen town, is illustrative.[35] Here, the fertility of the soil is made visible by the abundance of the fresh vegetables it yields, and thus the income it earns; this in turn has had a direct impact on population, since clansmen and diverse relatives from other parts have flocked to build their houses and gardens there, a pressure the inhabitants relate directly to fertility of the soil. They are pleased that they should have attracted so many to them. While an analogic relationship between human and non-human fertility is thus held constant, resources are also being compared with other resources and a direct relationship perceived between scale of the influx of people and scarcity of land. So people attempt to

[35] Visited in 1995; I am grateful to the British Academy for the research grant which made the visit possible. These observations are expanded in some of the essays in M. Strathern (1999).

make the land yield more. There were some old gardens being redug for potatoes to sell to the fish-and-chip shop in Hagen town. As the fine, black peat soil was turned over, the owner poured out several bags of white chemical fertilizer to ensure a really lucrative crop. The more money spent on land, the more it should yield.

COMPENSATION

What should we make of the fact that Papua New Guinea has apparently become a nation of landowners? The term 'landowner' (pidgin *landona*) is used by nationals in negotiating royalties on minerals or timber extracted from the land. But some go much further, generously applying their claims to loss of access to all sorts of resources such as enjoyment of future development. We might think that this reflects some primordial or spiritual value attached to land itself; or might see, in their confrontation with mining companies and other outside interests, the shrewd grasp that Papua New Guinea politicians have of the wider environment of competitive world markets. While nationals frequently evoke tradition ('custom') in appealing to the depths of their association with land, they are also calling themselves 'owners' in an international language that gives them negotiating power. It would seem that the term 'landowner' is only about ten years old, and has emerged hand-in-hand with a new concept of resource compensation.

In 1994, the Law Reform Commission of Papua New Guinea embarked on a study of compensation and resources in relation to land, and I draw on one of the contributions. It also happens to be one of the most incisive pieces of writing about contemporary development in the area I have seen. In it, Colin Filer describes the brief life of the concept of landowner.[36]

The background is simple. Witnessing the inroads of foreign commercial ventures, of which the most visible are land-based mining and logging, the thought of company profit prompts people to construe the counter-idea of recompense.[37] By staking a claim to land through the idiom of ownership, local politicians and businessmen are sometimes able to persuade companies that they should be entering into some kind of

[36] From Filer (1997); there was an older circumlocution (*papa bilong graun*) which did not carry quite the same resonances.

[37] I deliberately put it this way round: evidence of what others have attracted to themselves (profit) seems to trigger the counterclaim. Filer notes how the idea of customary landowners has also generated the idea that the salient social grouping must everywhere be the 'clan'.

reciprocal transaction with them. They may argue that what is at stake is nothing less than social welfare. While an economist might call this the opportunity cost of lost subsistence production, nationals voice their claims as 'compensation' that will ensure their future development and security.[38] People imply that the loss of future benefit is like the loss recognized in Highlands compensation payments, whether these were for bodily injury arising from warfare or personal body payments for nurture. A fitting cultural appropriation, an anthropologist might say, *landona* is a hybrid term, appropriate to the end of the twentieth century, produced both by the new demands of post-colonial economics and by attempts to conserve local communities through appeal among other things to reciprocities in relationships. Traditional values meet world capitalism.

Colin Filer would have little of that. He flatly states that what is locally promoted as a division between indigenous economic principles and those that govern modern capitalist enterprise obscures a crucial link. Current use of 'compensation' as a 'concept in the politics of national resistance to the world economy' goes hand-in-hand with 'the growing dependence of the national economy on that specific form of compensation which economists call "resource rent"'. He comments that the lack of realism in demands for compensation

should not lead us to suppose that they are founded on an incorrect assessment of the [current] forces driving the economy.[39] For the popular [Papua New Guinean] perception of 'development' as the collection of a resource rent reflects the real historical tendency for an ever-increasing proportion of the national income to be obtained in this form [from outside companies]. (Filer 1997: 172)

Colin Filer refuses, then, to agree with the actors' current equation of compensation and tradition—and not only the local actors. Expatriate developers may be doing their best to package their relationships with landowners in forms of caring reciprocity, including 'traditional' compensation agreements intended to function as signposts to their mutual obligations, while, Filer adds, indigenous landowners are seeking their own private ways and means to remove elements of balance

---

[38] Filer is quoting here from the Lihir Mining Area Landowners Association.

[39] He points to people's (developers and landowners alike) failure to address the issue of power: 'Papua New Guineans may place a very high value on the possession and circulation of money but still deny that money and power may properly be used in pursuit of each other. And this denial, I would argue, is due to the fact that 'power' is not (yet) conceived in the Western manner, as something which, like money, can be a legitimate form of personal property, but in the 'customary' way, as something which is properly avoided, dissipated, multiplied or neutralised by the efficacy of moral agents' (1997: 181).

from the relationships and either ask for favours or resort to coercive hostilities!

That aside, and agreeing that payments were always made for damage done to bodies in the context of reproductive payments, he argues that there was no real precursor in 'custom' to treating land in this way. Despite its appeal to bodily compensation, resource compensation is new. Moreover, when one looks into the demands, claims to social embeddedness seem to evaporate. The demands, negotiations, and payments are contained within a matrix of landowner–developer relationships that are hard to pin down:

> [For] when we try to investigate or conceptualise the substance of their mutual conduct, we may find that we are no longer dealing with any actual pattern of relationships between real individuals in concrete social settings, but only with snatches of rhetoric which, like the abstract opposition of 'landowners' to 'developers', are applied to 'development discourse' in a certain type of public forum.   (Filer 1997: 174)

We are left with the rhetoric. So where is its power?

Now Filer's critique depends on acknowledging scale. He looks, for example, to 'actual' social relationships to substantiate Papua New Guineans' claims about social relations, an exercise that requires discrimination between different orders of fact. Indeed, that is the power of his account, a scale-sensitive attack on the way people insensitively run things together. They ignore the difference between interpersonal and interinstitutional arrangements and observe no scale at all in translating, as they do, sacred landscapes into lucrative ones. Nonetheless, it is also here that we see why the idea of compensation has such runaway effect.

The demands draw on both dimension and comparison. On the one hand, the sums seem exorbitant to developers, and indeed may be constrained only by what nationals imagine the developers can pay; on the other hand, both sides are caught up in a spiralling set of constructs or images as the nationals draw in all kinds of comparisons to make their point. The very concept of compensation has undergone a kind of inflation. Not only must the same satisfaction be obtained at increased cost, but there are new arenas for satisfaction and more reasons for demanding it.

One could thereby talk of an inflation in the range of activities to which the concept of compensation applies. It is not just in dealings with outsiders that Papua New Guineans try to extend notions of recompense from body payment to resource rent. The same is happening internally. To return to Hagen again: the Pidgin (Neo-Melanesian) term '*kompensesen*' covers a wider range of payments than any indigenous category did.[40] Hageners linked recompense for bodily harm with recognition of the energy and work that went into nurture; not only is an implicit category now made explicit but it has expanded to include interactions of all kinds. Where before separate terms discriminated between different payments and different ways of discharging obligations, the new mode shows a generic tendency. It has the potential to cover almost any negotiation of relational responsibility simply because the fundamental idea of recompense for bodily exertion can be so widely applied. All that has to be kept constant is reference to the body and expenditure of resources. This expansion (of these ideas) is facilitated by money, and in Hagen nowadays numerous relational transactions can be conducted through the idiom of money payments. In relation to resources, and in situations where quantity becomes a dimension of value, this leads to one very simple outcome. Whatever commands a price also triggers an analogic calculation. There is a new interest in land as the object of investment that commands a price, for the wealth (company profits) extracted from it can be taken as evidence of the 'wealth' (ancestral fertility) that has gone into it.

There is inflation, too, in the way in which the concept of compensation has spread across Papua New Guinea. The reader will recall the restricted landscapes I evoked at the beginning, societies in which there was nothing equivalent to the scope of Highlands (as in Hagen) political transaction and where land is not objectified in the same way in terms of its products.[41] Yet there, as elsewhere across the country, the human body is held to reveal in its activities inner resources of some kind or other. This notion keeps constant pace with notions of expenditure. In short, the Hagen-type idea that extracting wealth from others matches what has been extracted from one echoes those other growth/depletion regimes focused on the body. The significance of recompense (i.e., taking in and giving out) remains in place. Conversely, what applies to the vitality of persons also applies to the fertility of land. By the very token that fertility, like vitality, is a hidden quantity until it is revealed, it follows that anything that the land yields—oil, timber, gold—can be taken as evidence of inner resources.

Colin Filer refers to an area[42] where local people 'blend received notions regarding powerful spirits with rumours regarding the finding

---

[40] See A. Strathern (1993) on differences here in Hagen and Duna (to whom I refer briefly below) usage, and see Modjeska (1982: 55).

[41] Vigorously argued by Gell (1992).

[42] The Duna; the quotation is from Stürzenhofecker (1994: 27). Duna are a border Highlands society with labour-intensive gardening practices but a relatively low production economic regime in Modjeska's (1982) terms.

of oil resources, in such a way as to move from a picture of a sacred
landscape, whose fertility must be preserved for the future, to a picture
of an exploitable landscape available for manipulation by a company'
(1997: 172). Here, we see the power of analogy-making that observes no
scales. For those leaps and extrapolations are not just vague rhetoric; it
is the capacity to jump scale which makes people willing to take on 'new'
things in the first place. So what might have been initial conditions for
this ubiquitous state of affairs?

The kind of inflation that characterized 1960s Hagen was both scale-
sensitive and scale-insensitive. Here we are thirty years on. What we see
today is possibly one outcome: the bifurcation that Filer describes in
Papua New Guineans' attitudes towards resource-compensation. On the
one hand, it is *scale-insensitive*: landowners attempt to extract recompense from outside interests through appeal to general community
welfare, keeping constant the ratio between wealth and strength.[43] On the
other hand, very *scale-sensitive* indeed, they compete with their peers in
the quantity of resources they handle, on the basis of a thoroughly econ-
omistic rationing of their own time, money and patronage. As Filer puts
it, ' "landowners" seek deliverance from the same web of social obligations which serve to justify and mobilise support for "compensation"
claims' (1997: 156).

You might think I have been singularly careless about letting my own
field area, Hagen, occupy centre stage in this account. The Highlands—
let alone Hagen—is not Papua New Guinea. Indeed, Filer states that
there is little evidence that 'compensation' was a traditional form of material transaction in other parts of Papua New Guinea. To the contrary,
and this is the point, nationals may nowadays point to the Highlands as
the origin of the present pan-island category.[44] If Highlands-style compensation was a particular version of a more general phenomenon, a
reproductive model of body expenditure, it is a version that has become
something of a norm. At the same time, the basic image of body process
as a ceaseless giving out and taking in of resources was itself widespread.
These were not just traditional ideas waiting for modernity. They comprised the creative set of conditions for people's capacity to move along
two different trajectories at the same time, now making scale relevant to
the size of things and now making it not. For that reproductive model,

---

[43] I have underplayed the role of feelings and emotions as a factor in compensation
satisfaction.

[44] Filer himself points to two historical pushes from the colonial state; one was the
payment of war damages compensation after the Second World War in many coastal areas,
while the second was the administration backing given to Highlands war compensation
payments to encourage peacemaking between previously warring groups that I have been
describing here.

embracing all manner of bodily activity, was able to cross scales, that is, it could be replicated in all kinds of contexts. Perhaps, indeed, this insensitivity to scale was in certain systems the doorway to letting in its opposite—sensitivity to scale expressed in Highlands-style reckonings of gain and profit.

In certain systems: I have just been focusing on one. Hagen interest in size took a particular transactional form. People measured what they put in by what was taken out, and their own power to extract wealth was measured by the power of those who had extracted it from them in the first place. Such measurements of human activity were 'external' to one or other party by virtue of the distinct social identities of each: as we have seen, recognition of one person's body expenditure came from another. The accompanying concept of 'compensation' entailed the further calibration of resources by resources. And that particular idea of recompense could translate the perception of new and unprecedented possibilities into the widespread body idiom of vitality, growth, and depletion. No wonder the nation of landowners do not pitch their price according to some preconceived value of the land but scale up their demands according to the developers' ability to pay.

CONCLUSION

This is not the juncture at which to reflect on the inflationary components of the anthropologists' double construct, 'culture'. Its current ubiquity needs no further comment. All that remains to be added is that if its double senses suggest a dualism, let me repeat that this pair (the two senses of the concept of culture) is not binary, dichotomous, or dialectical. Rather, each element has its own complex trajectory. For the sake of the present topic, I have characterized the two trajectories as sensitivity and insensitivity to scale change. And that is because I want to say two things at once. Both of them are rather obvious, but worth reiterating. On the one hand, scale matters: to perceive the effects of human activity on a world imagined as an outside or encompassing environment is to take responsibility for such activities. It is equally the case, on the other hand, that scale does not matter: imagining the dimensions of that responsibility draws, as it were, the environment within ourselves. It is also a precondition for drawing within our compass societies such as those of Papua New Guinea, not 'small-scale' at all in terms of the analogical insights they afford.

Let me condense this argument in a final pair of images, and return to the question of unpredictability. Why should Hagen-type (Highlands) compensation have become, as it has in recent years, a kind of Papua New Guinean norm? If one can trace 'compensation' back to 'inflation', then what were the initial conditions for that?

Part of the longstanding technology of production (and still in use) was the string bag or 'net bag', used for transporting crops from the gardens that feed both human beings and pigs. Similar working bags to that depicted from Hagen (see figure 2.3) are found in many areas, including the Telefomin described by Maureen Mackenzie.[45] The two areas present different landscapes and different regimes of horticulture, these being based on taro in Telefolmin and sweet potato in Hagen. Taro generally supports a lower population than sweet potato and a whole language group might be no more than the size of one of Hagen's dozens of internal political units.[46] At the same time, these string bags contain a very similar spectrum of values. In Telefomin, women carry everything from babies to taro; taro plants are likened to children who have to be coaxed to grow, just as the sweet potato vines picked for further planting in Hagen are a reminder that people are planted in clan territories. Bags taken empty to the gardens each day return full. Hagen women thus carry on their backs both the yield of the land and the instrument by which that yield contributes to the rounding of the body's contours.[47]

There is a second set of initial conditions here. In neither area do men wear bags in the manner of women, any more than men carry out the range of women's tasks. However, one could not predict from these pieces of information how men actually separate themselves off from women or for that matter the form that their distinctiveness takes. Rather, in the way in which men both separate themselves from women and constantly make comparisons of their respective powers, we see another interesting conjuncture of trajectories. The two conjunctures behave differently in the two areas; they have, we might surmise, taken different directions.

Telefolmin men do sport bags but wear them on the nape of the neck or shoulders. Men use them primarily for carrying hunted meat and

---

[45] The Telefomin material is taken from Mackenzie's (1991) study of peoples from the Mountain Ok region of Papua New Guinea mediated through the particular attention she pays to the string bags that women make.

[46] In the Mountain Ok region, the entire population amounts to only 30,000. There are internal variations in reliance on taro and sweet potato, in the part that hunting and the collecting of wild foods plays, in soil quality and fallow cycle, and in the densities of populations so sustained. Indeed, the Mountain Ok area can be divided into internal regions according to differing horticultural regimes on a local basis—it even has its own 'Highlands', as it is known in the literature (Hyndman and Morren 1990). Variation between regions internal to the Mountain Ok thus repeat on a small scale the kind of variation one finds between the area as a whole and other parts of Papua New Guinea.

[47] On the swollen form of belly/bag, see Mackenzie (1991: 143).

FIGURE 2.3 A young girl, soon to be married, carries back from the gardens two string bags of sweet potatoes, to feed both pigs and family; Mount Hagen, 1967. (Photograph by the author.)

personal possessions, and whereas women take pains in manufacturing these bags (they make both men's and women's), men attend to ways of decorating what then becomes special male attire. Grades in the Telefolmin male initiation cult are marked by the type of feather men attach to the outside. Hagen men do not wear string bags at all.[48] If one were looking for an analogue, it might be the feathers that Hagen men attach to their wigs, which they ordinarily cover with a string covering referred to by the same name as the women's string bag. Here we encounter a significant divergence. The Telefolmin feather-covered initiation bag signals promise of what it holds within. Like the Hagen headdress, it is both a display and points to the containment of secrets. But what *in addition* Hagen men have within themselves they also objectify as the external wealth of their houses and the size of their pig herd. They have no need to wear containers on their persons. And there is no metaphorical limit to what they may thus 'contain'.

Of these two modes of male distinctiveness,[49] only the latter seems to have become the basis for present-day ideas about recompense and 'compensation'. The modes are not equivalent. Telefolmin men conserve an analogy between the reproductivity of women (the string bags) and the vitality of men (the feathers); Hagen men both keep a similar analogy and turn it into one in which quantity also plays a key part. The Hagen man in figure 2.1 does not offer a complete picture in himself: he is completed by the amount of shells or pigs or money he can command, in short, by the scale of his resources. That external measure is realized through a concept of compensation which, over the last sixty years, seems to have unfolded with great creative potential.

REFERENCES

Arizpe, L. (1996). 'Scale and interaction in cultural processes: towards an anthropological perspective of global change', in L. Arizpe (ed.), *The Cultural Dimensions of Global Change: An Anthropological Approach*. Paris: UNESCO Publishing.
Bender, Barbara (ed.) (1993). *Landscape: Politics and Perspectives*. Oxford: Berg.
Biersack, A. (1982). 'Ginger gardens for the ginger woman: rites and passages in a Melanesian society'. *Man*, 17: 239–58.

---

[48] Apart from little 'pockets' or tobacco pouches for personal items, or bags carried on special occasions in the context of all-male rituals.

[49] Epitomized in the regional contrast between vitality and fertility, or between initiation cults and ceremonial exchange, not developed here; for a sketch, see M. Strathern (1988).

Biersack, Aletta (1995). 'Heterosexual meanings: society, the body, and the economy among Ipilis', in A. Biersack (ed.), *Papuan borderlands: Huli, Duna, and Ipili Perspectives on the Papua New Guinea Highlands.* Ann Arbor: University of Michigan Press.

Bloch, Maurice (1995). 'People into places: Zafimanary concepts of clarity', in E. Hirsch and M. O'Hanlon (eds), *The Anthropology of Landscape: Perspectives on Place and Space.* Oxford: Clarendon Press.

Casey, Edward (1996). 'How to get from space to place in a fairly short stretch of time: phenomenological prolegomena', in S. Feld and K. Basso (eds), *Senses of Place.* Santa Fe: School of American Research Press.

Donald, Merlin (1991). *Origins of the Modern Mind: Three Stages in the Evolution of Culture and Cognition.* Cambridge, MA: Harvard University Press.

Ellen, Roy (1982). *Environment, Subsistence and System: The Ecology of Small-scale Social Formations.* Cambridge: Cambridge University Press.

Feld, Steven (1982). *Sound and Sentiment: Birds, Weeping, Poetics and Song in Kaluli Expression.* Philadelphia: University of Philadelphia Press.

Feld, Steven and Basso, Keith (eds) (1996). *Senses of Place.* Santa Fe: School of American Research Press.

Filer, Colin (1997). 'Compensation, rent and power in Papua New Guinea', in S. Toft (ed.), *Compensation for Resource Development in Papua New Guinea.* Boroko: Law Reform Commission (Monograph 6); Canberra: National Centre for Development Studies, Australian National University (Pacific Policy Paper 24).

Gell, Alfred (1975). *Metamorphosis of the Cassowaries. Umeda Society, Language and Ritual.* London: Athlone Press.

Gell, Alfred (1992). 'Inter-tribal commodity barter and reproductive gift-exchange in old Melanesia', in C. Humphrey and S. Hugh-Jones (eds), *Barter, Exchange and Value: An Anthropological Approach.* Cambridge: Cambridge University Press.

Gell, Alfred (1995). 'The language of the forest: landscape and phonological iconism in Umeda', in E. Hirsch and M. O'Hanlon (eds), *The Anthropology of Landscape: Perspectives on Place and Space.* Oxford: Clarendon Press.

Gow, Peter (1995). 'Land, people and paper in western Amazonia', in E. Hirsch and M. O'Hanlon (eds), *The Anthropology of Landscape: Perspectives on Place and Space.* Oxford: Clarendon Press.

Gregory, Christopher (1982). *Gifts and Commodities.* London: Academic Press.

Harrison, Simon (1988). 'Magical exchange of the preconditions of production in a Sepik River village', *Man*, 23: 319–33.

Hirsch, Eric (1995a). 'The coercive strategies of aesthetics: reflections on wealth, ritual and landscape in Melanesia', *Social Analysis*, 38: 61–70. (Special Issue: ed. J. Weiner, 'Too Many Meanings'.)

Hirsch, Eric (1995b). 'The "holding together" of ritual: ancestrality and achievement in the Papuan Highlands', in D. de Coppet and A. Iteanu (eds), *Society and Cosmos: Their Interrelation or Their Coalescence in Melanesia.* Oxford: Berg.

Hirsch, Eric (1995c). Introduction to E. Hirsch and M. O'Hanlon (eds), *The Anthropology of Landscape: Perspectives on Place and Space*. Oxford: Clarendon Press.

Hirsch, Eric and O'Hanlon, Michael (eds) (1995). *The Anthropology of Landscape: Perspectives on Place and Space*. Oxford: Clarendon Press.

Hughes, Ian (1978). 'Good money and bad: inflation and evaluation in the colonial process', in J. Specht and J. P. White (eds), *Trade and Exchange in Oceania and Australia, Mankind* (Special Issue), 11.

Hyndman, David and Morren, George (1990). 'The human ecology of the Mountain-Ok of Central New Guinea: a regional and inter-regional comparison', in B. Craig and D. Hyndman (eds), *Children of Afek: Tradition and Change among the Mountain-Ok of Central New Guinea*. Sydney: Oceania Monograph 40.

Kelly, Raymond (1993). *Constructing Inequality: The Fabrication of a Hierarchy of Virtue among the Etoro*. Ann Arbor: University of Michigan Press.

Küchler, Susanne (1993). 'Landscape as memory: the mapping of process and its representation in a Melanesian society', in B. Bender (ed.), *Landscape: Politics and Perspectives*. Oxford: Berg.

Lemonnier, Pierre (1993). 'Pigs as ordinary wealth: technical logic, exchange and leadership in New Guinea', in P. Lemonnier (ed.), *Technological Choices: Transformation in Material Cultures since the Neolithic*. London: Routledge.

Mackenzie, Maureen (1991). *Androgynous Objects: String Bags and Gender in Central New Guinea*. Chur: Harwood Academic Publishers.

Modjeska, Nicholas (1982). 'Production and inequality: perspectives from central New Guinea', in A. Strathern (ed.), *Inequality in New Guinea Highlands Societies*. Cambridge: Cambridge University press.

Mosko, Mark (1983). 'Conception, de-conception and social structure in Bush Mekeo culture', in D. Jorgensen (ed.), *Concepts of Conception, Mankind* (Special Issue), 14(1).

Mosko, Mark (1985). *Quadripartite Structures: Categories, Relations and Homologies in Bush Mekeo Culture*. Cambridge: Cambridge University Press.

O'Hanlon, Michael (1989). *Reading the Skin: Adornment, Display and Society among the Wahgi*. London: British Museum Publications.

Schieffelin, E. (1976). *The Sorrow of the Lonely and the Burning of the Dancers*. New York: St. Martin's Press.

Strathern, Andrew (1971). *The Rope of Moka: Big-men and Ceremonial Exchange in Mt Hagen, New Guinea*. Cambridge: Cambridge University Press.

Strathern, Andrew (1993). 'Compensation: what does it mean?', *Taimlain*, 1: 57–62.

Strathern, Andrew (1994). 'Crime and compensation: two disputed themes in Papua New Guinea's recent history', *PoLAR* [*Political and Legal Anthropology Review*], 17: 55–65.

Strathern, Marilyn (1988). *The Gender of the Gift. Problems with Women and*

Problems with Society in Melanesia. Berkeley and Los Angeles: University of California Press.

Strathern, Marilyn (1993). 'One-legged gender', *Visual Anthropology Review*, 9: 42–51.

Strathern, Marilyn (1997). 'Pre-figured features: A view from the Papua New Guinea Highlands', in J. Woodall (ed.), *Critical Introductions to Art: Portraiture.* Manchester: Manchester University Press.

Strathern, Marilyn (1998). 'Social relations and the idea of externality', in C. Renfrew and C. Scarre (eds), *Cognition and Culture: The Archaeology of Symbolic Storage.* Cambridge: McDonald Institute for Archaeological Research.

Strathern, Marilyn (1999). *Property, Substance and Effect: Anthropological Essays on Persons and Things.* London: Athlone Press.

Stürzenhofecker, Gabriele (1994). 'Visions of a landscape: Duna premeditations on ecological change', *Canberra Anthropology*, 17: 27–47.

Tilley, Christopher (1994). *A Phenomenology of Landscape: Places, Paths and Monuments.* Oxford: Berg.

Weiner, James (1991). *The Empty Place: Poetry, Space and Being among the Foi of Papua New Guinea.* Bloomington: Indiana University Press.

3

Ways of Placemaking

Fred R. Myers

However absolute the 'dreaming' significance of places may seem,
they were also always constituted ... within and through the range
of practices which linked people with places.

Francesca Merlan 1998

THE MEANINGFULNESS of 'place' in Aboriginal Australian cultural
life—as an index of a distinctive relationship between Aboriginal persons
and their behavioural environment—has been of significant interest to
cultural critics, New Age writers, to anthropologists (Jackson 1995), and
to politicians. It is well-known that hunter-gatherers have been regularly
depicted, both in the popular imagination and also in scholarly writing,
as in some way 'closer to nature' than modern Western people. As Lee
and Devore (1968) famously put it, hunting and foraging comprised the
human adaptation for 99.9 per cent of our history, and a fascination with
hunters-gatherers as the archetypal humans probably underlay the significance that the largely ecological studies of such societies had in recent
anthropology, valorizing research on this category of societies (Asch
1979; Myers 1988a; Wilmsen 1983). This variously evaluated relationship

Acknowledgments. I would like to thank Faye Ginsburg for her critical reading of
various drafts of this paper. She is not, of course, responsible for its flaws. I am also
indebted to Francesca Merlan for many conversations and the privilege of reading her
manuscript. Finally, I want to thank Howard and Frances Morphy for their close reading
and editorial comments on the revisions for publication.
   Research on which this essay is based was done over a long period of time. Grants from
the Australian Institute of Aboriginal Studies (1973–5, 1979, 1980–1), National Science
Foundation (1973–5), National Institute of Mental Health (1974–6), National Geographical Society (1988), National Endowment for the Humanities (1988), John Simon Guggen-
heim Foundation (1988), Research Challenge Fund of NYU (1991, 1993) all contributed
to the research. Portions of this paper draw on various other published and unpublished
work of mine, especially 'Place, identity, and exchange in a totemic system: Nurturance
and the process of social reproduction in Pintupi society' (in J. Fajans (ed.) *Producing
Exchange: Exchanging Products*. Oceania Monographs 43. Sydney: University of Sydney
Press 1993) and 'What is the business of the Balgo business?' (unpublished MS. 1982).

to nature, sometimes seen positively and sometimes negatively, has been central in the representation of such societies, whether they were denied to 'own land' as property because they appeared simply to dwell *in* nature and to wander over the land, as occurred in the legitimation of the original British dispossession of Aborigines (see Williams 1986; Wilmsen 1989); or whether they are understood as having a respect for the environment and the land as a place of dwelling, as has occurred in what John Morton (1989) understands as a form of modernist 'totemism' (see also Sackett 1991).

The best-known example of the latter is Bruce Chatwin's *The Songlines* (1987), but there are a surprising number of such popular representations in circulation which have become cult classics for New Age devotees. These range from Marlo Morgan's *Mutant Message Down Under* (1994)—an amazing fabrication of a supposedly true encounter with telepathic Aborigines that even more amazingly held its place on the *New York Times* bestseller list for twenty-two weeks—to Robert Lawlor's *Voices of the First Day* (1991), which stresses natural wisdom and something like an unmediated relationship between Aborigines and the natural world. Quoting from yet another mysterioso (Cowan 1989), Lawlor draws attention to the words of Big Bill Neidjie, an Aboriginal from Kakadu:

I feel it with my body, with my blood. Feeling all these trees, all this country . . . when the wind blows, you can feel it. Same for country . . . you feel it. You can look, but feeling . . . that put you out there in open space.   (Neidjie, quoted in Lawlor 1991: 237)

Chatwin's rendering of Aboriginal place-relations as 'songlines' has been exceedingly wide in its impact. Projecting his identification with the nomadic way of being, Chatwin explains through the voice of his narrator and his admirable cultural mediator Arkady:

how each totemic ancestor, while travelling through the country, was thought to have scattered a trail of words and musical notes along the line of his footprints, and how these Dreaming-tracks lay over the land as 'ways' of communication between the most far-flung tribes.   (Chatwin 1987: 13)[1]

And in another passage, much cited in reviews, Arkady explains:

In theory, at least, the whole of Australia could be read as a musical score. There was hardly a rock or creek in the country that could not or had not been sung. One should perhaps visualise the Songlines as a spaghetti of Iliads and Odysseys,

---

[1] Anthropologists and others are aware that the source of Chatwin's image, if not his inspiration, is T. G. H. Strehlow's (1971) magnum opus, *The Songs of Central Australia*.

writhing this way and that, in which every 'episode' was readable in terms of geology. (Chatwin 1987: 60)

The whole process of Aboriginal placemaking is translated as poetry, naturalized in its similarity to birds singing their territorial boundaries. Who wouldn't be taken with this image of alterity?

Such attraction to alterity is, of course, more than the New Age *Zeitgeist* of the present. Accounts by anthropologists, such as Elkin (1964: 79–80; 1969: 95–8), Maddock (1972: 27), and W. E. H. Stanner (1965), also emphasized that the essential association of the Aborigines with their land was religious, a 'spiritual kinship with the land' that Europeans have sometimes expressed as one in which 'the land owns the people as much as the people own the land' (see Williams 1986). Clearly, this formulation constitutes a rhetoric of contrast in which the usual Western/modern forms of domination over the natural environment—the reduction of 'dwelling' to commodity value—are not supposed to exist. It was also, ironically, a formulation which at one time was held by legal authorities to deny to Aborigines anything like rights of ownership to land (see Williams 1986; Wilmsen 1989).

Thus, a fascination with the nature of the supposed Aboriginal relationship to land, and a concern over its representation has arisen in this period no less because of the struggle within the Australian nation-state over the recognition of indigenous claims to land. This struggle dates back to the 1960s particularly, with the Gurindji walkout from Wattie Creek (Hardy 1968) and strike for land rights and the request from Yolngu people in Northeast Arnhem Land that the Australian government recognize their title to their clan land in the Gove Peninsula (Williams 1986). This request ended in Justice Blackburn's 1969 finding *against* native title (Williams 1986),[2] which was followed by the Woodward Commission's (Woodward 1973) inquiry into Aboriginal models of land tenure, the subsequent Aboriginal Land Rights (NT) Act of 1976, and finally the Mabo Decision. In this broad context, debates over the nature and representations of 'Aboriginal relationships to land' have been many (Bell 1983; Keen 1992, 1993; Jacobs 1996; Merlan 1991; Povinelli 1995; Weiner 1996). As the cases of Coronation Hill and Hindmarsh Island demonstrate, no less than the struggles over the meaning of now-

---

[2] Quoting Blackburn's ruling, Williams argues that the finding against native title was strongly influenced by accepting the anthropological metaphor of 'spiritual kinship with the land' to stand for the far more complex relations involved. Thus, Blackburn wrote: 'As I understand it, the fundamental truth about the aboriginals' relationship to land is that whatever else it is, it is a religious relationship. This was not in dispute. It is a particular instance of the generalization upon which I ventured before, that the physical and spiritual universes are not felt as distinct.' (Blackburn 1971: 167, quoted in Williams 1986: 162)

urban places such as the Swan Brewery site in Perth, they are a matter of concern beyond strictly academic theorizing.

DWELLING OR PLACE?

In recent years, the question of 'place' has received considerable attention in anthropology (Myers 1986a, 1988b; Weiner 1991; Feld and Basso 1995; Hirsch and O'Hanlon 1995; Ingold 1996). This concern was focused initially on the significance of the contrast between different cultural understandings of the environment. In the early 1970s, I conducted my initial research with Western Desert Aboriginal people on 'the self and its behavioural environment', in a perspective developed in the work of my former teacher, A. Irving Hallowell (1955). But Hallowell's earlier work tended to emphasize culture as a kind of neo-Kantian filter or grid projected onto the world. My engagement was more specifically with *practices*—with territorial organization and relationship to place.

In the preliminary chapter of my monograph on Pintupi-speaking people of the Australian Western Desert (Myers 1986a), I loosely identified these processes as a form of construction, as a 'culturalization of space'. My intuition in using that phrase was contrastive, the need to draw attention to how different peoples might 'see' different places in the same 'place',[3] a project akin to Hallowell's delineation of the 'behavioral environment' for the Ojibwa (1969). The untheorized assumption of 'space'—the three-dimensional, infinite grid—was the background against which distinct ethnotheories ('theirs' and 'ours') might provisionally be expressed. My own concern more broadly in the book was not merely interpretive, not merely an accounting or translation of the meanings Aboriginal people found or constructed in their environment, their country. Rather, I sought to present and analyse the social and political processes through which places were invested with meaning and value.

Two recent thoughtful discussions of 'place' have taken issue with my representation, each relying on a 'dwelling' perspective drawn either directly from Heidegger 1977, 1979, or from phenomenology more generally, which questions the apparent primacy given to 'space' over 'place' (see Casey 1995; Ingold 1993, 1996). Casey, for example, criticizes the (Enlightenment) presumption of a pre-existing medium of space and time

---

[3] I am indebted to Deborah Elliston for this formulation. I also recognize that the emphasis on 'seeing' would conform to the problem of possibly imposing what Heidegger regarded as a modern formulation (the 'world picture') on a very different metaphysics.

within which 'place' is produced. Instead, he argues, the phenomenologically prior experience is of distinctive and particular places, with 'being-
in-place'. Indeed, the 'very idea of space', he insists, 'is posterior to that
of place, perhaps even derived from it . . .' (Casey 1995: 16).

Equally concerned with the implications of the phrase 'culturalization
of space', Ingold (1996) takes particular issue with the primacy given to
'culture' and 'construction', arguing that:

hunter-gatherers do *not*, as a rule, approach their environment as an external
world of nature that has to be 'grasped' conceptually and appropriated symbol-
ically within the terms of an imposed cultural design, as a precondition for effective action. They do not see themselves as mindful subjects having to contend
with an alien world of physical objects; indeed, the separation of mind and nature
has no place in their thought and practice.   (Ingold 1996: 120)

He suggests:

we reverse this order of primacy and follow the lead of hunter-gatherers in taking
the human condition to be that of a being immersed from the start, like other
creatures, in an active, practical and perceptual engagement with constituents of
the dwelt-in world. This ontology of dwelling, I contend, provides us with a
better way of coming to grips with the nature of human existence than the alternative, Western ontology whose point of departure is that of a mind detached
from the world and which has literally to formulate it—to build an intentional
world in consciousness—prior to any attempt at engagement.   (Ingold 1996:
120–1)

Ingold's concern to avoid the separation of mind and nature, of culture
and nature, is longstanding. The embrace of a Heideggerian dwelling-
perspective and a critique of the 'world picture' formulation in some
forms of cultural construction are continuous with his earlier effort to
force the recognition that the practical activities of foraging are also
distinctly human activities, and not simply a creatural infrastructure (see
Ingold 1987).

Let me now express my concerns, because they are not simply a rejection of phenomenology *tout court*. Phenomenological approaches *have*
had great value in the efforts of anthropologists to fathom distinctive
relationships to the world (see Merlan 1998; Munn 1970), especially in
challenging taken-for-granted (i.e., cultural) assumptions about subjectivity—as in critiques of the Cartesian *ego*, the so-called 'ghost in the
machine'. Much of the current phenomenologically inspired interest concerns the experience or senses of place, the dwelling in it. I have no doubt
that some component of what places mean to Aboriginal people can be
approached in this way. One of my informants, indeed, said it: 'I can close
my eyes and see that green place' (where he grew up).

The assumption of Ingold's argument is that if we 'follow the lead of hunter-gatherers', the concrete activities of hunting and foraging will have primacy. But as Munn (1970) pointed out, the experiences of 'country' are not innocent of social life: one of the significant concerns of Aboriginal social practice (at least in Central Australia) is in producing a particular mode of orientation to the world, a kind of subjectivity. People do not simply 'experience' the world; they are taught—indeed, disciplined—to signify their experiences in distinctive ways. Moreover, ritual life is highly valued as the means through which this orientation most adequately secured—an orientation in which 'what is' (to use the language of metaphysics) is interpreted as a sign of prior sentient, ancestral activity. Experience, or knowledge of the world, is therefore in part an effect of power. Furthermore, the insistence on the 'activities of hunting and gathering' has the danger of reproducing one of the most problematic assumptions of ecological anthropology's emphasis on 'the band' (Myers 1988a)—namely, ignoring the significance of what are, perhaps to the hunter-gatherers themselves, the more enduring, broader social categories, and spatial aggregates which are brought into being at any particular place.

There remains, therefore, a hint of primitivism in Ingold's provision of primacy to hunting and gathering as activities defining the experience of place. This is my second concern. Phenomenology also has a history, in Western European responses to rationality: one should be wary of a deployment of 'dwelling' that runs along lines that parallel the profound primitivist separation between modern/pre-modern, alienated/unalienated that occupied Heidegger's search for Being as much as our New Age contemporaries.

To be fair, it is not entirely clear to me how serious might be the deeper differences between Casey and Ingold's invocations of 'dwelling' and my account and those of others. Indeed, I fully endorse Ingold's formulation that 'it is through *dwelling* in a landscape, through the incorporation of its features into a pattern of everyday activities, that it becomes home to hunters and gatherers' (1991: 16).

At its most productive, Ingold's argument is against the separation of 'the activities of hunting and gathering, on the one hand, and singing, story-telling, and the narration of myth, on the other' within the terms of 'a dichotomy between the material and the mental, between ecological interactions *in* nature and cultural constructions *of* nature' (1996: 144). He argues against a view of the landscape as 'culturalized space [which] entails the naturalization of hunting and gathering. [In this view] only as represented in thought [i.e., a mind detached from the world] is the environment drawn into the human world of persons' (1996: 144).

As applied to what I wrote, however, these phenomenological critiques selectively concern only the most descriptive of the chapters. They do not address my analysis of the processes of projection, objectification, or construction which occur, in my view, within and through the social relations of Pintupi life (Myers 1986a, see also Myers 1988b). Moreover, by the particular focus they give to an individualized subjective experience, their discussions offer inadequate attention to the social mediation of 'place'—of 'place' as something *already* constituted in social relations. What is proposed in my approach is not the construction of 'pure culture'. It is, rather, a dialectical model of construction that I identify more with activity theory and Vygotsky (1962, 1978) or Piagetian notions of construction (see Turner 1973)—a construction that emphasizes operations and practices that mediate between a subject and the world. I find these models to be most productive for understanding how environment is constituted socially. In contrast, the reliance of a 'dwelling' perspective on the primacy of perception in the constitution of place seems problematic to me, insofar as sociopolitical mediation is ignored at *all* levels. The model of place-constitution we are left to ponder assumes a singular existential subject of perception—not the Vygotskyian subject who is himself or herself also constructed out of activities, nor even the subject whose perception is guided by the instruction or tutelage that Vygotsky's 'zone of proximal development' (1978) allowed.

Indeed, Vygotsky is famous for this emphasis on socially mediated learning. Ingold attempts to forestall the objection that he has 'taken no account of that vital component of knowledge that comes to people through their instruction in traditional lore' (1996: 142). But nevertheless I find his treatment of knowledge to be problematic. While I never claimed such knowledge should be understood as 'maps' in the direct sense, I do believe that my ethnography supports the view that stories, songs, designs, and the like provide components of an 'inner representation' of the country, instructing learners what to find. These *are* what one means by representations: understandings objectified and transmitted through a range of activities of kinship and social relations.

My principal concern is that the 'dwelling' approach, while potentially able to envisage the significance of activity, tends to suggest that such experience is largely unmediated by social processes of the sort that have occupied my research. Perhaps on the general significance of 'activity' we ultimately agree, although the only activities Ingold is concerned to mention are those of hunting and gathering as concrete labour. However, named places, or 'country' (as *ngurra*, 'camp', 'country', 'place'), are not only the environment of experience; they are also objectifications of previous experience and process. Such places and their value, I have argued, are also brought into being as objects of exchange (both hierarchical and equal) between social actors and as components of the socialization of persons. These processes may select or define as socially valuable particular dimensions of places. Generally speaking, I have taken the position that writers about Aboriginal societies—as well as other hunter-gatherers—have adopted an overly naturalistic position on the role of place/space/country, as territory, life-space, or dwelling. My own work emphasizes not, as Casey and Ingold each would appear to say, the 'culturalization of space' or cultural construction—as a projection of a culture's meanings onto unmarked, objective space.[4] Rather, I have insisted that place enters into Aboriginal social life in a fashion similar to other material forms, mediated by social action, as a potential formulation of similarity and difference, a token of identity and exchange.

In other words, the social mediation of place is always already constituted in social relations in Aboriginal societies of this kind. I want to argue that the danger of ignoring such mediation is not simply a theoretical one. In Australia, as in other settings for indigenous peoples, rights to land are premised on theories and understandings of cultural 'difference', particularly in regard to placemaking. Thus, my central concern is less to engage in academic debate, *per se*, and more to clarify what are the emerging understandings about the Aboriginal productions of 'place' and what their consequences are. Such understandings are the bases on which claims to land and culture are being debated and decided (see, e.g., Brunton 1992, 1996; Keen 1992, 1993; Merlan 1991; Myers 1986b; Weiner 1996; Wilmsen 1989). The nature of Aboriginal culture and the 'nature' produced in Aboriginal social life are serious issues in contemporary politics.

What, then, is the import of contemporary ethnographic knowledge of the Aboriginal relation to place? I now draw in more detail on my own research into ways 'place' is socially produced by contemporary Aboriginal people.

The focus of permissible Aboriginal land rights, for at least the past two decades and still in the popular imagination, emphasized the elaborate objectifications of people's relations to land in ritual and ritual knowledge, known as the Dreaming (see below). This was taken as 'unchanging tradition', divorced from the placemaking practices—based on an attitude to everyday dwelling—in which it was constituted and

---

[4] I have described an example of a case of placemaking in my monograph (Myers 1986a: 64) in which two men discover an odd formation. They attempt to fit it into the known narrative of mythological events in the area but must await an authoritative judgment from the older men who are the 'custodians' of the place. The consequent determination must be seen as a negotiation of their positions and relationships to each other.

reified. Ritual and ritual knowledge were turned into apparently
autonomous forms.

Ingold draws attention to the concrete activities of hunting and gathering as the relevant foundation of placemaking. No doubt such activities can come to carry the weight of such determination, and they surely
have been neglected ethnocentrically as simply the material basis of
human activity. But there is reason to believe that the separation of these
activities from others and an emphasis on their phenomenological prior-
ity is itself ethnocentric. Over the last ten years, my work, along with
that of Francesca Merlan (1998), Elizabeth Povinelli (1995), and Sylvie
Poirier (1995), has proceeded from the opposite direction to that taken
by Ingold and has insisted on the continuity between the more spectacular ritual objectifications (of collective ritual in relation to land and
ancestors) and the everyday practices of living, residing, dying on the
land that might be called 'dwelling' as activities through which place
becomes a significant bearer of social identity. The Pintupi example, as I
will show, *did* demonstrate this continuity of related practices between
the everyday social experiences of band life and the objectifications of
ownership. Because the relationships are discerned among people who
were still socialized in conditions of life strongly connected to the past,
the apparent coherence of these practices makes it more difficult for
readers to disentangle the processes and practices through which definitions of place and person are constituted, as Ingold and Casey certainly
failed to do. Among Aboriginal people in situations less typically
regarded as 'authentic', various of these processes and practices themselves have come to be central in the making and remaking of place and
people's identities.

THE DREAMING, KNOWLEDGE, PLACE

My research with Pintupi Aborigines in Central Australia began in
1973. It has taken place at a number of settlements and homeland
communities.

The vital conception of Aboriginal life, here as in so many other
regions, is The Dreaming (see Stanner 1979), constituting the very framework of Aboriginal society. Most Aboriginal ceremony is 'totemic' or
(more suitably), in Strehlow's (1970) terms, 'land-based'. Derived from
the mythological period—the Dreaming—in which powerful ancestral
beings gave the world its shape and meaning, Aboriginal ceremonies both
re-enact the events of the Dreaming and come *from* it (thus, their authenticity). Aborigines say that in performing the ceremonies they merely

'follow up The Dreaming' (Stanner 1979), sometimes called 'the Law'. Knowledge is restricted, and the ceremonies are revelatory: they present the story of what happened at a particular place and how it shaped the geography there. Thus, they make available knowledge of fundamentally important and invisible events and structures.

Almost invariably, Pintupi discussions of country are punctuated by descriptions of what happened in the Dreaming. Every significant feature is held to result from Dreaming events. Yumarinya, for example, means 'wife's mother-place'. The *yumari* of this case is the mother-in-law of a mythological Old Man, who travelled west from the Henty Hills, and who copulated with her at this place. Rock outcroppings, a rockhole, and various markings within a few hundred yards are interpreted as the result of the illicit actions of the mythological beings. The name signifies here a specific feature of the event, the involvement of the Old Man and his mother-in-law. (See figures 3.1–3.4.)

These kinds of stories and the places they endow or describe are *owned* by particular groups and controlled by men (and women) who have the right to display the ceremony. Where a myth in its entirety encompasses the travels of ancestors through a great number of places and many ceremonies, a Dreaming-track links several localized groups. It joins the

FIGURE 3.1 Yumari rockhole, Western Australia, 1975. (Photograph by Dick Kimber.)

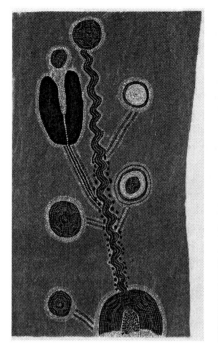 

FIGURE 3.2   Painting of Old Man Dreaming at Yumari, 1973 by Wuta Wuta Tjangala. Acrylic on board, 74 × 43 cm. (Collection of John Kluge.) (© copyright courtesy Aboriginal Artists Agency)
FIGURE 3.3   Painting of Yumari, 1979 by Wuta Wuta Tjangala. Acrylic on canvas board, 74 × 43 cm. (© copyright courtesy Aboriginal Artists Agency)

groups at one level and differentiates them within it. Because initiation (of men) is necessary both to gain a wife and to gain access to the religious knowledge which defines adulthood, access to religious knowledge (and its distribution) structures the defining social relationships of Pintupi social life—that is, the relationship of young men to old men and of women to men—just as it structures the relationships of locality. However, the meaning of these places, their value, must be understood as *constructed*—not by the application of some pure cultural model to blank nature, to which Ingold rightly objects—but in activities that constitute relationships within a system of social life that structures difference and similarity among persons, a system of practices for which 'land' is one medium. It is the neglect of such social processes as central to the production of value in place to which I object in the overemphasis on 'dwelling'.

FIGURE 3.4   Painting of Old Man Dreaming at Yumari, 1983 by Wuta Wuta
Tjangala. Acrylic on canvas, 242 × 362 cm. (Reproduced by kind permission of
the South Australian Museum.) (© copyright courtesy Aboriginal Artists
Agency)

PINTUPI PRACTICES/ACTIVITIES OF
PLACE: EXCHANGE

Pintupi Aborigines traditionally occupied an arid region south of Lake MacKay with an average yearly rainfall of 13 to 26 cm, a few permanent and semi-permanent waterholes, and significant seasonal variation of resources. (When I began studying them in 1973, they lived sedentarily in a small outstation near Papunya, where they had recently been settled.) To understand 'place' among the Pintupi, we must begin with how it is lived in bands, among those who share a camp. Pintupi live in a material world of practices that must produce itself with the resources of its environment but also reproduce the relations of production. The coordination of these practices, in kinship, involves the production of social persons—imaged in the Pintupi metaphor of 'nurturance' or 'looking after' (*kanyininpa*).

Band sizes varied from 10 to 25 persons during most of the year. As I have shown previously (Myers 1982b, 1986a, 1988b), an individual-oriented approach to these groupings, based on the indigenous concept of 'one countryman', is necessary insofar as society was potentially boundary-less, with individual networks and ritual links extending beyond any definable group. Individuals did not live entirely in one place or with a single set of people, even during the course of a year, much less a lifetime. Rather, bands were temporary residential groups that moved across the countryside as individuals affiliated or departed for varying lengths of time. In these movements, people hunted and gathered, collected seeds, shared food, performed ceremonies, eloped, bore children, fought, died, and so on. Such activities came to be associated or memorialized—for the actors and their relatives—in the places they occurred, and passage or residence through these areas invariably recalls the happenings. In this way, through human action, places acquire—or 'gather'—meanings from lived experiences.

Bands constitute a framework of social life, but they are not the simple defining units of any person's life. In the several life histories I collected, people demonstrated themselves to have travelled widely, not confining themselves to a single band's area. They moved, instead, to and through areas which they ascribed notionally to different named groups of people—such as 'the people from X place'. Yet the composition of these co-residential groups was itself, concomitantly, variable and fluctuating. Finally, an individual, like my informants Wuta Wuta Tjangala or Shorty Lungkarta, would consider *all the people with whom he regularly camped*—people who might view themselves as focused in different bands—to be his 'one countryman' (*ngurra kutjungurrara*, 'from one camp').

It is important to stress that there were regularities in movements and gatherings—around the exploitation of seasonal items and resources—and there are constraints on the movement of individuals and groups. But there is little usefulness here to the idea of a band as a group of definable individuals travelling together in a yearly round from place to place. People moved through the landscape for purposes of their own, saw evidence of other people nearby, went to visit, travelled with them for awhile, and then returned to their own countries. These everyday social realities are expressed in the concepts I gloss as 'country' (*ngurra*) and 'one countryman' (*ngurra kutjungurrara*). *Ngurra* is polysemic, as 'camp' or 'country'. A person's 'one countrymen' are those with whom he regularly camps (or can expect to camp), varying probably with each individual. The concept is egocentric, with each person's set being unique to him, including many who did not always live with the same residential group. These are people, one can say, with whom one 'used to travel'.

These are people with whom a fundamental identity is held to exist. The critical condition for participating in a band—that is, for residing in a 'camp' and taking part in the relations of production—is recognition of the others as *walytja*. This term, which can be glossed as 'relatives' or 'kin', is associated with the meaning 'one's own' and can designate the reflexive 'oneself' (as in *nyininpa walytja*, he is sitting by himself, or *palyarnu walytjalu*, he made it himself). The concept formulates kinship as the inclusion into one's own identity of those with whom one cooperates.[5] Those with whom one lives, with whom one shares a place, are kin.

Equivalent exchange takes place regularly between those who live together in the temporary residential groups that have been known to anthropologists as 'bands'. Those who live together in one place, a 'camp', must 'help each other'. This means that, upon demand at least,

---

[5] By 'identity' here, I do not mean a person's total or integrated conception of himself or herself. First, I am using the term to refer to bases for (or markers of) self-differentiation and self-relationship. While these markers do not need to be 'natural species', Levi-Strauss (1962, 1966) is correct to point out that the culturally recognized bases for classification *do* typically find their purchase outside of human social relations themselves. Second, I do not mean to say that these identities are necessarily permanent or enduring dimensions of a person's relation to *all* others, although they may be: as I have shown in more extensive presentation of the Pintupi case elsewhere (Myers 1986a), these markers may constitute a basis for *differentiating oneself from* others in some contexts but for *expressing relationship with* different others in other contexts. Finally, the degree to which any of these multiple, particular bases are synthesized into more context-independent formulations of selfhood and society is a problem for analysis and comparison.

co-residents should be willing to give food, clothing, and other material items or, as the case may be now, provide transportation or labour.[6] In Pintupi understanding, the distribution of valued objects and services reflects and creates relatedness. Thus, they insist, those who live—or have regularly lived—together, those who have shared a camp (*ngurra*, or a place) are *walytja*, which we can translate as 'relatives' or 'kin'. They must help each other, and such help, once given, should be reciprocated.[7] Conversely, one becomes *walytja* through participating in such dimensions of residential life. Shared identity derives from repeated exchange, shared concern and help.

Of course, the relations—the identity—with those from 'far away' whom one might visit must be sustained, and co-presence cannot be maintained.[8] Regular visiting is one such method[9], and through this

---

[6] The most ritually marked form of exchange is the distribution of large game (kangaroos, emu, etc.) from men's hunting. Appropriately cooked by someone other than the hunter, parts of the meat are given to those other members of the residential group to whom the hunter has obligations and with whom he feels himself to be closely related. Women's production (small game, vegetable foods) is also exchanged, although somewhat less formally than is the case for large game.

[7] Those who fail to reciprocate or neglect their campmates are said to be '*munuwalytja*', not kin. Faced with such neglect, people may threaten violence in assertion of their relationship or move away in recognition of its lack.

[8] It should be clear, then, that I advocate a return to a focus on the constitutive nature of exchange in sociality—as Mauss's (1904/1979) original work on seasonal variations among the Inuit brilliantly suggested—with a recognition of the *particular* (i.e., varying) political problematics of life in small-scale societies.

Examination of cycles of exchange in such societies usually reveals a variety of distinctive positions, particularities of identity, that are defined through exchange. One should think especially here of identity and exchange as media for sustaining the political relations of social life in material conditions that combine aggregation with dispersal. The relationships established through these identities and their modulations mediate contradictions imposed by the requirement of social action's being organized both immediately (i.e. at the face-to-face level), as well as in relation to others not immediately present (i.e. in its spatial and temporal displacements). Surely, there are many specific forms of the contradictions as well as mediations of them. Nonetheless, the various forms of exchange that are already well-documented in some of these societies—e.g. !Kung marriage, name transmission, rights of land tenure, and *hxaro* (Lee 1984; Wilmsen 1989); the complex reorganizations of Central Eskimo sexuality, names, and food-sharing—as systems defining distinctive social forms in summer and winter (Mauss 1904/1979)—must be understood as differentiating and recombining identities into broader systems of social action. At the same time, the media through which these contradictions are objectified, such as land as 'place' or words as 'names', acquire value by their position in such processes.

[9] There is another dimension of the problem of distance and shared identity, but I cannot discuss it here. I just note that various media allow Pintupi to extend this model of kinship as shared identity beyond the immediate relations of the camp, of existential co-presence. In other words, beyond the temporary residential bands, equivalent exchange also constitutes regular social relationships—culturally understood in the practice of 'exchanging' women between groups of kin as requiring reciprocity and resulting in a greater sense of kinship or shared identity. Here especially, the expectation of exchange as *ngaparrku* ('level', 'back and forth', or 'one thing against another') holds. That is, equiv-

coresidence individuals sustain their 'countryman' and 'relative' status in more than one band. These give them the right to forage with the group, in its area. Such bands would likely be those in which relatives of one's grandparents resided. Moreover, as we will see, regular residence in an area also gives one a claim to identification with—and potentially to 'ownership' of—the 'country' (*ngurra*), the named places where one lives. I refer to this process as a transformation of residence into ownership, of everyday experience into identification, an objectification of 'camp' into 'country'.

Elsewhere in Australia, Aboriginal people have articulately specified this potential of 'sitting on the land' as a form of labour invested in it, a mingling of substance (Povinelli 1995). Be that as it may, in the case of Pintupi practice, the key issue is gaining acceptance by others of one's claim of identification, and this is where exchange and other processes in the formation of social identity are critical.

LAND AS IDENTITY

What might be called 'ownership' for the Pintupi consists primarily in control over the stories, objects, and rituals associated with the mytho-logical ancestors of the Dreaming at a particular place. Access to know-ledge of these esoterica and the creative essence they contain is restricted, and one can acquire it only through instruction by those who have pre-viously acquired it. Thus, such rights exist only where they are accepted by others, and the possession of such rights as recognized by others, called 'holding' a country, is the product of other people's acceptance of shared identity with a claimant. I stress here that landownership is an embedded index of processes of exchange and negotiation of identity.

The bases for claiming such identities and rights are various. In Pintupi culture there is a range of relationships a person can claim or assert between himself or herself and a place, all constituting an identification with a country as one's 'own'. These include one's own conception at a place or at a place on the same mythological track as a place in question (i.e., coming *from* the particular Dreaming), as well as the conception or death of father, mother, and grandparent. Residence may, as I have said, also provide a basis for claim. These forms of identification provide the

alence and return constitute the necessary conditions for defining the relationship. The 'giving' of spears, or shields, or sacred objects provides another means of establishing and sustaining relationships with people who are not, temporarily or otherwise, co-resident. Such gifts, it is understood, are to be reciprocated. If not reciprocated, those who have delayed are said 'to have trouble'.

cultural basis for ownership of 'country' (*ngurra*).[10] Through this logic individuals can and do have claims to more than one country.

With each significant place, then, a group of individuals can affiliate, and the composition of the group may differ for each place considered. Many people may claim to identify with a place, but only a portion of these are usually said to 'hold' a country and to control its related rituals. These primary custodians are the ones who must decide whether to teach an individual about it, and they favour close relatives, those with whom they have had regular ties of equivalent or hierarchical exchange. Thus, groups are constituted essentially in the form of descending kindreds of persons who have *primary* claims to sites, but the exercise of continuing exchange ('giving') is essential in producing this organizational form. The process is one in which cooperative ties among frequent co-residents (i.e., 'those from one camp') may be transformed into a more enduring one. To summarize, one gets 'country' from those who 'held' one as a child (for details, see Myers 1986a: 127–58). 'Country' is objectified as the shared identity of a distinctive set of kin—relatives, or as they are known, 'one countrymen'.

One's identification with a named place is, in this sense, at once a defining of who one is and at the same time a statement of shared identity with others. People's joint relationship through time to a named place represents an aspect of an identity they share, however limited. The process through which membership is established is precisely one in which people attempt to convince others that they already *are* related. Each named place, then, commemorates, records, or objectifies past and present achieved relations of shared identity among participants. Each place, however, represents a different node of relations, and thus one's identification with each named place specifies a particular dimension of identity shared with others, although not the entirety of one's identity. The ultimate expression of this principle whereby shared identity among participants is projected out into the object world (and seen as deriving from it) is the way Pintupi verbally extend identification with a place, describing some important site as 'belonging to everybody, whole family', or, as they say alternatively, 'one country'. In reverse, one may read this as representing their sense of the Pintupi—people with no distinctive organization as a political entity—as 'all related' (*walytja*

[10] Since knowledge and control of country are already in the hands of 'owners' (my gloss for the Pintupi term '*ngurrakartu*' referring particularly to custodians of named place), converting *claims* to an interest in a named place requires convincing the owners to include one in knowledge and activity. One's identification with a country must be actualized and accepted by others through a process of negotiation.

tjurta). For the Pintupi, land is a sign that can carry expressions of identity and difference, even integrating these into complex regional systems.

'Holding a country' (*kanyininpa ngurra*) constitutes an important, perhaps the primary, dimension of enacting one's identity. Recognized identification with named places and the rights to related ceremonies, stories, and designs provide opportunities for a person to be the organizer of a significant event and the focus of attention. Thus, the performance of myth-based ceremonies—ritual re-enactments of the Dreaming at a place—by one group of landowners for others constitutes yet another form of 'giving' (*yunginpa*) between people (both men and women) who are equivalent to each other. Among men, whose case I know best, when such ceremonies are displayed for those who are themselves fully initiated, it is expected that the people who reveal and give their own ceremony—and thus, their own 'countries' or 'places'—will eventually be reciprocated with a display from those to whom they have 'given'. As an element in a cycle of exchange, the display makes those who see the ceremony, in a sense, distant co-owners. It extends a degree of identity to them as 'one countrymen' (those who hold a place collectively), signifying those who have recognized each other by giving their most valued items of exchange into the other's holding. Being an owner, having an identity with 'country', places one in a position to participate equally with other fully adult persons, in offering ceremonial roles to others (as part of an exchange) and sharing rights in ritual paraphernalia.

REPLACEMENT

This kind of giving should be distinguished from the revelation of ceremonies to young men who are not yet themselves fully initiated, and are therefore not fully equal. The focus on 'inheritance' and 'rights' does not capture the whole process. From the Pintupi point of view, the emphasis in these ceremonies is not just on getting rights, but as much on the social production of persons who can 'hold' the country. That is, Pintupi men and women are concerned with initiating young men and teaching men and women the ritual knowledge necessary to look after the country. The Pintupi image of social continuity is effectively one in which 'country' as an object is passed down—'given'—from generation to generation. They regard this 'giving' as a contribution to the substance and identity of the recipient, a kind of transmission of one generation's (or person's) identity to the next. But this is more than just a passing on of 'identity'. It is passing down, as well, of transformative power or agency, the wherewithal to socialize the next generation,[11] and to exchange (or *act*)—to establish relations with people from far away—within their own generation. People who 'hold the country' contain the generative principles of social reproduction, principles perceived as external to human life itself. In the Pintupi view, by learning about the Dreaming and seeing the rituals, one's very being is altered. People become, Pintupi say, 'different' and stronger.

As recipients become owners of particular sites, taking on an identity they share with others, they have also, as it were, acquired an obligation, a responsibility that they can repay only by teaching the next generation. Pintupi stress that men must hold the Law and pass it on. As men are enormously concerned to pass on their knowledge and identification with places to their 'sons' and 'sister's sons', ritual or landowning groups effectively represent those who previous owners have 'held' and raised up (i.e., the children of 'those from one camp') and to whom they subsequently 'give' knowledge of their country.

'Country' can be contrasted with other personal objects, which are dispersed at death and not allowed to carry the deceased's identity forward in time. Men particularly strive to pass on to their successors an identity formulated through ties to named places. My friend Shorty Lungkarta, now deceased, put pressure on his son Donald to attend his ceremonies and to learn, so that he could 'pass on' this country. What such fathers pass on, or transmit, in this way is not personal property that they have created or accumulated themselves, but an identity that is already objectified in the land. Recipients acquire an identity with a named place that has pre-existing relationships with other named places on its Dreaming track.

Named places function as formulations of identity so that personal relationships of 'nurturance' and 'equivalence' (in shared identity) are objectified through time. Elders consciously attempt to transmit their identity through time by creating the same identity in others, 'replacing' themselves (Weiner 1980) through time as 'holders' of country. One can see the process of replacement as a transmission of identity in which men give their country for their *katja* (sons or sister's sons) to 'grab'.

The best example I have of this is a trip I made to the Gibson Desert with an older man, the famous painter Wuta Wuta Tjangala, and several others. During the travel, Wuta Wuta decided he wanted to take us all to see an important place to the north, to *nintintjaku* ('show' or 'teach') his

---

[11] I owe the recognition of the importance of this distinction to Jane Fajans.

katja (a term that can mean both 'son' and 'sister's son'). By this, he included Ronnie (brother's son), Morris (own son), and Hillary (sister's son). Two other older men opposed this, saying they were afraid the young men would use the sorcery spells from this place when they were drunk. Keen for knowledge of his country, Ronnie framed his objections in a noteworthy fashion: 'All right', he said, 'then nobody will ever know about that place when you all die. If people travel around out here, they'll just go up and down this road only'. In other words, his irony suggested, the place would be lost. Wuta Wuta hoped to establish an outstation near the place where his father had died. His brothers, he told me, were nearly dead; only he was still strong enough—and he was concerned—to 'give the country, *katjapirtilu witintjaku*', for these descendants to hold. This would constitute for them a particular identity as holders of the country.

Dick Kimber has recorded how a few years later Wuta Wuta took some of his 'daughters' to a similar site, which I believe was his own Dreaming place, Ngurrapalangu, whose claypan is a source of the seed-bearing *mungilpa* plant. (See figures 3.5–3.7.) While they were not allowed to see in detail the most sacred/secret of the properties of the site, Wuta Wuta revealed to them where these were to be found, so that—one presumes—

FIGURE 3.5   Claypans and hills of Ngurrapalangu, Western Australia, 1974. (Photograph by Fred Myers.)

FIGURE 3.6   Painting of Ngurrapalangu, 1974 by Wuta Wuta Tjangala. Acrylic
paint and canvas board, 90 × 60 cm. (© copyright courtesy Aboriginal Artists
Agency)

they could pass on such knowledge to appropriate male kin (see Kimber
1990: 7).[12]

[12] Kimber writes: 'Uta Uta directed me to a site which had never previously been visited
by the three women who were with us. They were ordered to sit a short distance away
and observe, and also to take care of the children. Uta Uta then asked me to assist him to
dig in the sand until we found an object. Soon enough we had uncovered it and cleared
away all sand. The women and children could see its general shape and the women were
required to remember the site, but could not see close details of the markings on this
unusually shaped stone, know its name or learn the songs of association. However by
showing the women the site and the stone Uta Uta was ensuring that, in the event of his
death and that of the other few senior men of authority who knew the location, there were
sufficient people who could pass on the general knowledge to the correct men of the next
generation. These men would already know the secret-sacred men's details, but not
necessarily the locality. As Uta Uta explained, the old days of extensive "foot-walking"
were over, but without an adequate motor vehicle of his own, he was unable to instruct
his sons in all aspects of his own country'. (Kimber 1990: 7–8)

FIGURE 3.7   Painting of Jangala and Two Women at Ngurrapalangu, 1982 by Wuta Wuta Tjangala. Acrylic paint and canvas, 122.5 × 91 cm. (Reproduced by kind permission of the South Australian Museum.) (© copyright courtesy Aboriginal Artists Agency)

Just as in this example, the people most likely to replace seniors are those who were, as children, 'held' by them. Ultimately, seniors achieve their most significant status in this hierarchical exchange, just as they take on this position of 'holding' others. In the production of social persons, they give to younger men the capacity to establish extensive relations of equivalent exchange with each other and to become holders themselves. Such identification with place is a form of 'inalienable wealth' (Weiner 1992). One can take part in exchanges without really losing it. When one dies, these inalienable possessions, with which one has come to be associated in the course of one's life, remain in the landscape. The people to whom one contributed by 'growing them up' and by teaching are those able and obligated to carry on the responsibility for this country. This is the identity that endures and is reproduced in place.

Let me provide one extended illustration, since it is in 'practice' that place gains meaning and value. For simplicity, I will stick primarily to the case of a single individual, Wuta Wuta Tjangala, and the significance of the place known as *Yumarinya*—or 'Mother-in-law place'. This rock-hole is one of the places where Wuta Wuta used to live, prior to leaving the bush for a settlement in 1956. It was filled with his memories of experience, of life historical events, and it was very important to him.

So, how did he come to be identified with this place (and not only with this, as you will see)? His father was not from this area but came originally from the south, from the area near a sacred site known as *Yawalyurrunya* ('black bush currant place'). Yumari was part of his mother's 'country', her *ngurra*. His father had moved there when he married her, and he continued to live in the north, near Yumarinya with his wife's people, a common practice for a period after marrying. This father subsequently died at *Kalturanya*, nearby to Yumarinya, and is now known by the name of his place of burial. Wuta Wuta's mother was conceived near to Yumarinya, which means that her Dreaming is identified with the place—thus, providing a significant basis to claim ownership.

Wuta Wuta himself had *his* conception dreaming (i.e., was conceived through the essence of the Dreaming) at *Ngurrapalangunya*, a place associated with the activities of Two (ancestral) Women who were heading for Lake Mackay to the north, but who were frightened at this site—a hill and claypans—by the Old Man on his way to Yumari. According to Pintupi understanding, these figures left Wuta Wuta behind, hiding in a cave, from which he was eventually conceived. Wuta Wuta's older brother, Minpuru, was conceived at *Yawarrankunya*, a site identified with yet another Dreaming story (of Two Boys), to the west of Yumarinya. Yumarinya is tied in to places east and west, through sharing in the creative activities of this Old Man and his travels: one Dreaming.

Both men claim Yumarinya through their (shared) mother and her father (Wuta Wuta Tjapanangka) and through their own father, who is buried in the area, as well as through conception. Wuta Wuta also claims links to the south, through his father, at Yawalyurrunya in his father's country, which were recognized by his relatives there because he had been able to maintain his ties. He activated *these* ties and his identification with that place by marrying a woman from the southern area and moving there for a while—that is, through exchange.

Wuta Wuta also had important rights to the Pollock Hills in the west and also to *Tjitururrnga* in the east. These were places to which he regularly travelled, 'up and down' along the plain. They were 'one country' in respect to his residential habits; he 'sat' (camped) there. Marriage exchanges reinforced some of these—so that his sister's daughter was married to a man from the Pollock Hills. He can paint these designs and 'hold' that country in ceremony because these rights of identification were given to him by his one countrymen, recognizing in this manner their relationship. The shared identity is objectified in their mutual identification with the place and places.

In ritual exchange, and in controlling their sons for initiation and daughters for marriage, Wuta Wuta, Minpuru, and other brothers acted as a group—performing ceremonies as 'brothers'. The place Yumarinya is a vehicle of their shared identity, as 'sons' of the group of fathers. In terms of my argument, his identification with Yumarinya (and other places) provides Wuta Wuta with something he can exchange with other men—and in this sense, undergirds his identity as an autonomous, equal man. He probably acquired the knowledge necessary to do so post-initiation, as the film *Pintupi Revisit Yumari* (Sandall 1969) shows to be the case for some of his 'brother's sons'.

Wuta Wuta was associated with a range of places through the circumstances, experiences, of his life. This relationship is not necessarily a phenomenological expression of dwelling in a place, although this may be a basis for some of his claims (residence, conception). The larger process in which these dwellings take place suggest that place gains its significance through the value-making social processes of identity production, processes of kinship in the Pintupi sense, mediated by exchange. All of these associations to place are objectifications, projections through time, of various relations of shared identity.

One's country is a projection—in a sense—of one's movements and social relations, of kinship, converted to identity with place. 'Residence' or dwelling—living on the land, at a place—is very important in establishing one's identity with it and its meaning for one. But this fact is socially significant by virtue of a discursive valorization in making claims, as an acceptable basis of identity. In fact, if one does not live with those from the place or in the area regularly, one loses one's basis of claim: one is said to have 'nothing to do'. It is woven phenomenologically into the experiences of kinship and shared identity with other residents. If one cannot sustain ties through residence, exchange, and so on, one cannot be a one countryman or kin—and one's identification loses social recognition.

Let me try to summarize. I have delineated three fundamental aspects to the significance of 'country' or place as a cultural entity, all given form in processes of exchange. (1) With its origin in the Dreaming, 'country' constitutes a valued form of knowledge that is esoteric, transmitted (or

as the Pintupi say, 'given') to younger men, but restricted in access. (2)
At the same time, 'country' constitutes an object of exchange among
equal men (and women). For the Pintupi, 'country' provides an embodiment of identity that allows for the performance of autonomy in
exchange.[13] (3) Finally, it is important to remember that named place or
'country' is produced as an objectification of the transient formations of
'camps', as an iconic representation of shared identity that depends on
its indexical relations with the everyday practices of coresidence and
exchange.

This is related to a phenomenology. My concern is to show that the
identities produced as an experience of mutual caring among residents of
transient 'camps' (*ngurra*) are transformed into or objectified as relations
to enduring 'countries' (*ngurra*) as dreamings, and these objectifications
mediate social relations within a region. But there is an emergent dimension that enters experience. Such 'countries' are meaningful to Pintupi
cultural subjects as possessing the potential of exchangeability. My
concern is, therefore, to show that places acquire significance—or value—
in these social relations, and that a Pintupi cultural 'space' in the sense of
a synthesis of specific place–relations might be shown to emerge.

THE SOCIAL AND THEORETICAL
LOCATION OF PLACE

Central to my argument is a position enunciated by Tony Swain in his
book, *A Place for Strangers* (1993), concerning what one might call the
fundamentality of place in Aboriginal constructions of being. As Swain
puts it, 'Aborigines themselves do not, or at least once did not, understand their being in terms of time, but of place and space' (1993: 2).
Rather, 'Aboriginal understandings do not recognise the cosmos as a
unified arena in which events occur; one cannot speak of space of any
kind in the singular. The basic and only unit of Aboriginal cosmic structure is the place' (1993: 29). 'The basic totemic assertion is that all Lawful
existence emerges from the being of place . . .' (1993: 35).

While place may have paradigmatic status in Swain's conception as well
as my own (and others), I find it difficult on theoretical grounds to grant
its centrality to something like a culture's philosophical orientation
—which Swain does. To do so is to objectify 'culture', to give—as
Terry Turner (1980) once put it—the products of human activity an

---

[13] The possibility of handling 'country' in this way stems from initiation, which
also underpins the possibility of two other basic forms of autonomy through exchange,
marriage, and fighting—indicating the importance of treating 'country' as a sign.

autonomous existence and to substitute them for the original actors and their purposes as the objects of theoretical and political concern. Recent considerations of Aboriginal notions of 'place' in the Australian political arena argue cogently for the danger of separating 'what are in fact the products of human activity (e.g., society, culture) from the actors who produce them and the purposes for which they go to the trouble to do so' (Turner 1980: 17). Thus, I wish to reiterate here the embeddedness of such constructs within *social action*, stressing—in ways that I fear Ingold (1996) has not—both terms of that pair. The subject of place–experience is not prior to the social formation of what is to be perceived. Following Turner (1979, 1980), I have characterized the sociocultural system of Pintupi life as organized towards the production of social persons.

Pintupi understandings of kinship represent their society as a structure for the production of social persons, a structure formulated out of the cultural organization of significant acts of sharing, exchange, and protection. In Pintupi social life, the culturally defined course for the production of persons—the formation of significant identity—provides the structure that dominates the highest levels of the social system, and such production is defined by two sorts of exchange. Intergenerational, hierarchical exchange and intragenerational, equivalent exchange (see below) are both essential to and embedded in a larger cycle in the process of social reproduction through which individual persons acquire an identity. Such cycles of social action constitute 'kinship'.

My interpretation gives great weight to the significance of the Pintupi concept of *kanyininpa*—which I translate partially as 'nurturance'—in the formation of identity among Pintupi. It appears that the critical processes in the reproduction of Pintupi social life itself, at the most extensive levels, are those of producing social persons. This activity integrates 'growing up' people with 'looking after' (or reproducing) the places that contain the vital essence and identity of human beings.

To understand how 'place' conceivably figures within such a system, let me sketch an approach to its situation in social consciousness and its location in something we might call the 'environment'—perceived to be outside of social production, but in fact its product. In this view, which I adopt from Turner (1980),[14] social structures are to be seen as the hierarchical organization of productive activities. Here, the upper levels consist of reproductive processes which subsume productive processes as lower levels or components. Turner once discussed the relationship of these levels in Piagetian terms, as one of 'coordination', in which the

[14] Terry Turner has developed and extended his theorization of culture considerably beyond the simple form of this early paper, but its outline is clearest here (Turner 1980) as is its relationship to the practical consequences of culture's theorization.

higher level structurally expresses the commonalities of activities at the lower level.

Turner points out as well that such hierarchical organization can also be seen as a hierarchy of modes of social control. The lower levels consist of social forms and techniques for controlling processes of transformation. Higher levels are comprised of reproductive processes, consisting of relational mechanisms for controlling the production of primary processes and attendant social relations (e.g., marriage as a mechanism to reproduce the family). As one moves higher in such structures, he observes, differentiated social mechanisms of control and reproduction disappear:

A level is reached in every social structure in which production and reproduction are not directly controlled through specialized social relations or processes, but instead take place indirectly and as it were reflexively through the repetition of the institution, process or level of organization in question as a means of reproducing some lower level. (Turner 1980: 31)

Thus, for example, marriage is reproduced as a reflexive by-product of its use to reproduce the family.

At this point in the hierarchy of social processes, there is a change in the form of social consciousness from the viewpoint of actors. Relations and processes are no longer represented in cultural terms as products of deliberate social activity. 'Higher level processes, the reproduction of which is not directly under social control, tend to be represented not as artifacts of human activity but as products of natural forces or supernatural agencies' (Turner 1980: 32).[15] What are emergent properties of social action are discerned as invariant, natural. It is regarded as beyond the scope of social agency to create or change these processes which, Turner says, are

not seen as interdependent parts of a system of social relations and activities, but rather as normative entities with a reality of their own independent of the pattern of social relations that results from their enactment. They are objectified or reified, that is, considered as things-in-themselves that constrain behavior but are not constrained by it. [Turner 1980: 32]

Thus, Turner is interested in how social consciousness at higher levels of social structure tends to be alienated, tends to define the value attached to a level of organization as simply inherent in itself, rather than as a product of human social activity or of a system of interdependent relations among parts of a whole. This fetishized character of the collective

---

[15] For a similar argument, see Myers (1980).

representations constituting the society's form of consciousness of itself can become an obstacle in its reformulation.

PRACTICES AND NEW CONDITIONS OF PLACE

My concern here, pursued under the abstract sign of 'fetishization, is not immediately with the question of misrecognition so much as it is with the relationship between the qualities of 'place' and the cycles of social activity in which they are constructed. This is, I hope to have indicated, a rather different process of 'construction' than the one Ingold (1996) criticizes and attributes to me. It is one in which the value of 'places' is produced in their capacity to mediate relationships of shared identity and difference, of hierarchy and equality within a regional sociopolitical system. The process of placemaking is also to be understood as one in which the material properties made significant by movement or travel in the world—constituted through processes of aggregation and dispersal, in the traditional mode, and now through other vectors of movement— are marked as having distinctive value by virtue of their capacity to dif- ferentiate and combine. Indeed, we can see just such accumulation occur as new religious cults, such as *Tjulurru* or the 'Balgo Business' (see also Glowczewski 1984; Kolig 1979; Myers 1982a; Swain 1993) discover and discern new relations among places, recombining and even reformulat- ing them—as I have argued (Myers 1982a) and as Swain (1993) has shown quite brilliantly in his book. Indeed, in such relations of exchange, place becomes more 'generalized', a sort of currency, a generalization in fact which might result in something like the local creation of a more homo- geneous 'space', as seems to occur in some religious formulations which spread throughout Central Australia and the Kimberleys, where travel- ling religious cults have been traditionally a medium for formulating and reformulating relationships among people, between localities.[16]

My account insists, not on some simple application of cultural models to space but on the significance of social practices intervening between subject and the object world. This is what we certainly see in the broad-

---

[16] Such indigenous practices often reformulate the relationship among places in terms of newly revealed (or discovered) ancestral activities linking them. In that respect, they represent the discovery of new qualities in place, consequent to their integration of chang- ing supralocal regimes of order. Thus, the Warlpiri Gadjari (Meggitt 1966) cycle connects places of different local groups through the visits ('above the ground') of a unifying set of ancestors. Such an integration of distinctive places within encompassing relations of similarity and difference in larger systems is familiar in Arnhem Land, too, in various groupings of clans.

est sense with socialization, and now also it is possible to acknowledge
the way in which research in Aboriginal Australia has shown how
involvement in broader regional (and transregional) systems has led to
the construction of meaning in place. This is to insist on a semiotic mediation in place of originary meanings of dwelling: that experiences acquire
meaning and value within already extant regimes and relations of signifying practice. Even at its simplest, each individual subject does not infer,
deduce or even in any simple way invent the meanings of these places
through a process of 'dwelling' as some unmediated experience of the
place itself. Most of the meaning that places 'gather', so to speak, has
been taught, passed on through distinct processes of socialization, albeit
practices whose revelatory emphasis (on secrecy and disclosure)
promotes a distinctive mode of orientation to experience the world
(Munn 1970).[17]

Merlan's (1998) analysis of how an Aboriginal girl named Julie, living
in Katherine, came to understand an event of local construction as
the extraction of a rainbow serpent from the river-cave illustrates just
such a role of social mediation in understanding place. Subjects acquire
knowledge of the environment only partly through direct perception
or engagement: this environment is actively produced as meaningful, is
objectified and revealed, through the signifying practices of various
commentators and instructors—her mother and another older relative.
Even new discoveries, as they do occur in dreams or ritual innovation,
of what is 'in the country' must pass through procedures of legitimation
to become 'true'. The girl's sense of dwelling in Katherine is not constituted simply by the everyday experience of being there. It is constituted,
instead, by a range of objectified mediations through which a mundane
piece of roadwork instantiates an ontology of place as revelation. Julie is
walking down the street in Katherine to get an ice-cream cone but
her readiness to grasp the manifestation she has seen shows a sense of
relation to the place that is different overall, not just a matter of a single
experience.

Moreover, this signification of place–meaning is motivated by a range
of accompanying practices and social relations. Among these, according
to Merlan, is 'the faithful acceptance of the word of older people on such
matters as the particular meanings of place' characteristic of Julie and
others of her background (Merlan 1998: 59). The understanding of place,
furthermore, provides for Julie the self-assurance of the person who
belongs locally: she speaks of herself as a person on the scene, familiar

---

[17] For a recent attempt to develop this sort of point about secrecy, see Weiner's (1996)
discussion of the controversial Hindmarsh Island bridge affair in South Australia and
Brunton's (1996) response.

with Katherine town, and able to walk around it without a problem, given the personal relationships which anchor her.

PROBLEMS OF PLACEMAKING

There is more to the story Merlan provides, leading us to the next and final topic to be considered here—the importance of changing politics and relations of signification in defining the meaning of place. The uprooted rainbow serpent provides a distinctive image as 'an autochthonous force that assaults the unfamiliar' (1998: 70). In the story, then, the anonymous stranger is seen to uproot and destroy the native force which was the guardian of the difference between 'countryman' and 'foreigner'. Now, the unfamiliar, the stranger, is free to visit the town. Anybody can be here now, without fear of reprisal: a former 'place' has become part of town space, no longer a significant focus for Aboriginal objectifications of identity, either in general or more specific terms (1998: 74).

Merlan describes the development of a consciousness in which country and place are experienced as meaningful in a variety of ways, of divisions within the landscape. Some places are said to be 'just country', meaning Aborigines assume mythological associations exist but do not know them. 'Aboriginal people like Julie now live with a diversified consciousness of the possible meaningfulness of country and places' (Merlan 1998: 73). Such diversified consciousnesses, no longer (if ever) singular, require that they be placed within a framework of changing practice to be understood.

The processes involved in this Katherine placemaking are not entirely 'traditional', but represent what Turner (see above) also tried to theorize in his rejection of a focus on the *products* of human social activity (culture, society). The neutralization of town space is articulated through Aboriginal practices, but it is not anymore a 'place' of the same sort. No longer 'traditional', yet not simply 'Western', this relationship to the town centre shows the effects of whites' reorganization of the temporal and spatial dimensions of Aboriginal relations to places through work, modifying some of the sensitivities for relationships to places. A position that acknowledges the primacy of social practice allows us to see contemporary Aboriginal selfmaking and placemaking as continuous with earlier practices rather than abruptly disjoined. There has been, after all, considerable disputation about what might be authentic Aboriginal relations to place.

Merlan takes the contemporary situation of the Aboriginal people of Katherine as her problem, people whose relationships to their own historical cultural practices are quite uncertain—differing, therefore, from the case I have articulated for the less dislocated Pintupi people. Nonetheless, she seeks to explain the particularity of their contemporary production of place and their relationships to places through a consideration of the practices of residence, kinship, and politics they have carried from the past. This ought not to be seen as an absolute *cleavage* in their historical being, although the changing nature of their knowledge of the land through foraging is relevant.

I have tried to show that the meanings of places, even as 'the place where I forage', should not be thought of as existing outside of a set of social determinations that might well be founded in systematic relations beyond the local. This is not to ignore the experiences of the activities of hunting and gathering but to deny them a priori value or originary significance, any more than the association of places with significant emotional attachments to relatives can be understood outside of a broader system that gives them value.

This argument is necessary to pursue not only for theoretical reasons. To put the point briefly, the Katherine people are in a complicated position in relation to recent efforts within Australia to provide a place for recognizing 'Aboriginal culture', either through land claims in which people might be granted title to 'traditional' Aboriginal land, or more generally through the recognition of their contemporary cultural activity as 'Aboriginal'. The dilemma is best exemplified in three quite bitter cases—that of Coronation Hill (Merlan 1991), that of Belyuen Aborigines (Povinelli 1995), and the most recent case of Hindmarsh Island (see Weiner 1996)—where claims of Aboriginal 'inventions of tradition' and customs were used by the state to cast doubt on the authenticity of their claims to identity with the places. The standards through which Aboriginal culture has been judged by the state have involved the implicit understanding of 'tradition' as largely unchanging, ancient, and so on—viewing only such expressions as deserving of official respect by Australia's land rights laws.

Few of the people in Katherine, exemplarily of the situation, any longer practice the ritual re-enactments of the Dreaming which are typically identified as constituting a 'traditional Aboriginal relationship to land'. Rather than conceiving of the change as their having become less Aboriginal or more Western, or to have lost their culture, Merlan demonstrates that they have distinctive (and often contradictory) practices and ideologies of placemaking. These practices have objectified social groups far larger than the pre-contact 'local descent group' in terms of their relation to a 'tribal territory' that probably did not exist in this form earlier, representing the historical amalgamation of distinctive groups in their joint relationship to an extended country.

Merlan has pointed out the problems raised by questions of socio-cultural change, and the problematic concept of 'tradition' in public discussions of Aboriginal culture as 'ancient and unchanging' (1991: 341): opposing tradition to modernity, they formulate 'tradition' as purely cultural rather than in any sense social and historical. The current relationships of Katherine people to place are judged as 'non-traditional'. Such positions deny tradition's legitimate relevance to Aborigines today.

In a sense, the Aboriginal people of Katherine are caught up in the problems of the representation of their culture and social life by others. This is well-known in Australia, and elsewhere, and it first emerged most clearly in relationship to whether women in Aboriginal societies had rights to land—since anthropologists had emphasized men's ritual as the source of this relationship. But Merlan has a particularly powerful subsequent location in which to explore the effects—since one of the most important public controversies about the truthfulness of Aboriginal claims in Australia took place in her area, focused on the 'authenticity'—not only the Aboriginalness, so to speak, but also their identity with prior practice—of contemporary understandings of Coronation Hill as a 'place'. I wish to point out that a major issue in the contemporary attempt to sustain such Aboriginal understandings within the context of conditions set by the Australian nation-state has been how to overcome the emphasis anthropological representations of 'Aboriginal culture' and the religious relationship to the land have had in such judgements of what constitutes genuine Aboriginal culture. How to show that ceremonies need not be conceived as the only 'authentic' forms of Aboriginal recognition of place, how to allow for further construction, without calling it 'invented' or 'non-traditional'.

There is a problem in theorizing this process of construction, in not identifying the 'Aboriginal' with the emergent product—ritual objectifications—only. Rather, it would be necessary to recognize the activities through which people in Katherine continue to produce an identity for themselves in relation to place. Since this might not involve the hunting and gathering activities as primary in dwelling, to grant these originary value would be as problematic in the end as identifying the genuinely Aboriginal with ritual.

Thus, Merlan insists—as do I—on the centrality of *practices* which provide the foundation for the formulaic objectifications of traditional Aboriginal formulations of 'place' in terms of the Dreaming—which had been the only forms of relationship granted legitimacy in Australian law.

'However absolute the 'dreaming' significance of places may seem', she writes, 'they were also always constituted ... within and through the range of practices which linked people with places'.[18]

CONCLUSION

The crux of my argument has been that the practices of placemaking and the experiences of place, must be understood as socially and politically organized. This may or may not give primacy to the concrete activities of hunting and gathering, which I regard as an empirical point to be determined in any case. That is to say that I regard the process of 'construction' not as a projection of pre-existing cultural templates on to a tabula rasa world, but a dialectical engagement of socially and historically constituted schemas of practical activity with worldly circumstance. In this way, and perhaps only in this way, are we able to avoid removing Aboriginal people and their practices of everyday life from history—to see them as only now entering into the world of contesting discourse and

---

[18] Merlan names three anthropologists whose work is exemplary of this view: (Bell 1983; Rose 1992; Povinelli 1995). To this list, I would also add the important contribution of Sylvie Poirier (1995). As in the work of Bell, she emphasizes the potential of dreams while on the land to bring living people back into contact with the ancestral presence, to establish an identity with place. Focusing on the role of dreams, creativity, and innovation within the context of an ideological structure of permanence among Western Desert Aboriginal people, Poirier emphasizes the 'immanence' of the Dreaming (its place *within* everyday life), and its consequent availability for the formulation of new human arrangements without challenging the overall structuring of experience. The second contribution is her theoretical argument that the cultural organization of dreaming constitutes an important *structure* itself, mediating the contingent with the mythological realm of the Dreaming.

This is clearly an area that deserves to become the centre of studying an expanded Aboriginal sociality. The medium of dreams offers a space–time, she shows, in which the creative participation of individuals can be articulated with the ideological emphasis on permanence and continuity. It is a social medium of objectification. In documenting numerous examples of individual constructions of experience within the Kukatja lifeworld, *Les jardins du nomade* is able to show how the overarching structure of the Dreaming is mediated by acting subjects in daily life. The project of understanding (and explicating) the 'oneiric process' as a sociocultural form involves, as well, several quite singular reconsiderations of social process in Aboriginal life. She develops, for example, the idea of an apprenticeship in dreaming, through which individuals learn to manage the experience as a cultural medium; this formulates the activity of dreaming into a social one. Her discovery of the prevalence of dreams of death as a parallel to conception illuminates the outlines of the cosmological structure, partly apprehended by Aboriginal participants, in which dreams stand as the significant mediator of human reproduction. The cases she presents of the appropriation of dreams in Aboriginal practice provide a concrete basis for the claim that exegesis is always 'open', waiting for events, and an exploration of the practice of interpretation in egalitarian communities in which authoritative interpreters are lacking.

contradictory valuations. Any Pintupi subject must always have found himself or herself born to a location within an already existing spatially extended system of places and people.

The Katherine people are not hunters and gatherers living in a world of hunter-gatherers but are, then, like most people in the world forced to define themselves in relation to a variety of discourses that are not of their own making. These are practical conflicts with theoretical signifi-cance and conflicts in which the boundaries between theory and practice are breached.

As the discussion above shows, it would be impossible to separate anthropology from the rest of Western discourse. Theorizing is always a form of practical encounter with data, and therefore representations are necessarily inescapably part of a broader context. The attempt to make anthropological descriptions of Aboriginal social life stand absolutely for what they represent is also bound to fail. Yet, the act (and politics) of representation and the production of 'truths', far from being issues of academic concern, have come to be central material forces in the contemporary constitution of Aboriginal social life in their claim to land in the present.

Let me return, therefore, to my broader concern about the political context of placemaking. It is critical to remember that the representa-tional practices of anthropology and ethnography are inextricably caught up in the production and deployment of indigenous identities, making all of the philosophical and theoretical questionings of recent critique (the limits of representation, the problem of power/knowledge) intrinsic to description itself. As importantly, we are just beginning to theorize how one is to come to terms with the more subtle forms of 'difference' and 'cultural activity' that are instantiated in the new Aboriginal cultural for-mations. An approach that looks at Aboriginal practices contextually in historical process is very illuminating of the way in which meanings are reshaped and contested—whether in Katherine, Darwin, or the Western Desert. There is no question, too, that within the Australian context the local meanings Aboriginal people hold to exist about 'places' (sacred sites, and so on) have become the focus of national politics and contro-versy. Controversies about place, it would appear, are founded on the same dichotomous procedures of separating 'culture' from 'practice' (Merlan 1998; Turner 1980) or 'culture' and 'economy' (Povinelli 1995) that underlay an earlier anthropology.

A postscript might be in order. As Merlan has noted for the people in the Katherine area, the relationship of Pintupi people to their country is changing. I can see this with those I know best. Only a few remain who grew up hunting and gathering as a way of life. These men and women

knew the country, lived it, in a way those who were born in settlements
and missions do not. They knew the habits of each creature, the slightest features of the landscape, a landscape that is now travelled more typically by vehicle. In Alice Springs last July, I found out that my friend
George Yapa Yapa—born at Kumirnga, out past the Pollack Hills in
Western Australia—now lives in town full time. I cannot think of too
many people who can describe for me, eyes bright and glinting, how they
travelled in the old days, where to find water, shade, or food. George has
kidney problems, and lives in a camp on the southern end of Alice
Springs. In Alice, George and his remaining Pintupi friends are much
sought after by dealers for their paintings, and their pictures are displayed
by the paintings as tokens of authenticity. The paintings are all about the
country, but—so it seems to me—not many people are interested in the
sort of knowledge that George has, the detailed knowledge of all those
places that used to constitute one's identity. Will theoretical anthropologists, now focused on the transnational and the more universalizing
discourses of modernity, return to such knowledges, or will we pursue
the objectifications of Aboriginal country that have entered into worldwide circulation?

At the moment, this has again become significant, as the Ngaanyatjarra
Council has filed a claim on behalf of Pintupi people based on the Native
Title Act (based on the famous Mabo High Court Decision in favour of
recognizing native title) for the area of the Western Desert previously
long occupied by the Pintupi. For this claim, the knowledge of travels
that I recorded from Wuta Wuta, Freddy West, Yumpurlurru, and others
is again relevant. Travelling over the country is being converted, it is
hoped, into permanent title. Visits to this country, which have been
renewed in recent years, are teaching much about the way people lived
here and what sort of place it is.

The famous Tingarri site of *Ngunarrmanya*, about which I had heard
so much and which featured in the Balgo business, also has been revis-
ited, as part of the new understandings of native title constituted in the
Mabo decision. This Tingarri place, also known as '*Nyaru*' ('burned out
place') is said to have been a source of 'living water'. Under the ground
there, I was told, were sacred objects buried to protect them from the big
fire (at initiatory time in the story). Indeed, a researcher for the claim told
me what was discovered during this last visit to the site: digging into the
soakage, one finds red stone outcroppings under the ground, and from
this stone—these transformed sacred objects of the ancestors—leaches
out living water! Such instances clarify the inseparability of the sort of
phenomenological knowledge of dwelling and knowledge of environmental features that Ingold underscores as essential to placemaking, and

the socially mediated cosmologies classically associated with the Dreaming—both embedded in structural relations of social life. Our most difficult problem in theorizing the relationship to land has been the focus on an imagined uniform 'tradition' and the failure to conceptualize the potentially conflicting and disaggregated practices through which socially recognized identities with place and places themselves are produced. Our knowledge of these is mediated yet again in the political economy and legal culture that has framed Aboriginal lives in different ways for the last 220 years.

REFERENCES

Asch, Michael (1979). 'The ecological–evolutionary model and the concept of mode of production: Two approaches to material reproduction', in D. Thomas and G. A. Smith (eds), *Challenging Anthropology*. Toronto: McGraw-Hill, 81–97.

Bell, Diane (1983). *Daughters of the Dreaming*. Sydney: McPhee Gribble.

Brunton, Ron (1992). 'Mining credibility: Coronation Hill and the anthropologists. *Anthropology Today*, 8 (2): 2–5.

Brunton, Ron (1996). The Hindmarsh Island Bridge and the credibility of Australian anthropology. *Anthropology Today*, 12 (4): 2–7.

Casey, Edward (1995). 'How to get from space to place in a fairly short stretch of time: Phenomenological prolegomena', in S. Feld and K. Basso (eds), *Senses of Place*. Santa Fe: SAR Press, 13–52.

Chatwin, Bruce (1987). *The Songlines*. New York: Viking Press.

Cowan, James (1989). *Mysteries of the Dreaming*. Dorset, UK: Prism Press.

Elkin, A. P. (1964). *The Australian Aborigines: How to Understand Them* (4th edn). Sydney: Angus and Robertson.

Elkin, A. P. (1969). 'Elements of Australian Aboriginal philosophy'. *Oceania*, 40: 85–98.

Feld, Steven and Basso, Keith (eds) (1995). *Senses of Place*. Santa Fe: SAR Press.

Glowczewski, Barbara (1984). 'Manifestations symboliques d'une transition economique: Le "Juluru", culte intertribal du "cargo"'. *L'Homme*, 23: 7–35.

Hallowell, A. Irving (1955). *Culture and Experience*. New York: Schocken Books.

Hallowell, A. Irving (1969). 'Ojibwa ontology, behavior and world view', in Stanley Diamond (ed.), *Primitive Views of the World*. New York: Columbia University Press, 49–82.

Hamilton, Annette (1982). 'Descended from father, belonging to country: Rights to land in the Australian Western Desert', in E. Leacock and R. Lee (eds), *Politics and History in Band Society*. Cambridge: Cambridge University Press.

Hardy, Frank (1968). *The Unlucky Australians*. Sydney: Thomas Nelson.

Heidegger, Martin (1977). 'The age of the world picture', in *The Question Concerning Technology and Other Essays*. W. Lovitt, trans. New York: Harper Torchbooks, 115–54.

Heidegger, Martin (1979). 'Building, dwelling, thinking', in *Poetry, Language, Thought*. A. Hofstadter, trans. New York: Harper and Row, 143–62.

Hirsch, Eric and O'Hanlon, Michael (eds) (1995). *The Anthropology of Landscapes*. Oxford: Oxford University Press.

Ingold, Tim (1987). *The Appropriation of Nature*. Iowa City: University of Iowa Press.

Ingold, Tim (1991). 'Against the motion (1)', in *Human Worlds are Culturally Constructed*. Manchester: Group for Debates in Anthropological Theory.

Ingold, Tim (1993). 'The temporality of the landscape'. *World Archaeology*, 25 (2): 152–74,

Ingold, Tim (1996). 'Hunting and gathering as ways of perceiving the environment', in R. Ellen and K. Fukui (eds), *Redefining Nature: Ecology, Culture and Domestication*. Oxford: Berg, 117–55.

Jackson, Michael (1995). *At Home in the World*. Durham: Duke University Press.

Jacobs, Jane (1996). *At the Edge of Empire*. New York: Routledge.

Keen, Ian (1992). 'Undermining credibility: Advocacy and objectivity in the Coronation Hill debate'. *Anthropology Today*, 8 (2): 6–9.

Keen, Ian (1993). Aboriginal beliefs vs. mining at Coronation Hill: The containing force of traditionalism. *Human Organization*, 52: 344–55.

Kimber, Richard [Dick] G. (1990). *'Friendly People—Friendly Country': An Exhibition of Aboriginal Artworks from the Peoples of the Tanami and Great Sandy Deserts*. Victor Harbor, SA: Ambrose Press.

Kolig, Eric (1979). 'Djuluru: Ein synkretistichen Kult Nordwest-Australiens'. *Baessler-Archiv*, (new series), 27: 419–48.

Lawlor, Robert (1991). *Voices of the First Day: Awakening in the Aboriginal Dreamtime*. Rochester, VT: Inner Traditions Press.

Lee, Richard and DeVore, I. (eds) (1968). *Man the Hunter*. Chicago: Aldine.

Lee, Richard (1984). *The Dobe !Kung*. New York: Holt, Rinehart, and Winston.

Levi-Strauss, Claude (1962). *Totemism*. Chicago: University of Chicago Press.

Levi-Strauss, Claude (1966). *The Savage Mind*. Chicago: University of Chicago Press.

Maddock, Kenneth (1972). *The Australian Aborigines: A Portrait of their Society*. London: Penguin.

Mauss, Marcel (1979). *Seasonal Variations of the Eskimo: A Study in Social Morphology*, trans. by J. Fox. London: Routledge and Kegan Paul. (Original work published 1904)

Mauss, Marcel (1954). *The Gift: Forms and Functions of Exchange in Archaic Societies*, trans. by Ian Cunnison. Glencoe, IL: Free Press.

Meggitt, Mervyn J. (1966). *Gadjari among the Walbiri Aborigines*. Oceania Monographs. Sydney: University of Sydney Press.

Merlan, Francesca (1991). 'The limits of cultural constructionism: The case of Coronation Hill. *Oceania*, 61 (4): 341–52.

Merlan, Francesca (1998). *Caging the Rainbow*. Honolulu: University of Hawaii Press.

Morgan, Marlo (1994). *Mutant Message Down Under*. New York: Harper Collins.

Morton, John (1989). 'Black and white totemism: Conservation, animal symbolism, and human identification in Australia', in David Croft (ed.), *Australian People and Animals in Today's Dreamtime*. New York: Praeger, 21–52.

Munn, Nancy (1970). 'The transformation of subjects into objects in Walbiri and Pitjantjatjara myth', in Ronald Berndt (ed.), *Australian Aboriginal Anthropology*. Nedlands: University of Western Australia Press, 141–63.

Myers, Fred R. (1980). 'The cultural basis of Pintupi politics'. *Mankind*, 12: 197–213.

Myers, Fred R. (1982a). 'What is the 'business' of the Balgo Business? A Contemporary Aboriginal Religous Movement'. Unpublished manuscript.

Myers, Fred R. (1982b). 'Always ask: Resource use and landownership among the Pintupi of Central Australia', in N. Williams and E. Hunn (eds), *Resource Managers: North American and Australian Hunter-Gatherers*. Boulder: Westview Press, 173–96.

Myers, Fred R. (1986a). *Pintupi Country, Pintupi Self: Sentiment, Place, and Politics among Western Desert Aborigines*. Washington, D.C.: Smithsonian Institution Press.

Myers, Fred R. (1986b). 'The politics of representation: Anthropological discourse and Australian Aborigines', *American Ethnologist*, 13: 430–47.

Myers, Fred R. (1988a). 'Critical trends in the study of hunter-gatherers', *Annual Review of Anthropology*, 17: 261–82. Palo Alto: Annual Reviews, Inc.

Myers, Fred R. (1988b). 'Burning the truck and holding the country: Forms of property, time, and the negotiation of identity among Pintupi Aborigines, in T. Ingold, D. Riches, and J. Woodburn (eds), *Hunter-Gatherers*: II. *Property, Power and Ideology*. London: Berg.

Myers, Fred R. (1993). 'Place, identity, and exchange: The transformation of nurturance to social reproduction over the life-cycle in a kin-based society', in J. Fajans (ed.), *Exchanging Products: Producing Exchange*. Oceania Monographs, 43. Sydney: University of Sydney Press. 33–57.

Poirier, Sylvie (1995). *Les jardins du nomade: Cosmologie, territoire et personne dans le désert occidental australien*. Leiden: Lit.

Povinelli, Elizabeth (1995). *Labor's Lot: The Power, History and Culture of Aboriginal Action*. Chicago: University of Chicago Press.

Rose, Deborah (1992). *Dingo Makes Us Human: Life and Land in an Australian Aboriginal Culture*. Cambridge: Cambridge University Press.

Sackett, Lee (1991). Conservation/primitivism.

Sandall, Roger (1969). *Pintupi Revisit Yumari*. Film. Canberra: AiAS.

Stanner, W. E. H. (1965). 'Aboriginal territorial organization: Estate, range, domain and regime', *Oceania*, 36: 1–26.

Stanner, W. E. H. (1979). 'The Dreaming', in W. E. H. Stanner (ed.), *White Man Get No Dreaming*. Canberra: Australian National University Press, 23–40.

Strehlow, T. G. H. (1970). 'Geography and the totemic landscape in Central Australia', in Ronald Berndt (ed.), *Australian Aboriginal Anthropology*. Nedlands: University of Western Australia Press, 92–140.

Strehlow, T. G. H. (1971). *Songs of Central Australia*. Sydney: Angus and Robertson.

Swain, Tony (1993). *A Place for Strangers*. Melbourne: Cambridge University Press.

Turner, Terry (1973). 'Piaget's structuralism'. *American Anthropologist*, 75: 351–73.

Turner, Terry (1979). 'Kinship, household and community structure among the Kayapo', in David Maybury-Lewis (ed.), *Dialectical Societies*. Cambridge, MA: Harvard University Press, 179–217.

Turner, Terry (1980). 'Anthropology and the politics of indigenous people's struggles', *Cambridge Anthropology*, (winter).

Vygotsky, L. S. (1962). *Thought and Language*, trans. and edited by Eugenia Hanfmann and Gertrude Vakar. Cambridge, MA: MIT Press.

Vygotsky, L. S. (1978). in *Mind in Society: The Development of Higher Psychological Processes*, M. Cole, S. Scribner, V. John-Steiner, and E. Suberman (eds) Cambridge, MA: Harvard University Press.

Weiner, Annette (1980). 'Reproduction: A replacement for reciprocity', *American Ethnologist*, 7: 71–85.

Weiner, Annette (1992). *Inalienable Possessions*. Berkeley: University of California Press.

Weiner, James (1991). *The Empty Place*. Bloomington: Indiana University Press.

Weiner, James (1996). 'Anthropologists, historians, and the secret of social knowledge, *Anthropology Today*, 12 (3): 3–7.

Williams, Nancy (1986). *The Yolngu and their Land*. Canberra: Australian Institute of Aboriginal Studies Press.

Wilmsen, Edwin (1983). 'The ecology of illusion: Anthropological foraging in the Kalahari', *Reviews in Anthropology*, 10: 9–20.

Wilmsen, Edwin (1989). 'Introduction', in E. Wilmsen (ed.) *We are Here*. Berkeley: University of California Press, 1–15.

Woodward, A. (Mr Justice) (1973). *First Report of the Aboriginal Land Rights Commission*. Melbourne: Office of the Aboriginal Land Rights Commissioner.

4

Landscapes with People

Barry Cunliffe

TO ENTITLE my essay 'Landscapes with People' in a book devoted to 'Culture and Environment' might, at first sight, appear to be slightly perverse—an unnecessary playing with words perhaps. But not quite so—though I confess to believing that a title should, under no circumstances, give any indication of what a contribution is about lest a reader approach it with expectations. 'Culture and Environment' is, quite properly, a broad and widely embracing title designed to allow individual contributors ample scope to choose aspects of the interplay of the two concepts appropriate to their interests and expertise. My theme is more restricted. Instead of *culture* I intend to concentrate on the reaction of individuals, or groups of individuals, and instead of *environment* I will be considering that part of the cognitive environment that is more appropriately called *landscape*.

This gloss needs explanation. Environment is to landscape as *space* is to *place*. The American geographer Yi-Fu Tuan (1977) defined *space* as a continuum with no boundaries—that which is external to ourselves. Space can be measured and characterized in absolute terms in much the same way as environment can be described in terms of the interaction of lithosphere, biosphere, hydrosphere, and atmosphere. Environment, then, like space exists without dependence on the observer. *Place*, on the other hand, is specific to time and to people. It is enmeshed in a network of beliefs and values: it is a personal construct. One can fairly argue, as others have done, that a landscape is a network of personal places (Bender 1993).

Let us take an example. *Harvest Time 1860* is a typical Victorian landscape painted by George Cole in 1860 (figure 4.1). It is a product of its time, redolent with High Victorian values. We are overwhelmed with visions of industrious man and provident nature. But look more closely. The people are individuals interacting with each other within the constraints of their own social system. They do so in a landscape that is part

FIGURE 4.1 *Harvest Time 1860* by George Vicat Cole (1833–93). (Reproduced by kind permission of Bristol Museum and Art Gallery.)

nature (i.e., *environment*) and part artefact. It already has the patina of age. These are boundaries legitimized by time, thoroughfares along which people, goods and information flow, buildings with histories about which stories can be told and myths developed, underpinned by beliefs. The land is productive. It sustains but is fickle and wayward. It can yield in abundance or it can hold back and cause misery. It demands to be nurtured and propitiated. To each of these individuals the landscape is all of these things. As Tim Ingold (1993) has put it, 'The landscape is the world as it is known to those who dwell therein.'

But let us explore this further. It is perhaps a little more complex—there are degrees of cognition. *Mountain and Lake Landscape* painted in 1907 by Wu Shixian (figure 4.2) offers an informative example. Here we are presented with a foreground which embodies the activities of daily life: this is the present. There is also the background which is a place of potentials: herein lies the future. In looking upon this landscape we are invited to enter dimensions of time and to consider the prospect of things to come, half glimpsed at a great distance.

So, for people, their personal landscapes have many faces: they nurture through their productivity; they constrain and legitimize through their boundaries; they inform through their symbols; they instil awe through their waywardness; and they inspire through their distant vision of

FIGURE 4.2 *Mountain and Lake Landscape* by Wu Shixian (1907). Ink on paper. (Reproduced by kind permission of the Department of Eastern Art, Ashmolean Museum, Oxford.)

futures. In short, the physical *environment* (that is measurable and absolute) is a blotting paper into which the cultural images of *landscape* are absorbed.

It is one of the tasks of anthropologists and archaeologists to identify, untangle, and explain these images. The aims of the two disciplines are essentially the same but our methods of achieving them are different. The anthropologist can interrogate people about their landscape and is able to observe them react within it. The archaeologist has to decode the marks on the blotting paper, usually without the advantage of contemporary explanation, though for the most recent, tiny, fragment of the archaeological record our understanding may be enhanced by recorded anecdotes—the study of which is called *history*!

Some years ago I excavated a Roman palatial building at Fishbourne, near Chichester and discovered within the great central courtyard the physical remains of a contrived landscape, a garden (Cunliffe 1971). Using the range of techniques available to archaeologists we were able to produce a detailed plan of the layout of the bedding trenches for planting, the post-holes of the pergolas, the paths, and the water supply for the fountains (figure 4.3). By measuring the acidity/alkalinity of the soils

FIGURE 4.3   The Roman garden at Fishbourne reconstructed.

it was possible to determine the range of plants that could be grown, while pollen analysis added further details. Yet how people reacted to that garden and what it meant to them was beyond recovery. Contemporary wall paintings, like the famous garden scene on the wall of Livia's house on the Prima Porta in Rome, add the dimension and colour of the plants, greatly enlivening our vision of what it might have been, but it is the writings of the Younger Pliny, communicating with a friend about the charms of his country villa at about the time that Fishbourne was at its height, that allow us to begin to understand the delicate interaction of the man and his carefully contrived landscape. The passage is worth quoting *in extensio*:

The design and beauty of the buildings are greatly surpassed by the riding-ground. The centre is quite open so that the whole extent of the course can be seen as one enters. It is planted round with ivy-clad plane trees, green with their own leaves above, and below with the ivy which climbs over trunk and branch and links tree to tree as it spreads across them. Box shrubs grow between the plane trees, and outside there is a ring of laurel bushes which add their shade to that of the planes. Here the straight part of the course ends, curves round in a semicircle, and changes its appearance, becoming darker and more densely shaded by the cypress trees planted round to shelter it, whereas the inner circuits—for there are several—are in open sunshine; roses grow there and the cool shadow alternates with the pleasant warmth of the sun. At the end of the winding alleys of the rounded end of the course you return to the straight path, or rather paths, for there are several separated by intervening box hedges. Between the grass lawns here there are box shrubs clipped into innumerable shapes, some being letters which spell the gardener's name or his master's; small obelisks of box alternate with fruit trees, and then suddenly in the midst of this ornamental scene is what looks like a piece of rural country planted there. The open space in the middle is set off by low plane trees planted on each side; farther off are acanthuses with their flexible glossy leaves, then more box figures and names.   (Pliny to Domitius Apollinaris; Radice 1963)

It is all here, the light and shade, the colours, the contrasting shapes, the delight in feeling the sun upon the skin. Pliny's garden, like that at Fishbourne, was an attempt by people to enter into a dialogue with environment by creating landscape.

   The sophistication of Pliny's garden nicely contrasts with the stark vulgarity of the Stonehenge car park. Though a fascinating anthropological study in itself, what concerns us here is what was discovered beneath it when it was built. Here, archaeologists uncovered a row of five large pits, dug down into the chalk bedrock. They appear to have supported massive upright timbers which could well have stood to four or five metres above the ground. This surprising construction was dated to the Mesolithic period (about 7000 BC), and pollen analysis showed that building took place in a clearing in a forest dominated by pine and hazel. This much is demonstrable but what does it mean? Totem poles, perhaps, set up by a band of hunters and gatherers in their woodland habitat? Whatever the physical form of the construction there can be little doubt that the community involved was creating a *place* by modifying nature. They were beginning a dialogue with the environment which was to culminate five millennia later (about 2000 BC) with the final phase of the great stone monument we know as Stonehenge (figure 4.4). Admittedly, there is an uncomfortable chronological gap of some 4000 years between the erection of the row of timbers and the setting out nearby of the first circular ditched enclosure in the Neolithic period, about 3000 BC, but it is simpler to assume some form of continuity, once monumental manipulation of the environment had begun, than to accept the coincidence of two unique acts of social investment occurring in the same landscape without connection. In other words, the standing timbers put up by the Mesolithic hunters gave significance to the place. Once signified further monumentalization followed in an even more tangible and durable form and this very durability ensured that, as a place set aside, Stonehenge thereafter featured in every generation's landscape.

With its original meaning forgotten, later communities, realizing the antiquity of the monument, invented pasts for it in their own image and to meet their own needs. Thus, for the antiquary William Stukeley writing in the early eighteenth century, it was a source for endless scholarly speculation largely about the Druids. For Constable, a hundred years later, it provided a suitable subject for a romantic painting. Today neo-Druids and hippies use it as a focus to establish their identity, while for the new breed of professional heritage managers it provides endless lucrative consultancies. Each generation, as Jacquetta Hawkes so perceptively put it, gets the Stonehenge it deserves. The monument remains largely unchanged calmly reflecting back to us our own different perceptions.

Stonehenge is an example of a durable, created, landscape but not all anthropogenic changes to the environment survive into the landscapes of subsequent generations. An example is provided by fieldwork on the South Downs in the Hampshire parish of Chalton (Cunliffe 1973). Here, it was possible to plot the field systems, roadways, and settlements of the rural landscape in the Roman period over considerable areas. But a large blank exists in the middle of the map (figure 4.5). The reason for this is simply that this part of the Roman landscape was erased by the development of the medieval village and its surrounding fields. One generation wipes clean that part of its inherited landscape which has no

FIGURE 4.4 Stonehenge today. The ancient structure scarred by roads and tracks consolidated in the twentieth century.

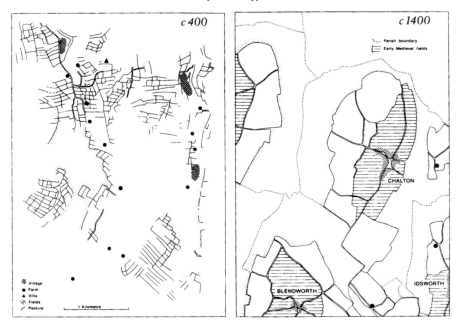

FIGURE 4.5   Chalton, Hampshire: two landscapes. The Roman landscape (left) with a gap in the centre where all trace of the early field systems has been destroyed by the medieval village and its fields.

significance for it. In this way the city fathers of many an English town removed their ancient city gates and walls as the pressure of traffic increased in the nineteenth century. Nowadays, in a fast changing world, these symbols of the past are much more highly prized, not for their beauty, but as essential points of reference in a time of destabilizing mobility. They provide a focus for pause and reflection, very different from their original legal and military functions.

Examples could be multiplied but enough has been said to show that not only does the interpretation of the landscape change over time but that the choice of what is retained and what is wiped away may depend, quite substantially, on changing social needs and perceptions.

It is, perhaps, on the chalklands of Wessex that we are able to come closest to understanding changing societies through changing landscapes. Taking the broadest overview of the developments over the last 4000 years BC it is possible to detect two very generalized cycles, the one merging into the other in the period 1300–800 BC. The early cycle, covering what is traditionally the Neolithic and Earlier Bronze Age, saw the

FIGURE 4.6   A Bronze Age barrow cemetery at Winterbourne Cross Roads just west of Stonehenge. The cemetery developed from the focus of a much earlier Neolithic long barrow (top left).

creation of a huge number of monuments involving hundreds of thousands of person–days of work. Among the earliest were the long barrows which we may assume to reflect the prowess of the lineage. Later came the massive ditched enclosures generally known, somewhat inappropriately, as henge monuments. The construction of each involved person power, and an order of coercion, of an impressive magnitude. These early monuments, whatever their immediate social use, provided structure in the landscape. They symbolized the relative power of the different lineages and polities and they acted as a counterbalance to the power of the wild. The monuments offered a sense of visual order and permanence in a world of natural chaos.

The later round barrows of the second millennium added more structure to the landscape (figure 4.6). A significant number of those interred were provided with valuable grave goods a knowledge of which, handed down from generation to generation, could not have failed to have endowed the landscape with a rich mythology. Thus, by the middle of the second millennium, 2,500 years of monument-building had created a familiar overlay to the land. Everywhere there were points of reference providing a sense of distance, identifying territories, glorifying ancestors, and offering an ever-present visual reminder of the long-established roots of the community. It is even possible that a knowledge of the different barrow types and the configuration of the cemeteries enabled an informed observer to measure time past and to identify social hierarchies thus providing a visual history to augment and make manifest the aural history which must surely have been re-enacted at social gatherings. The archaeologist's analytical approach to a barrow cemetery is far, far, removed from that of an inhabitant of Salisbury Plain 3,500 years ago. The monuments may be the same but our cognitive landscapes are very different.

In the middle of the second millennium BC a major shift away from monumentality can be identified. Instead, a new form of ordering becomes apparent with the creation of huge areas of regularly laid out fields often contained by linear earthworks. A good example of one such system has recently been studied on the western boundary of Hampshire near Quarley at a place with the unlikely local name of Windy Dido (figure 4.7). The fields were first identified in the 1920s when O. G. S. Crawford photographed them from the air. Since then, further air pho-

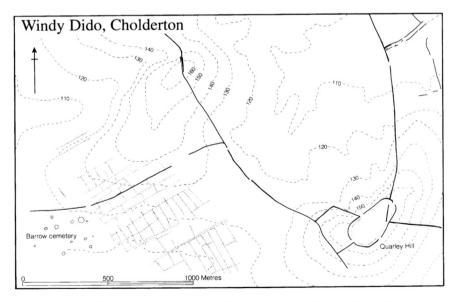

FIGURE 4.7 The second millennium field system at Windy Dido, Hampshire, planned from air photographs.

tography and ground surveys have shown that the system covers more than 90 hectares and was laid out within large rectangular blocks running downslope from a linear ditch occupying the crest of the ridge to the east. The magnitude of the scheme and the extreme order with which it was realized implies social organization at a high level motivated by a central coercive power.

The Windy Dido fields are not an isolated phenomenon. Other large tracts belonging to the same broad period have been identified in the vicinity of the later hillforts at Danebury and Woolbury to the east and are well known on the eastern fringes of Salisbury Plain and on the Marlborough Downs to the north (Palmer 1984; Gingell 1992). While dating evidence is not always precise, sufficient is now available to suggest that these allotments of regularly planned, coaxial, fields begin in the middle of the second millennium. Nothing like it was known before. This same period sees the establishment of the earliest linear boundaries, comprising straight runs of ditches slicing through the landscape, and small settlements of family, or extended family, size bounded by banks and ditches. Together, the impression given is that, over a comparatively short period of time, communities began to take control of the land to a degree never before contemplated and to impose themselves on it with a new and unaccustomed rigour. In place of the gentle trails of barrows following the contours of slope, a new rectilinearity scores the land, paying scant heed to natural land-form.

These changes may not have been too sudden—they may have spanned several centuries—but the overall visual effect would have been dramatic. We are witnessing the deliberate creation of a new landscape but one which appears to have complemented the old by leaving many of the ancestral barrow cemeteries intact in areas of pastureland beyond the boundaries of the arable.

Observing change in the archaeological record is not difficult but explaining it is seldom without problems. At a simple level one could argue that increase in population was the prime mover forcing society to take a more ordered approach to food production. This may well have an element of truth in it but the hypothesis is difficult to test. The need for greater efficiency in arable production could have brought about more far-reaching changes in society, forcing the community to focus more closely on the fertility of the land and the deities who controlled it. Once society had embarked on such a trajectory other things would have followed. Status, once made manifest in burial architecture, might now have been displayed in the ability of the lineage to control land by containing it within boundaries. A great expanse of ordered and well-tended fields is an impressive sight redolent of power. How much of this lay in the mindset of the Bronze Age inhabitants of Windy Dido we cannot say but at the very least the creation of an entirely new landscape over a period of a few centuries represents a social and economic transformation of considerable moment.

Towards the end of the second millennium another significant change to the Wessex landscape can be recognized with the creation of extensive systems of linear ditches carving up the landscape into huge blocks. These 'ranch boundaries' or 'linears' as they are called clearly represent a new concept of land allotment. Whatever practical functions they may have performed—in terms perhaps of livestock management—they were, above all, a symbol of social reordering on an extensive scale (Bradley *et al.* 1994). The sight of these thin white lines seared through the landscape will have impressed on the observer the centralizing power of the responsible authority. That many of the linears relate to prominent hilltops is a hint that the concepts of spatial organization behind them were really quite sophisticated (figure 4.8). Five or six centuries later some of these hilltops, like Sidbury, Clearbury, and Quarley were enhanced by enclosing defences, creating what are generally referred to as 'hillforts', a fact which suggests that the symbolism of the linears was being further reinforced at this time.

One, potentially revealing, observation is that some of the new linear ditches cut straight through the earlier field systems. How extensive was the dislocation to agriculture it is impossible to say since not all of the fields would have been put out of use but the act of scoring across earlier landscapes could well be thought to signify a cancellation of the values and authority inherent in the preceding system. The writing on the landscape is there for us to see but we can only guess at its message.

All this happened towards the beginning of what is traditionally called the Late Bronze Age, that is probably in the twelfth century BC or thereabouts. Elsewhere in Britain at this time equally dramatic landscape transformations were taking place. On Dartmoor, for example, a complex landscape of linear boundaries, enclosures, settlements, and fields, created in the middle of the second millennium, was widely abandoned (Flemming 1988) and similar large-scale abandonment is evident over much of the uplands of northern Britain. It has been conventional, until comparatively recently, to regard this large-scale dislocation as the direct result of climatic deterioration, the argument being that a slight increase in precipitation beginning in the middle of the second millennium started to accelerate about 1000 BC and reached a peak about 800 BC, the wetter conditions leading to the development of peat bogs particularly in upland locations. On Dartmoor, the blanket bog can be shown to have become

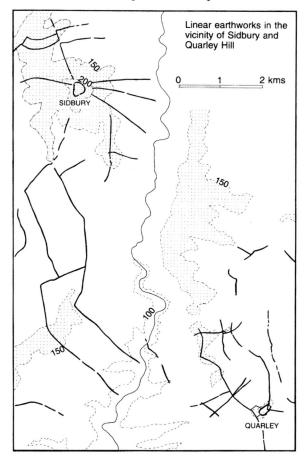

Linear earthworks in the
vicinity of Sidbury and
Quarley Hill

0   1   2 kms

SIDBURY

QUARLEY

FIGURE 4.8   Linear ditches of the Late Bronze Age in west Hampshire and
east Wiltshire.

far more extensive during this period (Simmons 1970) and accelerated
peat growth has been recognized in several western and northern
locations (Turner 1981). Coupled with this is the suggestion that there
was a 2 °C fall in overall mean temperature between *c.* 1300 and 900 BC
(Lamb 1981). Changes of this magnitude must have had a significant
effect on those communities who inhabited marginal upland regions. The
waterlogging of the soil and decrease in the crucial hours of warmth
needed for ripening crops drove out communities, leaving the land
desolate.

It is easy to understand how these environmental changes affected upland economies but what of congenial Wessex? The comparatively slight changes of precipitation and temperature were surely not significant enough to have caused large-scale desertification? We will return to this question in a moment.

Another catastrophe theory that has recently been explored is volcanic activity. In 1159 BC the Hekla volcano in Iceland enjoyed a major eruption. The event was first noted in the early 1980s by the Danish glaciologist C. V. Hammer who, in studying long cores from the Greenland ice sheet, identified a series of acid layers each representing an eruption. The twelfth-century BC event was later picked up by dendrochronologists and more recently *tephora*, that is volcanic dust, has been identified in relevant positions in northern Scottish peat bogs. Much of the crucial dendrochronological work has been carried out by Mike Baillie at Belfast using Irish oak (Baillie 1995). On three separate specimens Baillie was able to recognize a recurring pattern of a comparatively thick ring for the year 1160 BC followed by ten very narrow rings representing a decade during which there was virtually no tree ring growth. It is widely accepted that this 'biological catastrophe' was the result of dust clouds in the upper atmosphere caused by the Hekla eruption in 1159 BC but the crucial question which remains is how widespread and devastating were the effects of the eruption? Clearly, it affected Ireland and there was some fall-out in north-west Scotland but could there have been any significant impact further south? Opinion is divided between those who argue that dust clouds caused widespread devastation followed by plague throughout Britain and those who argue that the potential effects have been grossly exaggerated (Buckland *et al.* 1997). Until the relevant tree ring evidence is available from southern Britain in sufficient quantity the matter will remain unresolved.

This said, let us explore some possible scenarios. The archaeological evidence for Wessex suggests that a major reorientation in land apportionment took place at the end of the second millennium when a system of linear ditches was imposed upon the landscape. In a number of cases, the ditches ran across existing field systems rendering large tracts of arable land unusable. In social and economic terms this 'event' must have had a considerable impact—it was also an act which symbolized change in a highly dramatic manner for all to see. If the linear boundaries do reflect, as some would argue, a greater reliance on stock management as opposed to crop growing the explanation could lie in the failure of the large-scale agrarian system introduced, with so much expenditure of effort, in the middle of the second millennium. In seeking explanations for this, it could be that after five centuries or more of intensive use the thin downland soils showed signs of exhaustion. This might well have been exacerbated by an increase, however slight, in precipitation. Declining yields matched by a rise in population would have caused much social stress perhaps leading to a fear that the chthonic deities controlling fertility had ceased to favour humanity. Add to this the *possibility* of a decade of dust clouds in the upper atmosphere affecting the power of the sun and one can begin to picture the sense of foreboding that may have been generated requiring precipitate communal action. All the qualifying 'mights' and 'mays' must be underlined lest we begin to find the picture too compelling. What is offered by way of explanation is nothing more than a series of loosely linked possibilities. The fact, however, remains that there was a major transformation at this time which must have had a deep-rooted cause.

What followed is also, I believe, of direct relevance to our understanding of these events. Simply stated, throughout much of the first millennium BC in Wessex the archaeological record shows there to have been an intense, almost obsessive, focus on fertility. The first hints of this become apparent in the eighth and seventh centuries with the creation of huge middens like those recently identified and sampled at Potterne and East Chisenbury in Wiltshire (Needham and Spence 1997). The East Chisenbury midden is up to 2 metres thick and covers the astonishing area of 4 to 5 hectares giving it a rotted-down capacity of 65,000 cubic metres (McOmish 1996). Whilst, I suppose, a more prosaic explanation in terms of a thoroughly organized refuse disposal system is possible, such sophistication would be anachronistic at this time when populations seem to have been widely dispersed in family or extended family groups. Nor is the suggestion that the deposits were created solely by cycles of feasting entirely convincing, though periodic social gatherings of this kind may have played a part. We are forced to accept that refuse from settlements over a wide area was brought together and stockpiled. One plausible explanation for this is that the accumulation represents the desire to create communal control over society's midden material thus commanding the potential fertility embedded within it. One has only to look at the rich record of European peasant economies to see how important the midden was to the individual household not least as a measure of status. In earlier archaeological contexts in Wessex there is ample evidence of the use of domestic midden material in complex burial rituals. Thus, a context for midden creation and reverence already existed—what is exceptional about the eighth- to seventh-century Wessex middens is their scale and the degree of social cohesion that their construction implies. They must represent an intense, but comparatively short-lived, communal response to a perceived need in some way associated with an overwhelming desire to control fertility. That the midden represented power, not least as a manifestation of social cohesion, is a reasonable interpretation but how it was perceived and used at the time is impossible to say.

Another aspect of the increased emphasis on fertility is marl digging which becomes a widespread phenomenon in the first millennium. Shallow chalk quarries are frequently found on settlement sites, quite often as amorphous extensions growing out of the exposed edges of partially silted ditches. It may, at first sight, seem curious that quarried chalk was needed to marl fields on the chalk downs but many areas of the downland were covered with clayey acid soils which needed to be broken down and neutralized if they were to become productive. That some deeper significance lay behind marling is suggested by the fact that old chalk diggings were frequently used in Late Bronze and Early Iron Age Wessex for the disposal of the dead, who were deposited in small holes in tightly flexed bundles (figure 4.9). It is tempting to believe that some kind of reciprocity was inherent in this behaviour pattern, with the human body being returned to the earth which provided the fertility.

By the seventh century a more stable pattern of agricultural production was under way. Settlements now become evident and long-lasting after several centuries during which evidence of where people actually lived is somewhat sparse. It is also at this time that storage pits begin to appear in some number on all settlement sites and remain thereafter a common phenomenon until the aftermath of the Roman conquest. The use of an underground silo, believed to be for the storage of seed corn, is, on the face of it, a curious practice. Earlier views, that this was to protect the grain from raid, now seem unlikely not least because many of the settlements showed little evidence of significant defence and the grain for consumption was probably stored in highly visible above-ground granaries. Now, largely as the result of the careful excavation of a large sample of storage pits at the hillfort of Danebury (Cunliffe 1995) and the recognition of recurring patterns of propitiatory offerings after use, it is possible to offer a more plausible hypothesis that the deposition of seed grain in a storage pit was a deliberate act involving the placing of the seed in the protective custody of the chthonic deities during the dangerous liminal period between the time it was harvested and the moment it was sown. Once the pit had been emptied and the seed was in the soil, the pit became the focus of acts of propitiation, involving the structured deposition of parts of animals (figure 4.10), sets of artefacts, and other material. It is possible that these acts continued up to the time of the harvest and may have coincided with seasonal festivals (Cunliffe 1992).

FIGURE 4.9   The Early Iron Age burials at Suddern Farm, Hampshire, inserted into a quarry dug to provide chalk for marling.

It is tempting to suggest that all this emphasis on fertility, coming first into archaeological vision with the monumental community middens of the eighth and seventh centuries and continuing with the use of midden material and marl to enhance soil fertility and the careful storing of seed corn in below-ground silos, was a social response to some distant folk memory of times past when the land had become malignant and ceased to provide. The strategies designed to make sure the crisis did not recur were, as is so often the case, a mixture of the pragmatic and the superstitious: the land itself and the deities who controlled it had both to be attended to.

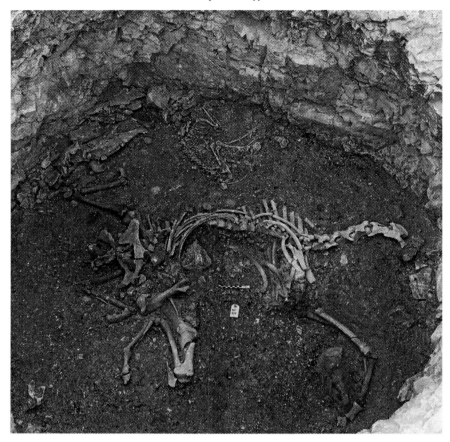

FIGURE 4.10 Propitiatory offering on the bottom of a storage pit in Danebury hillfort. The small animal (top) is a dog. The larger is a horse which has
been partially dismembered, its head and one foreleg being placed separately
against the pit side.

By the middle of the first millennium a stable state had been reached
and Iron Age societies living in Wessex were now creating new landscapes
with extensive field systems once more, overseen by large 'hillforts'
capping the dominant hills (figure 4.11). In the hillforts, whatever functions they were designed to satisfy, we are seeing a statement redolent of
assurance and control. Is it too fanciful to see in the emergence of these
now-familiar symbols an assertion that the land had now been brought
back under control?

FIGURE 4.11   The hillfort of Danebury, dominating the Hampshire downland.

Finally, let us stand aside from the detail of our millennium of Wessex. The last ten years or so have seen a significant change in our perception of ancient landscapes. There is a growing awareness of the complexity of human behaviour borne of a much closer rapport between archaeology and anthropology. This has emboldened archaeologists to move beyond the simple description of ancient environments and the categorization of subsistence strategies in an attempt, through identifying patterns of behaviour, to discover some of the belief systems and values of past societies. In this way we can hope to begin, albeit dimly, to see the landscape through the eyes of the people whose constraint and construct it was.

REFERENCES

Baillie, M. G. L. (1995). *A Slice through Time. Dendrochronology and Precision Dating*. London: Routledge.

Bender, B. (1993). *Landscape: Politics and Perspectives*. Oxford: Berg.

Bradley, R., Entwistle, R., and Raymond, F. (1994). *Prehistoric Land Divisions on Salisbury Plain. The Work of the Wessex Linear Ditches Project*. Archaeological Report 2. London: English Heritage.

Buckland, P. C., Dugmore, A. J., and Edwards, K. J. (1997). 'Bronze Age myths? Volcanic activity and human response in the Mediterranean and north Atlantic regions', *Antiquity*, 71: 581–93.

Cunliffe, B. (1971). *Excavations at Fishbourne*: Vol. I. *The Site*. London: Society of Antiquaries.

Cunliffe, B. (1973). 'Chalton, Hants.: The evolution of a landscape', *Antiquaries Journal*, 53: 173–90.

Cunliffe, B. (1992). 'Pits, preconceptions and propitiation in the British Iron Age', *Oxford Journal of Archaeology*, 11: 69–83.

Cunliffe, B. (1995). *Danebury. An Iron Age Hillfort in Hampshire*: Vol. 6. *A Hillfort Community in Perspective*. Research Report 102. York: CBA.

Flemming, A. (1988). *The Dartmoor Reaves*. London: Batsford.

Gingell, C. (1992). *The Marlborough Downs: A Later Bronze Age Landscape and its Origins*. Monograph 1. Devizes: Wiltshire Archaeological and Natural History Society.

Ingold, T. (1993). 'The temporality of landscape', *World Archaeology*, 25 (2): 152–74.

Lamb, H. H. (1981). 'Climate from 1000 BC–AD 100', in M. Jones and G. W. Dimbleby (eds), *The Environment of Man: The Iron Age to the Anglo-Saxon period*. BAR British Series 87, Oxford, 53–65.

McOmish, D. (1996). 'East Chisenbury: ritual and rubbish at the British Bronze Age–Iron Age transition', *Antiquity*, 70: 68–76.

Needham, S. and Spence, T. (1997). 'Refuse and the formation of middens', *Antiquity*, 71: 77–90.

Palmer, R. (1984). *Danebury. An Iron Age Hillfort in Hampshire. An Aerial Photographic Interpretation of its Environs*. RCHM England Supplementary Series 6. London.

Radice, B. (trans.) (1963). *The Letters of the Younger Pliny*. Harmondsworth, UK: Penguin, 5.6.

Simmons, I. G. (1970). 'Environment and Early Man on Dartmoor', *Proceedings of the Prehistoric Society*, 35: 203–19.

Tuan, Y.-F. (1977). *Space and Place. The Perspective of Experience*. Minneapolis: University of Minnesota Press.

Turner, J. (1981). 'The Iron Age', in I. G. Simmons and M. Tooley (eds), *The Environment in British Prehistory*. London: Duckworth, 251–61.

5

The French Nineteenth-century Landscape

John House

A CRUDE historical vignette—of three moments, and three texts—will outline the historical framework for an exploration of French nineteenth-century attitudes to landscape. In the broadest terms, early in the century the prime concern was for the preservation of historical monuments, premised on the assumption that the landscape itself was safe; by the 1860s, technological change had begun to threaten the landscape, and by the end of the century the monuments were for the most part safe, but the countryside itself, and the whole way of life for which it stood, were believed to be facing extinction.

In 1820, in the first of the pioneering volumes of *Voyages pittoresques et romantiques dans l'ancienne France*, Charles Nodier insisted on the national significance of France's monuments, not only as objects of beauty, but also as salutary reminders of the imprint of France's history, made all the more vivid by the recent events of the French Revolution and the massive destruction of historical monuments that followed it. His was not a work of antiquarianism but rather 'a voyage of impressions, if one may describe it like this'. Nodier recognized what the 'superb countryside' might offer the landscape painter; but this first volume, devoted to Normandy, focused on historical monuments because it was the monuments that were then at risk of destruction:

The title of these *Voyages* might seem to promise that we will be concerned with the picturesque sites of which there are so many in our beautiful country. Indeed, this was our original intention. . . . However, the general description of sites . . . is not an urgent matter. They remain; their forms change little, or they are

This essay, and the lecture upon which it was based, developed in part from my research for the exhibition catalogue *Landscapes of France: Impressionism and its Rivals*, London: South Bank Centre (Hayward Gallery), 1995 (also presented as *Impressions of France*, Boston: Museum of Fine Arts, 1995–6), and in particular for my essay 'Framing the Landscape' in this catalogue. Greg M. Thomas, Art and Ecology in Nineteenth-century France: The Landscapes of Théodore Rousseau, Princeton University Press 2000, was published after this essay went to press.

embellished when they change. By contrast, the monuments disappear; they disappear rapidly, particularly when they belong to the old institution of the State, when the new institution, impatient to renew everything, joins in a conspiracy with the effects of time to destroy them. . . . Our descendants, happy inhabitants of these beautiful country regions, will perhaps have enough leisure to paint them. But we, the last travellers in the ruins of old France, which soon will no longer exist, we want to depict only those ruins whose history and mysteries will be lost for the next generation. We will only turn our eyes away from the works of art that the centuries do not respect and scrutinise the natural scene whose imperishable beauty is not altered by the passing centuries when a picturesque site recalls a historical moment. . . .[1]

In the second volume of the series, on the Franche-Comté, landscape played a larger role, because the Jura region had fewer monuments than Normandy and its scenery was more spectacular. Moreover, geological formations of the region, such as the celebrated Grottes d'Oselles, might be regarded as part of the history of the land. However, at one point, it is acknowledged that human intervention was already spoiling one of the most 'picturesque' sites; amid a rapturous and rhetorical evocation of the Source of the River Loue (a site later painted by Courbet), the authors note: 'Yet the form of some of the cascades is changing. Man's industry, which has little respect for picturesque beauties, has constructed locks, iron-works and saw-mills next to these marvels; it has levied tribute-money on God's creation, and has mutilated the torrents in order to enrich commerce'.[2]

By 1866, this issue has become urgent for the geographer Elisée Reclus. His essay 'Du sentiment de la nature dans les sociétés modernes', published in the *Revue des deux mondes*, is a fascinating amalgam of views. At the outset, he celebrates man's wish to conquer mountains, and especially the English and German tastes for mountaineering.[3] However, when he turns to French views of nature, he focuses on the French taste for the 'humanized' landscape. This cannot, though, be appreciated by everyone; he insists that the countryside can only be truly valued by those with education and '*délicatesse*', whereas peasants and bourgeois 'exploiters of the soil' only measure it for its utility.[4] He warns of the

[1] Ch. Nodier, J. Taylor, Alph. de Cailleux, *Voyages pittoresques et romantiques dans l'ancienne France: Normandie*, i, Paris: Didot, 1820, 1–8 (quotation from 7–8); on the *Voyages pittoresques*, see especially Jean Adhémar, *La France romantique: Les lithographies de paysage au XIXe siècle*, Paris: Somogy, 1997 (illustrated reprint of 1937 publication), and Bonnie L. Grad and Timothy A. Riggs, *Visions of City and Country: Prints and Photographs of Nineteenth-Century France*, Worcester (MA): The Worcester Art Museum, and New York: The American Federation of Arts, 1982, 15–78.
[2] Ch. Nodier, J. Taylor, Alph. de Cailleux, *Voyages pittoresques et romantiques dans l'ancienne France: Franche-Comté*, Paris: Didot aîné, 1825, 1–10, 160–3 (quotation from 162).
[3] Elisée Reclus, 'Du sentiment de la nature dans les sociétés modernes', *Revue des deux mondes*, 15 May 1866, 353–65.   [4] Ibid. 365–71.

vast damage currently being inflicted on the countryside. Here, the villains are fourfold: tourists and visitors, who leave their débris everywhere; speculators, who divide up beautiful areas of the landscape into small plots for their own benefit; industrialization, which pollutes the air with factory smoke; and engineers, who impose ugly bridges and viaducts on to the natural scenery.[5] Yet at the end Reclus is able to bypass these pressing threats, and to praise man's desire to find solace and regeneration in unspoiled nature, in contrast to the decadence of urban society.[6]

By the end of the century Nodier's initial priorities had been comprehensively reversed. The countryside, and the whole way of life it embodied, were seen to be at risk, as the result of agricultural decline and modernization. André Theuriet's *La vie rustique*, published in 1888, was a lavish presentation of a way of life that he saw as disappearing (figure 5.1). After a brief invocation of the harshness of peasant labour, Theuriet turned to a paean to the 'charm' and 'picturesque qualities' that artists and poets found in the countryside. His book was a monument to what he saw as the imminent loss of this lifestyle, already foreshadowed by the invasion of industry into the environs of Paris, 'diminished, vulgarised, polluted by the factories'. As he presents it, though, Theuriet seems to be mourning the loss of a mythic image rather than of any social reality.[7]

These changing perspectives in attitudes towards monuments and countryside were reflected, too, in the history of French conservation organizations. The post of *Inspecteur général des monuments historiques* was established as early as 1830, quickly followed in 1834 by a Commission charged with the protection of historical monuments. By contrast, the *Société pour la protection des paysages de France* was founded only in 1901, and followed in 1906 by legislation on the protection of 'sites and natural monuments of an artistic character'.[8]

Of course, these changing perceptions of the condition of the countryside were an expression of material changes. New modes of transportation, notably the railway, created a wholly new type of mobility. The train provided the conduit that enabled the greatly expanded distribution of agricultural produce beyond the immediate area of its production. Moreover, the city increasingly appeared to offer possibilities of self-advancement, encouraging a process of rural depopulation that, by the end of the century, was viewed as a crisis that imperilled the future of French agriculture and of the countryside itself. At the same time, rural

[5] Ibid. 377–80.   [6] Ibid. 380–1.
[7] André Theuriet, *La vie rustique*, Paris: H. Launette, 1888, III–VIII.
[8] See Yves Luginbuhl, *Paysages: Textes et représentations du siècle des Lumières à nos jours*, Paris: La Manufacture, 1989, 186–9.

FIGURE 5.1   Léon Lhermitte, frontispiece for André Theuriet, *La vie rustique*, 1888.

areas were opened out to urban influences and ideas, and tourism extended into even the most remote corners of France.[9]

There were changes, too, in the patterns of tourism. Early in the century, the intrepid travellers who braved France's horse-drawn coaches were primarily interested in ancient monuments and sites with historical associations—the interests that the *Voyages pittoresques* volumes so clearly expressed. By the mid century, though, there was an increasing interest in what Nicholas Green has described as 'nature tourism', focusing on the sensory experience of the sites themselves, as refuges from the pressures of urban life.[10]

These historical patterns are crucial as the context for our subject. However, the issue of tourism brings us to a central issue in this essay: the notion of 'landscape' itself. Here two points must be stressed: first, the idea of landscape was not simply a matter of choosing to look at or to paint the countryside, but it involved a particular way of seeing; and second, for many thinkers in the nineteenth century this way of seeing might actively seek to exclude the presence of those who lived and worked in the countryside.

The notion of landscape itself, like that of landscape painting, is not simply a question of subject matter, but involves a way of seeing that views the outdoor scene *as* a landscape; the 'landscape' itself, as W. J. T. Mitchell has recently insisted, is 'already a representation in its own right',[11] and, as Reclus's text made clear, this way of seeing was socially and culturally constructed, depending on education and temperament. The immersion of the nature tourist or the landscapist in the countryside was of a totally different order from the involvement of peasant or farmer with his land; to see the land as landscape is to adopt a position that is by definition that of an outsider. Many texts of the period insist that those involved in working the land cannot view it as 'landscape', whether because, as proprietors, their view was dominated by financial interest, or because, as peasants, their lack of education and the sheer physicality of their contact with the soil made them unable to view it from outside.[12]

---

[9] Among the vast literature on the changes in rural France during the nineteenth century, see, recently, James R. Lehning, *Peasant and French: Cultural Contact in Rural France during the Nineteenth Century*, Cambridge University Press, 1995.

[10] Nicholas Green, *The Spectacle of Nature: Landscape and Bourgeois Culture in Nineteenth-Century France*, Manchester: Manchester University Press, 1990, 80ff. Green's book is of fundamental importance for the understanding of cultural attitudes towards the countryside in the period.

[11] W. J. T. Mitchell, 'Imperial Landscape', in W. J. T. Mitchell (ed.), *Landscape and Power*, University of Chicago Press, 1994, 14–15.

[12] See e.g. Reclus, 1866, 368, 378; Theuriet, 1888, III.

Daumier made the distinction between the peasant's view of the countryside and that of the landscapist very clear in a cartoon in 1864: a landscapist is sitting in a field, painting a fruit tree, while a peasant looks on,
saying to his companion: 'There's a strange fellow . . . making a portrait
of a tree that doesn't produce any apples . . . he must be crazy!'.[13] Monet
wittily played on a similar contrast in *The Beach of Sainte-Adresse* of
1867 (Art Institute of Chicago), where the fishermen in the foreground
turn their backs on the 'landscape' that we and the bourgeois couple on
the beach (the man with his telescope) are scrutinizing.

The distinction appears most starkly in a passage by Ralph Waldo
Emerson (1836), quoted by Mitchell:

The charming landscape which I saw this morning, is indubitably made up of
some twenty or thirty farms. Miller owns this field, Locke that, and Manning
the woodland beyond. But none of them owns the landscape. There is a property in the horizon which no man has but he whose eye can integrate all the
parts, that is, the poet. This is the best part of these men's farms, yet to this their
warranty-deeds give no title . . . you cannot freely admire a noble landscape, if
laborers are digging in the field hard by.[14]

The reparative function of landscape—whether visited or painted—
depended on the omission of those who inhabited and worked it and the
elimination of signs of change or of the invasion of modernization and
urban influences. In 1864 Léon Lagrange explained why he preferred
landscapes without figures: '. . . reduced to its very own elements, nature
still speaks to anyone who wishes to listen to it in a language full of
elevation. It even seems that the absence of man lends nature's voice
still more resonance.'[15] In 1861, Maxime du Camp was still more explicit
about why he wanted to cleanse the landscape of its human occupants:

The painters of landscapes and marines do not generally realise how much they
harm their pictures by loading them with useless little people. What one loves
in the forests, in the meadows, by the edge of the sea, is the absolute solitude
which allows one to be in direct communion with nature; if a peasant or a sailor
appears, the spell is broken, and one is grasped again by the humanity that one
had wanted to escape; what is true in reality is also true in fiction; a landscape
only has grandeur if it is uninhabited . . .[16]

This is a 'nature' stripped of signs of human life and labour, presented as
a spectacle for solitary contemplation. Du Camp's wish to banish the

[13] Published in *Charivari*, 9 December 1864; see Loys Delteil, *Le Peintre-graveur illus-
tré*, XXVIII: *Daumier*, IX, Paris: Loys Delteil, 1926, no. 3428.
[14] Ralph Waldo Emerson, 'Nature' (1836), quoted in Mitchell, 1994, 13–14.
[15] Léon Lagrange, 'Le Salon de 1864', *Gazette des Beaux-Arts*, 1 July 1864, 6, 9.
[16] Maxime du Camp, *Le Salon de 1861*, Paris: Librairie Nouvelle, 1861, 145–6.

figure was also an attempt to defuse the threat of other, potentially potent, ways of seeing the places—not as spectacle, but as habitat and workplace.

It may seem to be a significant shift from the idea of landscape as a way of viewing an actual place to the landscape as an art form. In some senses this is a vital shift, but in others less so. The French word *paysage*, like the word landscape, refers to both things—the visual representation of an outdoor scene and the scene itself. Time and again, in the critical writing about landscape painting in nineteenth-century France, these two meanings were elided. When discussing the landscapes exhibited at the Paris Salon, critics frequently wrote as if the paintings transported the viewer from the exhibition halls into the open air:

The critic feels a sense of joy and refreshment when, having examined the history paintings, the mythologies, the sentimental scenes and the portraits, he sees, in the middle of his voyage through the exhibition, these green meadows, these deep woods, these solitary valleys where the landscapists allow him to stroll and to breathe at leisure.[17]

Often, too, individual pictures were described as if they were transparent—as if the scene itself was being described. Landscape painting occupied a similar function to the idea of landscape itself; the idea of landscape could be reparative in three ways: through visiting the place itself, through armchair memory or imagination, or through engaging empathetically with a pictorial representation.

Art critics repeatedly speculated on the reasons why landscape had become so popular in the mid to later nineteenth century. Whatever their analysis of contemporary art and society, one theme kept recurring: the taste for landscape was seen in opposition to the experience of modern urban life—as a refuge from its mental and physical pressures. Landscape was essentially an urban art form. It was exhibited and sold in cities. Few of the viewers and buyers of landscape in nineteenth-century Paris belonged to the rural landowning classes. Their idea of landscape stood in contrast to their own experiences of life in the city; and the countryside, and 'landscape', were commodities that could be consumed in many forms: through antiquarian and geographical tracts, through popular magazines and novels, through topographical prints and exhibition paintings, and through actual travel and tourism.

But there was a further crucial dimension in fine art—the status of the 'fine art' object itself. Paintings shown at the Paris Salon were made to be viewed and judged as fine art and in relation to other paintings; their viewers were invited to assess them in relation to artistic conventions and

[17] Paul Mantz, 'Le Salon de 1863', *Gazette des Beaux-Arts*, 1 July 1863, 36–7.

criteria, as well as to the idea of a 'real world' lying beyond the picture. These factors did not apply equally to all visual representations; as we shall see, other visual media, such as the engravings that appeared in travel guides, were not always subject to the same constraints.

In fine art practice in the early part of the nineteenth century, a landscape subject needed to fulfil certain requirements to be worth painting—to be considered, in the artistic terminology of the nineteenth century, as a *motif*. The site needed to be significant, either through the elements in the scene or through its associations, and the forms of the landscape needed to be arranged in such a way as to give the scene a coherence and dignity—according to criteria loosely based on the conventions of the classicizing landscape painting of the seventeenth and eighteenth centuries, by painters such as Poussin, Claude, and Valenciennes.

From 1820 onwards, the magnificent lithographic plates in the volumes of *Voyages pittoresques* established conventions for the representation of the French countryside. Alongside plates showing details of individual buildings, many of the illustrations in them presented historical monuments in their natural surroundings, emphasizing the interplay between natural and man-made monuments as the essence of 'old France'.[18] In paintings, too, painters such as Paul Huet (who also made lithographs for the Auvergne volume of the *Voyages pittoresques*) and Jean-Baptiste-Camille Corot focused on similar themes, of medieval castles on hills or cathedrals in valleys.

Alongside this, from the 1830s onwards, there was a growing interest in paintings of secluded rural scenes, especially in subjects from the Forest of Fontainebleau, by painters such as Jules Dupré and Théodore Rousseau (figure 5.2); these images clearly correspond in some sense to the growing taste for 'nature tourism' in these years. In them, the forest is presented as a remote refuge, unpeopled except by the occasional small peasant figure who appears as if part of the natural scenario, overshadowed by the grandeur of the forest trees.

At first sight this may suggest that there was a relatively straightforward correspondence between artistic interests and the types of engagement with the countryside itself outlined at the start. But in two distinct ways this relationship was more problematic than it might at first appear. First, tensions might occur in actual physical terms, in conflicts between landscape painters and other users of the countryside. The second problem concerns the interpretation of paintings: putting it crudely, should the historian view landscape paintings primarily as expressions of

---

[18] See Adhémar, 1997 and Grad and Riggs, 1982, as cited in n. 2.

FIGURE 5.2   Théodore Rousseau, *The Forest of Fontainebleau, Morning*, 1850.
(Reproduced by kind Permission of the Trustees of the Wallace Collection,
London.)

an attitude to the physical scenes they depict, or rather in terms of the
ways in which they use and manipulate artistic conventions?

At one and the same time, the rising tide of 'nature tourism' was an
expression of a desire to find seclusion and solace in nature and a threat
to that desire. Rousseau's engagement with the Forest of Fontainebleau
was in explicit opposition to the touristic development of the forest.
While he was living there, Charles-François Denecourt was opening the
forest out to visitors, publishing guidebooks, and creating walks through
the forest itself that offered the visitor an easy path and interesting view-
points. In a sense, this allowed the forest to be seen as 'landscape'; but
Rousseau and other painters opposed these developments, seeking to
exclude the tourist hordes and to preserve its pristine wildness as a site
for solitary contemplation, as Rousseau presented it in his paintings.[19]

Other guidebooks of the period, such as the widely circulated Guides
Joanne, followed Denecourt's lead in publicizing his walks:

[19] See Green, 1990, 118–19, 167–81, 211 (n. 81), and Steven Adams, *The Barbizon School
and the Origins of Impressionism*, London: Phaidon, 1994, 71–7.

FIGURE 5.3   *The Forest of Fontainebleau, View at the Gros-Fouteau*, engraving from Adolphe Joanne, *Fontainebleau*, 1866.

This revelation of the forest to the thousand curious visitors who flock from Paris to Fontainebleau has displeased the artists who have been disturbed in their oases that had till then been solitary, where they pitched camp like gypsies. But this impression has been erased; and now the goodly Denecourt [the modern personification of Sylvain, the benevolent deity of the forest] is the object of sympathy from all those who know that it is thanks to him that they can so readily ramble through the most beautiful sites.

However, the vignette illustrations in the Joanne guide to the forest do not show these walks (e.g. figure 5.3). Ironically, they adopt conventions far closer to Rousseau's paintings, presenting the forest as an untouched refuge.[20] Was this because the enormous number of fine art paintings of forest interiors made it impossible to visualize the forest in any other way? Or because such guides to the forest were meant more for armchair travellers than for serious walkers? Or because the forest—whether in imagination or when actually visited—was expected to evoke aesthetic and poetic reverie that would be excluded by matter-of-fact vignettes of Denecourt's promenades? There are no clear answers here; but this is an

[20] Adolphe Joanne, *Fontainebleau*, Paris: Hachette, 1867; on Denecourt, 138–43 (quotation from 143); see engravings on e.g. 135, 147, 167, 185.

example of the complex interrelationships between different types of imagery and the social practices that lay behind them.

By the 1860s, there was widespread concern that material changes in the countryside were imperilling the artist's vision of 'nature'. The landscapist Frédéric Henriet vividly expressed these fears in his book *Le Paysagiste aux champs*:

The landscapist . . . admits with sorrow that all the savage and grandiose aspects of nature are being erased, as science exploits every richness in the soil, and civilisation . . . makes everything uniform: customs, costumes, social practices and habitations! Every conquest of industry and every material improvement involves some sacrifice of the poetry of memories or of picturesque beauties . . . Poetry! it is in the heart of the artist . . . We would say to the devotees of pure art . . . Immerse yourselves again ceaselessly in life-enhancing contact with nature . . . There still exist remote footpaths and forgotten corners where your inspiration will not risk breaking its wings against the factory chimney, the telegraph pole or the black funnel of the locomotive.[21]

If Rousseau and other painters opposed the development of the countryside in the 1850s and 1860s, Monet found himself in a different sort of conflict with his neighbours in the 1890s, when his ambitions to develop his water-garden met robust opposition from the local farmers, who feared that the exotic lilies and other water-plants that he planned to plant would pollute the local water supply.[22] Now, it was Monet's artifice that seemed to put the countryside at risk, rather than the invasion of outside developments threatening the purity of the painter's vision of 'nature'. Ironically, today it is the development of Monet's garden as a site of mass tourism that has transformed the local environment and economy of Giverny, since its restoration and reopening in 1979.

However, the key issues about the relationship between the imagery of landscape painting and attitudes towards the landscape itself emerge in a different context, in paintings that directly engage with the material changes in the countryside. The 'new' forest that Rousseau rejected made its appearance in painting in Monet's project for a vast *Déjeuner sur l'herbe* of 1865–6 (fragments in Musée d'Orsay, Paris; sketch in the Pushkin Museum, Moscow), in which a forest glade is the site for a lavish bourgeois picnic. But this image can be read in two ways: it can be seen in social terms, as a celebration of the practices of the tourist, or viewed in the field of fine art, as an explicit counter to the conventions of stock

[21] Frédéric Henriet, *Le Paysagiste aux champs*, Paris: A. Lévy, 1876, 96–7 (a version of this part of the book was first published in 1866).
[22] Daniel Wildenstein, *Claude Monet: Biographie et catalogue raisonné*, III, Lausanne and Paris: La Bibliothèque des Arts, 1979, 50, and especially 274–5, letter from Monet to the Préfet de l'Eure, 17 July 1893.

images of the forest such as Rousseau's. Both of these options need to be left in play, while we explore other examples where issues about the state of the countryside seem to come up against questions of the politics of painting. These issues come most sharply into focus in the scenes of the environs of Paris painted by members of the Impressionist group during the 1870s. Many of these paintings present a landscape that has been overtly invaded by just the signs of change and modernization that conventional landscape imagery so determinedly excluded.

Renoir's *The Harvesters* (Bührle Foundation, Zürich), exhibited at the first Impressionist group exhibition in 1874, presents a very common theme in the imagery of the countryside at the period.[23] However, instead of showing the harvest as a seemingly timeless ritual framed by the beauties of nature, he relegates his harvesters to the right side of the picture, juxtaposed with a cabbage patch on the left, a modern villa on the horizon, and an unexplained pair of figures approaching down the central path. The very summary, sketch-like technique, too, denies the harvesters the dignity conventionally given to fieldworkers in the art of the period. Clearly by exhibiting his picture Renoir was attacking the stock conventions; but does this reveal his attitude to the scene itself—to the raw materials out of which he made this iconoclastic 'landscape'? We might argue, instead, that the critique was essentially pictorial—both in his attack on the conventional picturesque, and in his parading of a virtuoso sketching technique. This technique would have seemed a travesty of fine art to most viewers, but, for Renoir's supporters, it was this that would have made his picture transcend its ungraceful subject.[24]

The work of Pissarro and Monet in the 1870s and 1880s will illuminate these issues further. In the mid 1870s Pissarro painted a sequence of pictures of the banks of the river Oise in which a factory on the river bank plays a prominent role.[25] This intrusion of contemporaneity is an overt rejection of the conventional imagery of the banks of the Oise, as

[23] See *The Passionate Eye: Impressionist and Other Master Paintings from the Collection of Emil G. Bührle, Zürich*, Washington: National Gallery of Art and London: Royal Academy of Arts, 1990–1, no. 50.

[24] In Louis Leroy's comic review of the 1874 exhibition (*Le Charivari*, 25 April 1874), the imaginary academic painter M. Vincent, driven to madness by the Impressionists' technique, criticizes the figures of Renoir's harvesters for being 'too studied', treated with three brushstrokes where one would have been enough; no reviewers singled the picture out for special praise, but the supportive commentators on the show viewed their sketch-like technique as the ideal means of conveying fleeting effects of light and atmosphere (e.g. Philippe Burty, *The Academy*, 30 May 1874, 616). The reviews of the group exhibitions are reprinted in Ruth Berson (ed.), *The New Painting 1874–1886: Documentation*, San Francisco: Fine Arts Museums of San Francisco, and Seattle: University of Washington Press, 1996; for Leroy's and Burty's comments, see I, 25–6, 10.

[25] On Pissarro's factory paintings, see Richard R. Brettell, *Pissarro and Pontoise*, New Haven and London: Yale University Press, 1990, 73–97.

popularized by the paintings of Charles-François Daubigny, which present the misty rural riverbank as an unspoiled retreat. Though at first sight Pissarro's factory paintings are comparable to Renoir's travesty of the stock vision of the harvest, there is a vital difference. In the Renoir, the central issue is his decision to formulate the subject of harvest in such an anti-picturesque form; with Pissarro, the disruption is caused by a physical intruder into the landscape itself—the factory on the river bank. In Reclus's 1866 essay, it was just such developments in the countryside that were seen as a threat to its potential as refuge and renewal.

But should we use Pissarro's picture as evidence for his personal attitude to this invasive presence in the rural scene? He could of course have avoided painting it, and chosen a different view, or he could have simply left it out. But can his choice to paint it be interpreted as a criticism of the industrialization of the landscape? The answer to this question is complicated by the very different ways in which he presented this factory in different pictures. In *Banks of the Oise, Pontoise* (Indianapolis Museum of Art) it is relegated to the background, though it is still a key element in this humdrum panorama of everyday life on the banks of an unpicturesque stretch of the river. In *Factory near Pontoise* (Museum of Fine Arts, Springfield), by contrast, it is the central feature, its sheds and smoking chimneys dominating the scruffy remnants of 'nature' around it; here, an ecological reading, in terms of its destruction of the landscape, might seem appropriate. Yet in a third canvas, *The Oise on the Outskirts of Pontoise* (Clark Art Institute, Williamstown), it is seen from further away, and framed by trees, bushes, and flowers, now seemingly a benign presence in the landscape.[26]

This group of paintings, all painted in the same year, 1873, is a salutary reminder that we cannot directly read off social attitudes from fine art images such as these. The differences between the effect and mood of the paintings are the result of Pissarro's choices—of weather and viewpoint; and these are part of his artistic project, not an expression of a view about the landscape itself. Taken as a whole, his project suggests that the presence of the modern can assume many faces in the landscape: a truly modern type of painting should bring together just those contrasting elements that traditional landscape imagery had kept categorically separate.

Likewise Monet, in his paintings of Argenteuil in the same period, explored the widest variety of different tonalities and moods. Sometimes he presented the place in more conventional guise, as if it were a rural village; more often, the signs of modernity obtrude, but these are extremely varied: factories and railway bridges appear, but so do suburban

---

[26] See Brettell, 1990, 82, 85, 87.

FIGURE 5.4   Claude Monet, *The Railway Bridge at Argenteuil*, 1873. (Reproduced by courtesy of Helly Nahmad Gallery, London.)

villas, riverside chalets, and sailing boats. And the tone of the pictures varies constantly, as he explored the place in all seasons and all weathers.[27] A regatta may be presented in overcast stormy conditions, and the railway bridge in radiant sunshine (e.g. figure 5.4); there is no correlation between the overall tone of the picture and the elements that are included in it. He immersed himself in the widest range of visual effects, rather than standing outside them to pass a verdict on them. As with Pissarro, Monet's project seems to have been to explore the multifarious processes of modernization that were transforming the environs of Paris, and thereby to challenge the conventions of picturesque landscape painting.

Here, another contrast between media is helpful. A sequence of Joanne guides published from the 1850s onwards follow the new railway routes out of Paris; the engravings in them actively celebrate the train's path through the landscape—not only the bridges across the rivers, but also the spectacular viaducts (e.g. figure 5.5).[28] Here, there may be a trace of

[27] For discussion of Monet's Argenteuil paintings, focusing primarily on the material sites he depicted, see Paul Hayes Tucker, *Monet at Argenteuil*, New Haven/London: Yale University Press, 1982.

[28] e.g. Eugène Chapus, *De Paris à Rouen et au Havre*, Paris: Hachette, 1855. For a reproduction of another of the engravings in this guide, see Robert L. Herbert, *Impressionism: Art, Leisure and Parisian Society*, New Haven/London: Yale University Press, 1988, 223.

FIGURE 5.5   *The Mirville Viaduct*, engraving from Eugène Chapus, *De Paris à Rouen et au Havre*, 1858 edition.

an aesthetic argument, and indeed figures of artists sketching appear in several of the engravings; but essentially this was a form of advertising: an incentive to tourists to follow these tracks—and doubtless to buy another Joanne guide at their destination. One type of social history might pinpoint the similarities between Monet's paintings and the Joanne images; the present account would rather highlight the differences between the projects, in their means and aims, and in the interests they served. The type of image that fitted readily into a tour guide might become bizarre or subversive when transposed into the sphere of 'fine art'.

Few critics directly addressed the Impressionists' choice of landscape subject matter, but Charles Bigot, reviewing the third Impressionist group exhibition in 1877, argued that the sites that the group chose to paint were a travesty not only of landscape painting but of the very idea of nature itself:

In the final analysis, it is not true nature that they have looked at and have tried to render, but rather the nature that one encounters on outings in the great city or its surroundings, where the harsh notes of the houses, with their white, red or yellow walls and their green shutters, come up against the vegetation of the trees and form violent contrasts with it. How much better have ... our modern landscapists, the Rousseaus, the Corots and the Daubignys, understood how to express not only the poetry but also the truth of nature! How much better have they represented the countryside, with its waters, its woods, its fields and its meadows, with its distant and calm horizons![29]

By contrast, another critic at the 1877 exhibition, Frédéric Chevalier, saw that even discordant elements such as these might be understood as a coherent world view: subjects and technique together could stand for the idea of modernity:

The characteristics which distinguish the Impressionists—the brutal handling of paint, their down to earth subjects, the appearance of spontaneity which they seek above all else, the deliberate incoherence, the bold colouring, the contempt for form, the childish naiveté that they mix heedlessly with exquisite refinements—this disconcerting mixture of contradictory qualities and defects is not without analogy to the chaos of opposing forces that trouble our era.[30]

Chevalier's comments introduce an overtly political dimension to the discussion. Under the 'moral order' régime that followed the disasters of the Franco-Prussian War and the Paris Commune of 1870–1, the State was seeking to foster a reassuring, seemingly timeless image of the French countryside, presenting the landscapes of *'la France profonde'* as the stable backbone of the nation, as in Charles Busson's *The Village of Lavardin*, purchased by the State at the Salon in 1877.[31] The fragmented modern world that Chevalier found in the Impressionists' canvases was in stark contrast to this deeply conservative vision.

Monet's career around 1880 gives us a further warning against reading directly from landscapes like these to social or environmentalist concerns. He left Argenteuil early in 1878, and later in the year moved to Vetheuil, on a remote bend of the Seine forty miles north-west of Paris, where he painted village scenes that were similar in subject (if not technique) to many paintings shown at the Paris Salon, showing the old village crowned by its medieval church or the humble cottages of Lavacourt on the opposite bank of the Seine. Monet's move has been attributed to environmental reasons—that the increasing pollution and industrialization at Argenteuil undermined the idyllic view that he had held of the

[29] Charles Bigot, 'Causerie artistique: l'exposition des "Impressionnistes"', *Revue artistique et littéraire*, 28 April 1877, 1046, reprinted in Berson, 1996, i, 134.
[30] Frédéric Chevalier, 'Les Impressionnistes', *L'Artiste*, May 1877, 331, reprinted in Berson, 1996, i, 139.
[31] See *Landscapes of France*, 1995, 128–9.

place earlier in the decade.[32] An immediate problem with this argument is that the first paintings that he made after leaving Argenteuil, on the Ile de la Grande-Jatte, nearer to Paris, were among the most heavily industrialized scenes that he ever painted.[33]

However, Monet's change of direction around 1880 needs to be seen in broader contexts, and from two further points of view. First, it came at a moment when he was seeking to make sales through commercial art dealers, and he may well have felt that less overtly modern subjects would sell better to private collectors. But it also coincides with a major political shift: in 1879, the Third Republic dramatically changed direction. After the social and political repression of the mid 1870s, in the aftermath of the Franco-Prussian War and the Commune, elections in 1879 introduced a liberal expansionist democracy. State artistic politics in the 1870s had favoured the most traditional forms of rural landscape; the new regime actively encouraged the depiction of contemporary scenes.

In the same years the countryside itself became the focus of heightened anxieties. The concerns about the impact of the railways and industrialization were longstanding, as Reclus's 1866 article shows; but the 1880s were the years of the 'great agricultural depression', precipitated by technological underdevelopment, agricultural diseases such as Phylloxera in the vines, falling prices as a result of international competition, and continuing rural depopulation.[34] These concerns lay behind Theuriet's *La Vie rustique*, with its deeply conservative yearning for a disappearing past.

How then might we read Monet's withdrawal? Was it a new-found distaste for modernity itself, precipitated by pollution? Or was it because such modern subjects, under the new expansionist regime, had lost their power to shock? Or was it a smart market move for a forty-year-old artist seeking to establish a career on a firm economic footing? It seems likely that it was a combination of the last two. This point has been explored here at some length because it highlights the difficulties of making straightforward links between subject matter as it is presented in paintings and attitudes towards the material subjects themselves.

We do find word of environmentalist concerns expressed by one former member of the Impressionist group; in 1902 Cézanne lamented the changes at the port of L'Estaque, near Marseille on the Mediterranean coast, that he had painted earlier in his career: 'I well remember the once so picturesque coastline at L'Estaque. Unfortunately, what we call progress is nothing but the invasion of bipeds who do not rest until they have transformed everything into odious *quais* with gas-lamps, and, what

[32] Tucker, 1982, 176–86.   [33] See *Landscapes of France*, 1995, 244–5.
[34] cf. e.g. Gabriel Désert, 'La grande dépression de l'agriculture', in *Histoire de la France rurale*, ed. Georges Duby and Armand Wallon, III, Paris: Seuil, 1976, 387–407.

is still worse, with electric light. What times we live in!'³⁵ Cézanne's concerns did not, though, extend to the factory chimneys at L'Estaque, which
he had been willing to include in many of his paintings of the place in
the 1870s and 1880s, playing off their verticals against the broad expanses
of the bay beyond.

Pissarro's paintings of the later 1880s offer a further reminder of the
problems of reading social attitudes from art images. At first sight, a
painting like *The Gleaners* of 1889 (Dreyfus Foundation, Kunstmuseum,
Basel), with its monumentalized peasants gathering the abundant left-
overs of the harvest, presents a very similar scenario to the illustrations by
Léon Lhermitte in Theuriet's *La Vie rustique* of 1888 (see figure 5.1). Pissarro's canvas might well be assumed, like Theuriet's book, to be a lament
for a passing way of life, and a monument to it. But Pissarro's own comments about his social views and his aims in his art make it clear that his
rural idyll should rather be seen in terms of the utopian anarchism of
writers such as Kropotkin—as an image of a future decentralized rural
society, rather than as nostalgia for a mythic past.³⁶ There is nothing in the
image itself that can lead us unequivocally to such a reading; without
background knowledge it would seem quite reasonable to interpret it in
terms similar to Lhermitte's illustrations. Yet the contextual information
reminds us of the very different readings and meanings that idyllic rural
imagery could invoke in late nineteenth-century France.

Landscape painting played a central part in debates about the countryside in France in the nineteenth century, and at times offered a vivid
expression of wider concerns about the values for which the countryside
itself stood, and the threats that endangered these values. Yet the central
theme of this essay is that we cannot view the imagery of the fine art
landscape as a reflection or a direct expression of attitudes towards the
physical environment; the conventions of fine art painting, and the heated
debates of the period about its purpose and justification, must be our
primary concern in looking at these paintings. Certainly, the patterns
of artistic development intersect in significant ways with the history of
attitudes towards the countryside itself; but they are not facets of a
single history.

³⁵ Letter from Cézanne to Paule Conil, 1 September 1902, in Paul Cézanne,
Correspondance, ed. John Rewald, Paris: Grasset, 1978, 290.
³⁶ See e.g. letter from Pissarro to Octave Mirbeau, 21 April 1892, in Janine Bailly-
Herzberg (ed.), *Correspondance de Camille Pissarro*, III, Paris: Editions de Valhermeil,
1988, 217, in response to Mirbeau's recently published *La Conquête du pain*; see also
Martha Ward, *Pissarro, Neo-Impressionism, and the Spaces of the Avant-Garde*, University of Chicago Press, 1996, especially 179–80.

6

Technology and Text: Glass Consciousness and Nineteenth-century Culture

Isobel Armstrong

A PIECE of common nineteenth-century window glass, held up to the light, is likely to display small blemishes—the blisters of air bubbles, and spectral undulations, almost invisible striae which slightly distort the vision. Such material, cylinder glass, or sheet glass as it was often termed, is different from the float glass produced in the computer-controlled factories of today. It was the commonest form of mid nineteenth-century glass, superseding the crown glass manufactured earlier, and preceding plate glass. Plate was in general use in the later part of the century even though, like crown, it was being made in the 1840s. The production of both overlapped with that of sheet. But sheet was dominant. It was blown by the human breath as massive four to six feet cylinders before being cut and flattened to produce pieces of glass up to twenty feet square.[1] In seven- to ten-hour sessions or 'journeys' before the furnace, a team could produce up to eight hundred feet of sixteen-ounce glass (the weight for common use). In other words, when you looked through glass in the mid nineteenth century, as often as not you looked through the residues of the breath of an unknown artisan. You literally looked through, and by means of, somebody else's breath. This is how *the* innovative material of the nineteenth century was made.

Glass is one of the earliest artificial materials in the world. It goes back well before 2000 BC. But a revolution in production in the nineteenth

---

[1] Crown glass was spun on a rod, not blown, which produced large circular tables of glass. Its disadvantage, despite its superior lustre, was that it was wasteful, as the centre of every piece, where the rod was attached, had to be cut away. This limited the size of the resulting glass panels, as did the circularity of crown. Plate glass was manufactured throughout the century, but displaced sheet only when it became less heavy, and less expensive to manufacture. A terminological confusion arises because when polished by a process invented at the Chance factory sheet was called 'polished plate'. The best account of sheet glass production is by Henry Chance (Chance 1883), which derives from an 1856 paper read at the Society of Arts.

century, when the techniques of industrialization were added to the
atavistic process of glassblowing, produced virtually a new artefact and
a culture of mass transparency never before experienced. The result was
a revolution in seeing and the transformation of people's bodies and
minds as they used glass to imagine with. New cultural meanings and
iconography emerged, but glass transformed consciousness itself by
creating new physical conditions. A new play of light and matter came
into being, different possibilities for light and shadow.

This unique glass consciousness, and the 'optical unconscious' (Walter
Benjamin's term) which went with it, is the subject of this essay
(Benjamin 1969: 237). I shall discuss glass production, going on to debates
on greenhouses and windows—things so common we take them for
granted—and explore the convergence of technology and text in some
nineteenth-century fiction. But first, some preliminaries on the transformation of mass-produced glass.

The translucent world of the nineteenth century is often traced to the
lifting of the glass tax in 1845 and the gradual removal of the window
tax. It is also appropriate to trace the origin of mass-produced transparency to one man, Robert Lucas Chance; one place, Chance's factory
in Spon Lane, Smethick; and one year, 1832, the year Chance introduced
French and Belgian *souffleurs* to blow cylinder glass for the first time in
England. Chance's hegemony was such that he produced all the 300,000
panels of blown sheet glass for the Crystal Palace in 1851. In January
1851, his factory produced 65,000 panels in a fortnight (Chance 1919: 52).
More of Chance later.

Two consequences arise from the mass production of glass. First, the
universal use of glass is inaugurated. A rare luxury becomes common. By
1852 it was possible for a contributor to a popular journal to write:

Considerable quantities of pressed or moulded glass are sold in London and the
principal towns, in the shape of drinking vessels, decanters, ornaments for
candles, &c. It is, of course, much inferior to cut glass, both in quality and
appearance, but its extreme cheapness has rendered it available for numerous
purposes for which glass has not hitherto been used; and so popular has it become
since the reduction of duty, that what was before a comparative luxury, has
happily become a necessity, in the houses of the humblest cottagers. (*The Illustrated Exhibitor and Magazine of Arts* 1852: 71)

An almost overwhelming *jouissance* of the eye is apparent as the very
surfaces of the world scintillate, offering glittering colour in a reflective,
shape-changing environment of anamorphosis and perspective play. The
same journal carried an article on silvered and coloured glass, which
creates an 'Alhambra' of 'Eastern Style' objects, in a temperate zone

appropriating the plumage of the humming bird or the carapace of the tropical beetle.

When the [coloured] glass is cut, the brilliancy of the effect is heightened, and the soft floating character of the lights is broken up into countless scintillations. On the other hand, by grinding the glass surface, the reflection is dispersed, and the appearance of frosted silver and the delicate lustre of the pearl are produced. With coloured glass, a wide scale of metallic hues is obtained. These dazzling tints may be compared to the plumage of the humming birds and the wing-cases of the buprestidae and other tropical beetles. Indeed, there is not one of the gorgeous metallic tints with which the insect and feathered kingdoms are adorned, that may not be closely copied by this process. (*The Illustrated Exhibitor and Magazine of Arts* 1852: 259)

Silvered glass combines the contradictory pleasures of minute reflection and distortion simultaneously.

spheres of glass of all diameters and capacities ... are formed and silvered in this way ... so great is their power of reflection, that the entire details of a large apartment are caught upon them with surprising minuteness and clearness of definition, and in the amusing perspective which is peculiar to spherical substances ... in whatever shape it may be fashioned it [silvered glass] contributes beyond any known material to the effect of artificial illumination, reflecting back unimpaired nearly the whole of the light that falls upon it. (*The Illustrated Exhibitor and Magazine of Arts* 1852: 259)

A second consequence of mass-produced glass is suggested by the dual pleasure of reflection and distortion described above. This is the inauguration of the first era of a scopic culture, a culture of seeing, prior to our own. This first phase, in which hypersensitivity to sight becomes prominent, lasted from approximately 1830 to 1890 and was generated from just two components, the glass panel and the lens. The prefabricated glass panel as window, either domestic or commercial (from the time it was a privilege to have a window to the time it was not), as conservatory wall, as photographic plate, opened untold possibilities. The lens extended the technologies of high science—the telescope, the microscope, the lighthouse—to popular optical toys such as the magic lantern, stereoscopic and anamorphosic games, transparencies, mirror play, the kaleidoscope, perspective games, the diorama and the panorama, which depended on mechanized repetition and the prosthetic eye.[2] This first phase of scopic culture leapfrogs print culture and literacy.[3] It was well advanced before

---

[2] For an account of optical toys see Stafford 1991.

[3] Ruskin's attack on the fallacy of the *trompe l'oeil* and the 'mean and paltry surprise which is felt in jugglery' in *Modern Painters* (1843) is an example of hostility to the visual pleasure of low forms of imitation. See Cook and Wedderburn 1903–1912; III, pt. 1, s. 1, ch. 4.

the Education Act of 1870 and shocked intellectuals. It can be marked off from our own, second phase of scopic culture, which begins with the moving image, and which is dominated by the screen, whether of film or computer. Production still depended on the body and not on automated technology and electronic media, just as the dissociated eye took precedence, rather than the dissociated voice of the phonograph or telephone.

Whereas our perceptual problems turn on virtual reality and the simulacrum without original, those of the earlier scopic phase turn on transparency itself, that is, on the simple transitive nature of glass—you can see through it. This transitivity generated a number of problems. Glass can be seen through, but only because of its invisible intervention between gazer and seen. Heat, sun, and light pass through it, so that glass is both barrier and medium. Glass is the element of reflection and refraction, but it can produce an ideal image which does not converge with matter. It bends light and distorts images, so much so that Ruskin used the physics of glass as an image of pathological modern consciousness (Ruskin 1851–3).[4] A world of multiple transparency very quickly became a highly mediated world, generating different kinds of epistemological confusion out of the very lucidity of glass. Just as the artisan's breath was invisible so also was the fact of mediation, as the invisible shaped experience. To what extent is one in control of one's experience? An index of such a concern is the appearance in fiction of moments when the accidental reflection of one's body in the urban phantasmagoria becomes a matter of betrayal or exposure. A former lover's image appears momentarily but ambiguously in the glass of the Crystal Palace in Thomas Hardy's 'The Fiddler of the Reels' (1893). The bigamous Victor Radnor in Meredith's *One of Our Conquerors* (1891/1975) is appalled to believe that his wife might have seen his reflection in a mirror of the chemist's shop they both frequent. This supposedly lucid or limpid substance assumes the structural function of mediator. This cannot be willed away, though there is often an attempt to do so. The dialectic of glass in the nineteenth century is about mediation, about transitivity and its implications.

The intense cultural work (I take this phrase from Michel de Certeau) provoked by glass and its mediating function raises some appropriately reflexive questions of method for anyone attempting to grasp it.[5] How

---

[4] Vol. xi, iii, 179.

[5] Michel de Certeau argues that a broad definition of cultural work, which can be exercised in many contexts and environments by individuals and groups, is preferable to a hierarchical model of cultural production or one which emphasises the passivity of the consumer. See de Certeau 1984.

do technology and text converge and how is this relationship to be conceptualized? How does a *material* enter a text? How is a material to be 'read' and in what way can one speak of its language? Was the mode in which glass was produced in any way a determinant factor in discourses about it? And what of the invisible workman's breath? Is there any way this lives on in the dialectic of transparency, however dimly?

CHANCE AND THE PROMOTION OF GLASS

Robert Lucas Chance, who had run his father's glassworks at the age of fourteen, being known as 'the little Master in the jacket', and who perpetuated a glassmaking dynasty by marrying a cousin from another glassmaking family, took an enormous financial risk in turning over to cylinder glass in the deep recession of the 1830s. This move was hotly contested by his brothers. Already in debt, and dependent on George Bontemps for advice and contracts for French and Belgian glassblowers once he added sheet to his manufactures, he met obstructions: he found that the men refused to pass on their skills to British workmen (Chance 1919: 6, 7). One flattener wanted 10,000 francs for teaching an English worker. Circumstances did not look promising, except that excise levies were more favourable on sheet, and a greater quantity could be made with less wastage than with either crown or plate.

In fact, the decision to make cylinder glass guaranteed Chance's hegemony in glass manufacture for twenty-five to thirty years. But this would not have occurred without two additional forms of action. First, ceaseless political campaigning and second, ceaseless *personal* vigilance over and control of the immediate conditions of production. In other words, the Chance family not only produced glass: they had to produce and 'manage' themselves as the primary manufacturers of glass at a national level, presuming upon a commercial reputation before it was actually made. Robert Lucas Chance had ambitions to be the Wedgewood of glass manufacturers. In some ways the family literally performed the status they intended to achieve, one such performance being the occasion of a visit to Birmingham by the Duke of Wellington at the Chances' invitation.

Either intuitively or by analysis the Chances saw that their business could be promoted by using local politics to reach the national hierarchies of government. Robert Lucas Chance, the driving force of the firm, remained a dissenter and a seemingly retiring intellectual (he had been a friend of Coleridge in London) who was not active except as a quiet philanthropist in local affairs. But this did not prevent him from leading a delegation of manufacturers to lobby the Chancellor of the Exchequer in

1831 for the removal of the glass tax. His brother William, on the other hand, who ran his own export business, but who came on to the Board of Chance Brothers, became an Anglican and took public office. His Anglicanism also enabled William to send his brilliant son, James, to Cambridge, and later James incorporated the expertise of a senior wrangler into the firm. William became High Bailiff of Birmingham and prepared for the Chance fortunes to rise by inviting the Duke of Wellington and Sir Robert Peel on a 'non-political' visit which culminated in a dinner hosted by William Chance—and a near riot. In this year of the sound of breaking of glass all over Europe it was almost a convention of protesting crowds to break the windows of public buildings—Birmingham papers announced revolutionary action in Belgium, Saxony, Brunswick, and Hapsburg in September 1830, the month of the Duke's visit—and the Chance family came in for a share of breakage. All the lamps outside the hotel where the dinner took place were smashed.

The dinner provoked the rage of local groups. The *Argus* for October 1830, a satirical monthly which was not so much radical as sceptical of interest groups of all kinds, reported the visit with exaggerated irony and hostility: 'The Duke of Wellington has paid a visit to Birmingham and we question if he will soon forget it'. Commenting on the Duke's lavish attentions to Mrs Arbuthnot, his female companion, it questioned whether 'the gallantry of the military sexagenarian Romeo' was appropriate. 'Would she not have been better at home, than in company with this man of war and love, who "loves the wives of others?" This pretty pair stopped at Drayton. Is Lady Peel blind?' But the fiercest ridicule is reserved for William Chance:

The party above-named first visited the Society of Arts. 'The High Bailiff [William Chance], and other gentlemen', joined them there. The rooms were full. The High Bailiff—whose perpetual 'bowing' reminded us of the advice of a certain *Sir Pertinax Maesycophant*, seemed to feel the influence of the great man's presence, for he bowed 'as if by instinct.' His conversation *to* not *with* the Duke ran thus:—Ladies and Gentlemen! don't crush his Grace. Your Graceship (!!) must be annoyed by the crush? They are so very anxious to see your Grace. Allow me to carry your Grace's hat: it must tire your hand. Pray don't crush his Grace! Mr Low Bailiff, keep the people off, they incommode his Grace. Is your Grace incommoded? Let me carry your hat, your Grace. Look at that picture, your Grace. 'Tis as natural as life. I wish, your Grace, you'd let me carry your hat. Prey don't be pressing on his Grace. *Do* let me carry your hat, your Grace. Every 'Your Grace' was accompanied by half a dozen bows, and, finally, at the fourth 'time of asking,' the hat was given to Mr Chance, by the desire of Mrs Arbuthnot, and he carried it (as a flunkey would) while the Duke was in the exhibition room.

On leaving the Society of Arts, the party were loudly hissed, hooted, and groaned—as they went down the Canal, in a boat, the like symptoms of unpopularity were repeated—*ditto* at Thomason's, in Church Street, *ditto*, *ditto* on their return to the Royal Hotel! During the dinner the mob outside became very violent: the Duke was called for: the lamps of the Hotel were smashed: and everything was done to show 'His Highness' that he was decidedly unpopular. (*Argus*, October 1830: 210)

As a final volley of satire, the embarrassed and inept Chance is termed a 'toad-eater, hat-holder, and Court-Leet slave', a typical example of '*Brummagem breeding*'.

The Duke's boat journey along the canal was, of course, to Smethick, where his party saw the Chance glass factory and the Duke professed himself 'astonished' by what he saw. (Did he perhaps see a demonstration of the making of early examples of cylinder glass, which Robert Lucas Chance was already investigating?) But this alone is not sufficient to explain the animus of the commentator. The Duke was at the height of his unpopularity in 1830, which accounts for the rage of the crowds outside the hotel. But some of Chance's guests inside the banquet room were also enraged with him. Chance broke the conventions of a private ducal visit to protest against the lack of parliamentary representation for manufacturing towns, provoking a long and injudicious speech in his support from a local county MP, Charles Tennyson. Reading between the lines of *Aris's Birmingham Gazette*, a Tory paper, the speech became inaudible as much from noise inside the room as outside it.[6] The great Wellington dinner was seen as a fiasco by many. The protests were provoked not so much by the violation of hospitality and the demand for representation in itself, for this was a pressing demand in Birmingham at the time. William Chance, however, had advanced these claims on his own initiative, whereas there already existed a body committed to making such demands, the Birmingham Political Union, founded in 1829, from which William Chance had dissociated himself. This was an affiliation of middle class and working class groups. Chance appropriated the agenda of these groups while spurning them in favour of the privileged manufacturers whom he hoped would influence government. That he was using the principled campaigns of local groups while bypassing them for his own advantage, and seeing local politics instrumentally as a means of furthering his interest, seems to have been behind the fury which greeted his invitation to Wellington. Birmingham was not incorporated until 1838. But local politics were subordinated to national aggrandisement, at

---

[6] *Aris's Birmingham Gazette*, 27 Sept. 1830; 'but owing to the impatience which the company was beginning to manifest we were unable to gather anything but detached sentences'.

least in the eyes of Chance's critics.[7] The Wellington visit was, as we shall see, in its instrumentalism and the unintended collisions arising from the failure of its instrumentalism, in some sense a paradigm of the ways the business seemed to operate.

By 1851, as we have seen, the Chance firm was in a position to be the sole supplier of glass for the Crystal Palace. Robert Lucas Chance was on the main prize-awarding jury of the glass section, and though this disqualified him from winning prizes, his work was highly commended in all areas of glass production. How was this achieved? By a relentless drive to technological improvement and investment, by the driving down of wages wherever possible, by the standardizing of the work process, eliminating specialized family teams and encouraging the versatility of skills—blower and flatteners worked interchangeably by 1845—and by a combination of force and paternalism. The firm planned and set up a school over the years 1837–42 to educate its workers. Its evening classes were fully subscribed. A census of workers in 1842 seems to have been undertaken with the object of discovering literacy levels in the works. It offers graphic evidence of the family work patterns which still clung on, and the dominance of French workers. The thirty-nine-year-old Gaspard André and his fourteen-year-old son were both marked as being able to read and write.[8]

There was another element driving the works which must be called passion. Passion, peripeteia, and drama dominate the history of the factory, facts exposed rather than minimized by the blandness of its family historian. Robert Lucas Chance's intensity, fanatical energy, and obsessive attention to detail, his intimate understanding of the many kinds of disaster which can strike in the glassmaking process, his constant vigilance over and understanding of the shortcomings of individual workers, dominate the history of the factory until his death in 1865. Characteristic is a thirty-nine point memo to his son, John Homer, in 1850, when he first took responsibility for areas of the factory. It is filled with injunctions: 'you must pay special attention . . . you must take special care . . . be especially watchful . . . go constantly . . . see him constantly . . . take every possible pains'.

It will be an important part of your duty to see that the workmanship of each man is good, and there fore you will make yourself thoroughly acquainted with

[7] The *Argus*, Oct. 1830: 201, reported that William Chance as High Bailiff and Chief Magistrate had refused to call a 'Town's Meeting' and that in January, 1830, he had refused to preside at the formation of the Union, earning the criticism of Attwood, its founder.

[8] 'Workpeople employed by Chance Brothers', Dec. 1842. Chance Archive, Pilkington Glass, St. Helen's, Pilkington Archive (ZZ) 21. I would like to thank Dinah Stubbs, Information Management and Storage, Pilkington Glass, for her invaluable help.

what constitutes good work, for which purposes you must visit the warehouse daily and examine every man's work for yourself, and report to each manager the defects of each workman.   (Chance 1919: app. II, 57)

Absenteeism (on Mondays a fall-off of workmen exasperated Chance) was not to be tolerated. Chance advised his son to visit malingering workers in their houses. The tasks of individual workers are allocated and checked with vigilance. Parish, Thompson, and Oakes must alternate between blowing and flattening (point sixteen of his thirty-nine points); the highly paid Zeller must work on shades, which required a skilled worker (Chance 1919: app. II, 58).

Crisis, panic, and wild trade fluctuations engendering abrupt policy changes were the conditions of running the factory. Chance never found the true 'master's man' he valued, or the managers and foremen he wanted. A running dispute with the Hartley cousins, his managers, culminated in a breach in 1834. In 1846 he was thwarted by another recalcitrant manager, Withers, in the engagement of men. He was confronted with foreign competition from low-waged Belgian glassblowers in the 1840s, and believed that protectionism was the only answer. His agents searched for markets as far afield as Constantinople and even China [Chance 1919: 19–21 (dispute with Hartley brothers); 41–2 (Withers); 28, 36 (competition)]. When the glass tax was removed, internal competition increased as the number of glassworks grew from fourteen to twenty-four in 1847, and his skilled workers were poached by Tyneside: 'This losing of men annoys me beyond anything' (Chance 1919: 36). The removal of the tax occasioned a frantic attempt to double the number of blowers. The family scoured Europe in 1845. James Timmins Chance, William's son, was recalled from his honeymoon to negotiate in Namur. Zeller, once dismissed, returned. But £40,000 had been laid out in excess in the glass boom, and in 1848 wages were reduced and foreign workers were laid off or, like the Andrés, re-engaged on lower terms (Chance 1919: 37). But not long after this increased demand precipitated a renewed search for foreign workers in 1850.

'Our profits are no longer to be calculated upon; we must have about us a set of scoundrels' (Chance 1919: 39). Internal as well as external problems beset the firm. Theft was common. Drunkenness and malpractice, such as the common-shop system, where a foreman would allocate work only to men who bought groceries from a shop owned by his relations, had to be guarded against.[9] Petitions for wage increases and strike threats had to be dealt with. In 1847, Chance attempted to enforce

---

[9] Letter to James Chance 26 October 1860, concerning Joseph Neale's operation of a common-shop system. Chance Archive, Ibid. (note 8), CB (ZZ) 21.

a speedier rotation of work on the crown glassworkers, who were already disadvantaged because their skills were becoming obsolete. They threatened a strike and James Chance took their part against his uncle, though he did not refuse to work the scheme: 'we injure both the men and ourselves . . . [who are] not mere machines, but have sensitive feelings like ourselves'.[10] But the crown workers did strike in 1850, and the furnaces were put out.[11]

These instances of political work and factory administration bring one to some rather unexpected conclusions. The most striking discovery one makes in pursuing the history of the Chance factory is the presence of a violence and intensity of feeling which seems out of all proportion to the business of glass production and profit-making. The energy invested in it seems in excess of what was needed for success. It is a kind of managerial *pathos*. Above all, Chance appears to have been locked in an obsessive, driven, claustrophobic intimacy with his workers, drawing his sons and nephews into the same cycles of feeling. Extremes of emotion—fury, exasperation, satisfaction—are above all conveyed in the documents which record the day-to-day running of the business.[12]

It seems increasingly the case, as one considers the fortunes of the Chance firm, that none of the existing models of economic structures and relations which we commonly accept is quite apposite to its workings. Neither the model of the market and the free trade of Adam Smith's *Wealth of Nations*, nor Marxist accounts of capital and labour, nor Foucauldian accounts of the transmission of power, satisfactorily represent the working conditions of the Chance dynasty. Self-regulating free trade, the oppressions of economic power relations, the conduit of power through the techniques of surveillance—elements of all these models exist in the patterns of work and production at the Chance factory, but none of them quite matches the desperation and exasperation we encounter, the level of fury and *frustration* apparent in Chance's dealings with the circumstances created by trade and the workforce.

I shall try out another model. It would need to be elaborated, but even the small body of evidence offered so far in this paper appears to support it. It goes something like this: the Chance factory seems to alternate wildly between attempting to see its workers in terms of *pure* alienated labour, which is absolutely instrumental, and which makes their mediation invisible, by regulating it into abstract, standardized formulas which do not recognize the specific, particular nature of human labour, and a

---

[10] Letter to R. L. Chance 26 October 1860, 42.   [11] Ibid. 51.
[12] Ibid. e.g. 20 (bad work); 21 (attack on Hartley); 34 (bad work and 'blow up' with Withers); 57 (on George Bontemps). In the hunt for foreign blowers after 1845, Robert Lucas Chance accused his nephew of losing the firm money while he was on honeymoon.

quite different form of recognition. This different recognition acknowledges workers as workers, as individuals, and as unique labourers with bodies and minds. The workers are 'not mere machines', said James Chance, 'but have sensitive feelings like ourselves'. The system itself seems to produce this situation. That is, the recognition of the humanity of labour is not a compensatory act for depersonalization, such as we see in the Chances's generous administration of charity, but built into the structure of working relations. The knot, the insoluble contradiction or aporia of production is that one moment labour is transparent, invisible; at another it is a visible obstruction—the factory owner comes up against it. He comes up against it whether workers steal, or get drunk, or are needed for specific tasks only they can perform, or whether they have 'sensitive feelings'. Part of the uniqueness of this pattern is that glass manufacture was peculiar, requiring highly skilled artisans at the same time as it satisfied the demands of mass production.[13] I dwell on this knot because it is not only the peculiar characteristic of glass production but reappears as a characteristic of glass itself. Almost wherever glass appears in the nineteenth century its nature as invisible medium contradicts its tangible material reality and presence. Hence the epistemological confusion I have mentioned—you see through glass as if it is not there, and yet it alters body and mind and controls the environment.

Interestingly, nineteenth-century discussions of glassmaking do recognize labour, but they romanticize it and turn it into magic, so that it effectively disappears. Ruskin, for instance, said that the only noticeable aspect of the gigantic 'cucumber frame', the Crystal Palace, was its testimony to labour (Ruskin 1851–1853).[14] The popular journal from which I have already quoted, describing 'A visit to Apsley Pellatt's flint glass works', commented that 'it is frightful to witness the sufferings of the

[13] The peculiar nature of the glass industry, its dependence on skilled workers, and the many occasions for crisis, such as the timing of accurate regulation of furnace temperature and the possibility of breakage at every stage of manufacture, clearly created situations of high tension. Even as late as 1965 a Managing Director of Thomas Webb and Sons is quoted as saying, 'It is, in my opinion, an industry which can be very exhilarating one day and most depressing the next; such are the vagaries of making crystal glass' (Mr E. A. Stott) Woodward 1978: 27. During the same period the firm of Pilkington experienced labour problems similar to those of Chance, even bringing legal cases against workers who broke contracts. See Barker 1977: 81–98. Maxine Berg argues for the diversity and variety of industrial structures and modes of production in the nineteenth century, challenging monolithic Marxist models of factory organisation. Berg 1994: 182–8. Perhaps because glassmaking was organized as a 'vertical' hierarchy of skill, whereas other manufactures, such as printing, depended on a chain of 'horizontal' interaction among workers, it was particularly prone to upset. In a collection of documents on labour in the nineteenth century Berg quotes W. Glenny Cory, commenting in 1876 on the smooth running of a print factory, 'The whole place is orderly'. Berg 116–21, 118.

[14] Vol. IX, app. 17, 455–6.

workmen exposed to the radiation of the flames' of the open furnace when a new pot is being set to produce molten glass. But like Dickens, who spoke of the 'diabolical cookery' conducted by 'swarthy', muscular men, the writer sees a romanticized inferno—'dark figures flit by him, each bearing a mass of living fire' (*The Illustrated Exhibitor and Magazine of Arts* 1852: 58). The glassmaker was a kind of magician, we 'watch the workman as one would a conjurer, and the results are quite as surprising in the one case as in the other' (71). The more ingenuity, skill and dexterity is recognized, the more it disappears. 'This operation [the making of a wine glass], so long in telling, and apparently so complex, is the work of about three minutes!' (70). Glassmaking discloses the 'dexterous movement which occupies less time than we do in describing it (71). The 'minutiae of this operation eludes the eye' (71). That thousands of identical objects, such as wine glasses, could be made so rapidly, is a magic that guarantees, in a curious way, their disappearance as *made* artefacts.

In her *The Glassworkers of Carmaux: French Craftsmen and Political Action in a Nineteenth-Century City* (1974), Joan Scott quotes the apostrophe of a glassmaker to one of the bottles he has made, 'The Adieu of the Glassworker' (1899), by Maurice Maugré. 'You drink my blood', the poem ends. 'Again and again I blow glass from dawn till dusk, always. . . . With my part of the sky [the air] I shape contours, as the breath of my lungs brings these bottles to life . . . their colour was made with my energy'. This worker testifies to the invisibility of his labour, as the bottles which drink the oxygen in his blood reverse the usual act of consumption and obliterate him.[15]

GLASS HOUSES

Bearing in mind the invisibility of glass and its nature as medium, we can turn to the construction techniques and the politics of the glasshouse, for the two are involved with one another. The genius of the glasshouse was John Claudius Loudon. He was the substantive innovator of this form. Unlike Paxton, who used wood, Loudon pioneered the ridge and furrow and iron and steel construction, inventing curvilinear astragals or iron bars in which to slot panels of glass. This opened out the possibility of domed and rounded hothouses and an infinite variety of crystalline rotunda and curved walls. He also took forward the ambitious use of steam heating and artificial rain, for he envisaged a world of glasshouses

[15] Epigraph, in Joan Wallach Scott 1974.

which would literally change the environment and democratize the hothouse by making its pleasures available to all. With the hothouse, rural experience and controlled environments could be transported anywhere.

Loudon's schemes, popularized from the late 1820s through the encyclopaedias and journals he edited, such as *The Gardener's Magazine*, open out acres of glass-covered, steam-heated landscape. His obsession with the glasshouse, whether the ensuite range of hothouses running from the drawing room of a rich man's house to the central dome of a tropical palmhouse, or the artisan's lean-to conservatory, appears in everything he wrote. He designed hothouses for rich men and aristocrats and wrote the most scholarly hothouse treatise of that time (1817).[16] He reconciled his populism with his services to aristocratic privilege in a somewhat bizarre way by strategically combining an archaic customary culture, which emphasized aristocratic duty and the rights of access of the poor to aristocratic support, with a Benthamite republicanism which led him to write on the abolition of the monarchy and to invent the first comprehensive school.[17] He could do this because he believed in *luxury* as an essential democratic necessity. It activated the desire which emancipated people from subsistence level.[18] If the Duke of Devonshire could set 3,000 pots of strawberries at Chatsworth and have grapes 'at table all the year round', there was no reason why ordinary people should not have such expectations. When he wrote of his visits to the grounds and gardens of great aristocratic houses in *The Gardener's Magazine*, he assumed that these existed for the pleasure of the public. In 1831, though he was later to praise the great 'cathedral of Paxton's new palmhouse', he attacked Chatsworth under Paxton for not being well enough maintained for the 'public' to view. By implication, the glasshouses there were built to unsound and archaic principles. But Chatsworth, at least, admitted visitors. In the same issue he criticized the Earl of Shrewsbury for terminating general visits to Alton Towers. The Earl was 'being by far too

[16] *Remarks on the Construction of Hothouses* 1817, was followed by *Sketches of Curvilinear Hothouses* 1818. *The Suburban Gardener and Villa Companion* 1838, contains numerous instructions for the creation of hothouses and conservatories. For an account of the variety of Loudon's interests see John Edwards Gloag 1970.

[17] 'The Great Objects to be Attained by Reform'. Letter to the Editor of the *Morning Advertiser* (1830); 'Parochial Institutions; or, an Outline for a Plan for a National Education' (1829).

[18] See *Encyclopaedia of Agriculture*, 1835: 1225. Loudon insisted that agricultural workers should not be paid at subsistence level or be persuaded to be content with mere necessities. Apathy follows such a policy, whereas the poor have an entitlement to civilized enjoyment. This is not a wholly altruistic argument, although Loudon's ideological passions were clearly invested in improvement. To restrict the possibility of growth as human beings is to restrict energy for work and the circulation of money for goods.

162 Isobel Armstrong

aristocratic' in excluding all but liveried carriages from the grounds and, of course, from the magnificent conservatory:

The conservatory of the house, with its plants, trays of choice flowers, sculptures, candelabras, vases of alabaster, stained glass windows at the extreme ends, chandeliers with coloured burners, exotic birds in magnificent cages, &c., surpasses anything of the kind we have ever seen, and forms a suitable approach to the splendidly furnished gallery into which it opens. (*The Gardener's Magazine*, 1831, VII: 395)

It was this democratic impulse which later made the radical *Westminster Review* demand, in April 1850, well before the notion of a glass building had been officially mooted for the Great Exhibition of 1851, 'a grand metropolitan conservatory, or winter garden . . . thrown open to the poorest', so that even (a pessimistic note) the 'large invalid class of our population' could enjoy, like the Duke of Devonshire, a balmy summer in winter (*Westminster Review*, 1850 April: 92).

But there were problems in the search for the pure transparency of the glasshouse, which would facilitate the management of light, to which Loudon was blind. They turn on the invisibility of glass and its nature as a medium. Loudon's vision of unmediated Utopian experience produced by a crystalline environment is contradicted and obstructed by the transitive nature of glass itself. This happens in three ways. If the glasshouse was a nursery, it was also a forcing house. Its claims to produce an artificial environment made it the agent of social control as much as of social change. The taxonomy of the glasshouse depended on naturalizing the colonial order in a temperate context, for it was organized round the arrangement of tropical plants imported as exotica.[19] But the refusal to understand the implications of this displacement, a repression of difference exacerbated by Loudon's new, non-Linnaean scheme of classification of plants, meant that the 'place' of the colonial in the political unconscious was actually transposed to the poor, the barbarians of the city's heart of darkness (Briggs 1963/1990: 61–4). All of these problems carried over to the Crystal Palace, the culmination of the glass building, and into urban glass structures. The paradoxes of the Crystal Palace perhaps originated in its Benthamite beginnings, the Panopticon, a prison. The central lodge of the panoptical Inspection House was to be 'almost all window', Bentham had written (1791: 1, 19). His brother, who

[19] The subtitle of John Claudius Loudon's *Green-house Companion* 1824, indicates that the greenhouse was to be organized round a 'natural arrangement' of plants, i.e. a taxonomy depending on visual similarity of elements rather than the Linnean analysis of structural affinities. The new edition of Loudon's *Hortus Britannicus* 1839, contained both a Linnean (pt I) and a 'Jussieuan Arrangement' (pt II) of plants, i.e. a nonstructural taxonomy.

designed the Panopticon, worked in Russia as an engineer, where he had perhaps seen the imperial glasshouses in St. Petersburg, to which the Benthamite Loudon had also made a pilgrimage.

Two texts about rich business men, one written prior to the building of the Crystal Palace, Dickens' *Dombey and Son* (1848/1970) and another written after it, Meredith's *One of Our Conquerors* (1891/1975), suggest the complexities of the glasshouse discourse—complexities Loudon did not immediately recognize.

Dombey oversees his orphan son's fostering by making the wet-nurse, Polly, walk, holding his baby, in a conservatory or 'little glass breakfast room' leading from the gloomy sitting room or study in which he broodingly watches her perambulations. Outlined against the light as she is, he can see her, she can't see him: she 'walked for hours together . . . sensible that she was plainly to be seen by him'. Polly, we remember, is imported from the heart of darkness, the London poor, who, I have argued, stood in for the colonial other. Exercising the prerogative of the greenhouse taxonomist, Dombey has already exercised peremptory control over her by reclassifying her (literally) and converting her name from Polly (Poorly) to Richards—she is rich because she is nursing his baby, in an alien environment. Now he watches her as the overseer of a Panopticon prison might watch a prisoner exercise. The regime of discipline is timed by a bell:

a bell was rung for Richards to repair to this glass chamber, and there to walk to and fro with her young charge. From the glimpses she caught of Mr Dombey at these times, sitting in the dark distance, looking out towards the infant from among the dark heavy furniture . . . she began to entertain ideas of him in his solitary state as if he were a lone prisoner in his cell, or a strange apparition that was not to be accosted or understood. . . .   (Dickens 1848/1970: 176)

The brilliance of this scene comes about because of the convergence of both intimate boudoir and torture chamber in the word 'chamber', so that the place of nurture and the 'gothic' prison house converge sinisterly. But its virtuosity does not consist simply in the fact that Dombey is fiercely satirized as the Benthamite overseer staring at the prisoner silhouetted against the light, all the more powerful because unseen. On the contrary, this model of oppression is under scrutiny. The power of the unmediated gaze is under question. For one thing, it *is* mediated, by the light and shadow constituted by the very glass room itself. For another, the gaze is not one-way: Polly gazes back, so that a reversal in which *Dombey* seems the prisoner occurs. More profoundly, Dombey becomes for Polly an apparition, neither accosted not understood. It is not so much that this gives him power, but that Dickens is considering the dangerousness of a situation when power is *assumed* to be a mere shade. It is her sense of the unreality of Dombey's power which enables Polly to disobey his edicts by taking the children with her on a visit home, a transgression which unleashes all the violence he can command, her banishment, with real material consequences for her and for his own children. After this, Paul becomes sickly.

The misprisioning of mediation is at the heart of another conservatory scene in Meredith's *One of Our Conquerors*, only this time the misrecognition is about the nature of transparency itself. Because invisible barriers can be erected, it is possible to assume that they are simply not there. Victor Radnor, successful English business man and bigamist, takes a party of friends to an ostentatious new house where they picnic in the domed conservatory: 'And admirable were the conservatories running three long lines, one from the drawing room, to a central dome for tropical growths'. (In the first serial publication in the *Fortnightly* this is described as a quarter of a mile of glass.) Such a sweep of glasshouses is exactly that recommended by Loudon. A conversation on the dangers of miscegenation occurs during this visit, reminiscent of the creation of hybrids inside the conservatory, which is suggestive, for the experiments of classification inside the conservatory intimate transgressive violations of category beyond it. During the picnic lunch hail rattles ominously on the glass dome (those in glasshouses are subject to the assault of 'natural' weather conditions, hailstones from outside the artificial environment they have created). But the weather clears, and though his companions are inclined, with inadvertent tactlessness, to see the fluffy clouds metaphorically as an array of judges' wigs, Radnor himself prefers to see them in an idealized way as 'a radiant mountain-land', 'A range of Swiss Alps in air'. It is not that Radnor is exposed, or seen through, at this point, rather the opposite. Through his bigamous marriage he has manipulated the law, behaving as if obstructions and barriers are invisible. Thus the changes of category made inside the glasshouse can be made to occur outside it by fiat. Radnor changes space and time through metaphor, that shapechanger of categories, which converts the clouds into the Swiss Alps (Meredith 1891/1975).[20] It is significant that William Whewell had conceived the almost traumatic effect of the Great Exhibition in 1851 as the collapse of the categories of space and time, as materials from all over the world were abstracted from their different histories and contexts to converge on the Crystal Palace. In assuming that he has the freedom to manipulate the law (as one *can* in a conservatory) and in recognizing no obstruction, Radnor is creating a fallacious transparency. In refusing to

[20] p. 84, note 32.

admit obstacles he is a genuine idealist, head in the clouds, resisting the imperatives of the literal, material world around him. Human activities are mediated through humanly made institutions, which cannot be unilaterally annulled. Yet, in ignoring such mediation Radnor is, Meredith suggests, only following the impetus of his culture. The glasshouse of English business and aristocracy is a driving analogy in the novel.

Meredith's novel takes us from the rural to the urban glasshouse via a walk taken through London by Fenellan, Radnor's aide, and a companion. Their walk from the city, place of trade and commerce, to the West End, from Drury Lane, through Covent Garden, down to Trafalgar Square and on, leads us to the more sinister urban greenhouse. It is exactly the route, chosen on three occasions in a decade, for the site of the glassing over of London. Serious proposals made to parliamentary committees and envisaged as being financed by share capital were made between 1845 and 1855, first by Frederick Gye, then by Paxton and subsequently by William Mosely. *The Builder* of 1855, reviving the Gye plan in the light of more recent proposals, described his proposal for the relief of congestion created by the flow from East to West in the city. Massive glass arcades, 70 feet high, were to be raised on arches over existing buildings and routed over existing traffic, from the Bank of England to Trafalgar Square. Though 'the structure will not be in one straight line', it will form an unbroken unit and will 'present a series of direct arcades, crescents and rotundas, forming one uninterrupted covered promenade'. Branch avenues to churches and to rail stations would be created. Over property of 'inconsiderable value' the promenade can expand into 'several magnificent galleries or halls'. Baths, cafés, shops, excepting those shops 'unfitted' for such an environment, and an extensive flower market (residue of the conservatory origin of the arcade) would be built in this covered area of communication with a 'spacious and luxurious facade' (*The Builder* 1855: 603). There is no doubt of the excitement, the incitement, of this glittering ambition. But when one puts this together with Mosely's plan for a similar arcade along an almost identical route, and with Paxton's proposal for an atmospherically controlled crystal girdle, again seventy feet high, and ten miles in circumference, the 'Great Victorian Way', to be raised over central London along with eight railway lines running four on either side, one begins to see the sinister aspect of these plans (Chadwick 1961). The intention was to build a secondary city in the air, a glassy thoroughfare to preserve the untroubled flow of people and commodities which would keep in the protected and keep out all that troubled urban planners—the pollution of metropolitan water, the stench of the Thames, the mephitic vapours of putrefying graveyards, so overcrowded that they leaked into the sewers adjacent to them, and the poor themselves. The invisibility of glass is to engineer a transcendent city superimposed on the existing one, which is negated. The controlled environment of the conservatory has reached the point of creating, not transformation, but a double city. By a strange catachresis the invisibility of glass is to make what is outside it invisible, so that what it excludes cannot be seen. Transparency becomes something you cannot see through and loses its transitive nature in the act of asserting its utopian possibilities. Nevertheless, this townscape was not in essence emancipatory. It would have to be called dominated space, in the expression of Henri Lefebvre, whom I shall mention again later. We have to compare it with the anarchic aesthetics of later glass architects, such as Bruno Taut and Paul Scheerbert, and their anti-utilitarian projects such as glassing over the Alps. 'Glass dome in Portofino—Open halls with changing views of the sea. Built completely out of solid glass.... Yes! impracticable and without profit! But has the useful ever made us happy?' (Taut 1972: 125).

There is no doubt that the opposing impulses of the glasshouse converged on the Crystal Palace, though it is not possible to expand upon this here. I will simply note that it recapitulated the contradictions I have considered—the place of nurture and the forcing house, the artificial environment as a site of therapy and democratic transformation along with social control; scopic delight, and the pleasure of the eye, coexisting with the making strange of production and consumption, rendering them exotic in the taxonomy of display. As William Whewell argued, the simultaneous juxtaposition of materials and artefacts from all over the world collapsed space and time into one another, contracted space and produced synchronic experience, voiding history and institutions of mediating power.[21] Thus it was an epistemological shock, not just the biggest trade fair ever. Perhaps Elizabeth Barrett Browning summed it up in her *Casa Guidi Windows* of 1851. The 'Fair-going world' generated around the Crystal Palace was a diversion from international problems. Luxury, commodity display, and the magic of consumer goods persuaded people to literalize the invisible hand behind trade relations metaphorized by Adam Smith and made them believe that consumption was an unmediated experience. Such failure to recognize how our physical consumption comes to us denies material conditions and thus turns us into ghosts who walk 'Inaudible as spirits, while your foot/Dips deep in velvet roses'. The ostensive definition of this magical condition is the limpid glaze of the wine glass—'Here's goblet-glass, to take in with your wine/The very sun its grapes were ripened under./Drink light and juice

[21] William Whewell, 'Inaugural lecture, November 26, 1851. The general bearing of the Great Exhibition on the progress of art and science', London, 1851. This 16-page lecture is one of the central documents relating to the Exhibition.

together' (Kenyon 1914: 348). You can drink light because the glass is so transparent that light seems to pass unimpeded into the wine, the epitome of the unmediated experience, or rather, invisible mediation.

WINDOWS

The windows, in order to light a room cheerfully, should be brought down as low as the nature of the occupation of the room will allow, and be carried up as high nearly as the cornice. None of the sashes should be fixed; and particularly all the upper sashes should be made open. . . . Unfortunately, in houses occupied by the poor, the sashes are seldom hung; and the close, unwholesome air is therefore never effectually dispersed, even when the windows are opened. (Loudon 1838: 43)

The vertical window, an oblong aperture in a wall, seemed the obvious building type, as it did to Loudon, throughout the nineteenth century, until it was challenged by modernist architectural theory. Le Corbusier's assault on the vertical window revealed it and the environment which it created as ideological forms. For Le Corbusier, structural changes in modern building techniques made the necessity for high ceilings and comparatively limited slits in external walls unnecessary and made possible the horizontal window's transformation of domestic space. A horizontal window up to eleven metres long could bring 'the immensity of the outer world into the room, the unadulterated totality of a lake scene'. Such a scene, 'stuck' on a window, suggests release from constraint.[22] There is nothing to stand between viewer and viewed, no segmented panes, no frame, no organizing of the individual's perspective. A pure functionalism insists on doing away with the limitations of the mediated, privileged gaze organized by the vertical window. It is highly questionable whether the optical orgy of the untamed eye is not *more* about possession and consumption of the landscape, more about violent appropriation, than the gaze from the bourgeois interior figured in the vertical window. But the controversy around the merits of the different types of window revealed the cultural meaning of the vertical window as it was experienced by its defenders. For August Perret it was the measure of vertical, upright 'man' himself (Reichlin 1984: 71). The mute dialogues with street and sky created by the gazer offered the illusion of an unproblematical interaction between self and world in a dialectic of inside and outside. The primacy of the self and the movement to a transcendent 'beyond' is the model of seeing conjured by the vertical window.

[22] For the Le Corbusier–Perret controversy over the merits of the vertical or horizontal window see Bruno Reichlin 1984: 65–78.

It is not surprising, therefore, that a poetics of the window dominates
nineteenth-century texts. The insistent and most lyrical trope in fiction
and poetry is a figure at the window, gazing at the beyond, and, in spite
of Perret, that figure is usually a woman. The window is a site of intense
longing and desire. Charlotte Brontë's Jane Eyre flings open a window
when a longing for freedom overcomes her at the moment she decides to
leave the servitude of Lowood School. Her eye travels along the 'white
road' of release to the 'boundary' of the mountains: 'It was those I wished
to surmount' (Leavis 1847/1985: 117). In Margaret Oliphant's story, 'The
library window', a young girl is made sick with consuming desire for
spiritual experience figured as a dim male shape, a divine father figure,
behind an illusory window. The window is as much a barrier between
self and world as it is an enabling space: the seer often gazes from one
window to another. Baudelaire's prose poem, 'Fenêtres', meditates on the
woman at the window glimpsed from the outside as the *flâneur* gazes
across roofs to its mysterious, intriguing space. The enigma of the invisible screen and blank space is oneiric, an incitement to erotic dreams and
fantasy.

Pathological longing consumes the dying speaker of Mallarmé's
window poem, who would force a way through the crystal 'at the risk
of falling throughout eternity'[23] (Barbier and Millan 1983: 144–5). It is
noticeable how often the window is associated with extremity, trauma,
violation, and pathology. It becomes a site of danger and risk. So much
so that, to gain some understanding of this phenomenon, it is appropriate to shift attention from the gazing subject's seeing through the barrier
of the window, to how the window makes the gazer see, to shift from
autonomous viewer to the frame that mediates the gazer's gaze.

The window attracts two kinds of ambiguity. The first is spatial. At
the periphery of the house, a threshold but not an exit (though windows
can be doors), it is at the intersection of inside and outside but also at the
point of their dissolve, becoming the junction of owned and unowned
space. It is such an intense hermeneutic space, an interpretative enigma,
because here different kinds of space converge and question ownership.
You can look out of or into a window without it belonging to you.
Windows participate in what Henri Lefebvre has termed, refusing the
more simplistic categories of public and private, dominated and appropriated space. A window partakes, as an outlet on to the world, of public
space, but that space is constructed either by the state or civic or private
capital and generally through means of technology—even Jane Eyre's
white road. Even if you own the land outside there are always elements

---

[23] Thanks to Helen Carr for discussion of the translation.

of the external which you do not own. Indeed, as an aspect of technology a window is always made by someone else. But it is also a private view, an owned private view, often endowed with strong aesthetic meaning and affect. Round the window individual decorative choices can be made, forming an extension of the owner's identity. (Hence Loudon's glorying in the many different ways windows could be 'dressed' and curtained.) Thus, the domestic window is always at the junction of contradictory meanings, where individual and socially organized space converge.

A generic ambiguity also clings to the window—it is equally peepshow, proscenium arch, camera (as the presence of shutters sometimes confirms), and lens. Thus, the window becomes assimilated to the array of popular new optical phenomena, gadgets for playing with sight, often though not always lens-based, descended from the 'classic' philosophical instruments of high science, which I have already mentioned. The miniaturizing toys, the kaleidoscope, and stereoscope, or the larger-scale optical arrangements, such as diorama and panorama, all have something in common. They introduce a layer of tertiary mediation to experience. They do not relate to the self's primary labour on the world, the activity which leads to self-creation through work on the physical environment. Nor do they belong to the secondary mediations of money and property which make exchange possible. For while the optical toy might require both money and property in order to circulate, you need not own them. A temporary and tenuous relation with them is possible. The urban spectacle often provides them free and fortuitously, naturalized into the environment. And yet these optical instruments organize the vision, coming between it and the world. George Eliot described the novelist's vision as a medium, a 'delicate acoustic or optical instrument'. The nature of a prosthetic aid such as this is to be manipulated by the user but to remain independent of him or her. Tertiary mediation creates and is the creation of transitive objects, but offers an ambiguous transitional contract to the user, because it moves ambiguously between the control of subject and object.

Some moments in nineteenth-century fiction will gloss what I have just said. Lockwood in Emily Brontë's *Wuthering Heights*, breaking a window rather than accepting that it controls his way of seeing, perhaps epitemizes the trauma around windows at this time. Threatened in class status, his fragile masculinity shaken by Heathcliff and the coercively violent environment of the Heights, he dreams of the young Catherine, the dream Heathcliff himself is longing to have, and, with the audaciousness of dreamwork, steals the dream of his rival. When in his dream he peremptorily breaks a window-pane in order to seize 'the importunate branch' which had been knocking on the window all night, the sexual and genealogical punning of dreamwork—Catherine is indeed a branch of the family with a claim on the Heights—figures his need to displace Heathcliff by breaking through the imprisoning frame of the Heights and asserting his own control over experience. But this is an episode with too many ramifications to explore here. To end this discussion I will turn to two window episodes, drawn respectively from Charles Dickens and George Eliot, one which discloses the ambiguous space of the window and one which discloses its ambiguous genre. Both suggest how the window controls the experience of the viewer.

In Dickens' *Bleak House* (1851), Lady Dedlock looks out of a window on to a rain-saturated landscape at her residence in Lincolnshire:

The view from my Lady Dedlock's own windows is alternately a lead-coloured view and a view in Indian ink. The vases on the stone terrace in the foreground catch the rain all day; and the heavy drops fall, drip, drip, drip, upon the broad flagged pavement, called, from old time, the Ghost's walk, all night. On Sundays, the little church in the park is mouldy; the open pulpit breaks out into a cold sweat; and there is a general smell and taste as of ancient Dedlocks in their graves. My Lady Dedlock (who is childless), looking out in the early twilight from her boudoir, at a keeper's lodge, and seeing the light of a fire upon the latticed panes, and smoke rising from the chimney, and a child, chased by a woman, running out into the rain to meet the shining figure of a wrapped-up man coming through the gate, has been put quite out of temper. My Lady Dedlock says she has been 'bored to death'.   (Page and Miller 1985: 56)

Her vision is mediated by the window and the rain and these together by an aesthetic construction of the scene as a drawing in either pencil or pen and ink—the lead-coloured view and the view in Indian ink alternate with one another but are scarcely differentiated. These might be the 'views' or sketches such as a lady might produce, and the scene is at three removes from the things seen, sketched in the colourless tones of deep depression. Fleetingly, the terms suggest figure and ground, lead panes and the inky black seen through them, like the bars of a prison. The turn to the window is an attempt to block memory and desire, and the window scene becomes a screen to distract Lady Dedlock from the concerns which haunt her. But the window actually forces her to see what she wants to repress. The lead of the panes calls up, through the mortal rhyming of lead with dead, the dead in the churchyard, the buried Dedlocks who reproach her with the failure to produce an heir. And the window opens on to a domestic scene in lead or pen-and-wash as a child runs to greet its father, imaging her own lost child. Remorselessly, the screen of the window makes her see in spite of herself, making her see in particular the limits of her ownership. She owns the lodge and employs its keeper, but she cannot control its inmates, nor, despite the monotone 'view' created by both the weather and her own mind, can she control the glowing aura of the other window she looks upon.

A doubled window, a window looking out upon another window, puns on reproduction, both on biological and technological reproduction. The glass and lead of her 'own windows' are reproducible in a technological sense, as the age of the window makes them become the property of many. And these particular windows will become different windows as they become someone else's 'own windows', passed on to another heir who will inherit and propagate. So windows can be reproduced, or their privileged 'views' appropriated by others, just as Guppy 'views' the portrait of Lady Dedlock herself, an event leading to recognition of the suspicious likeness of herself and Esther and the eventual disclosure of her secret. Lady Dedlock is in a world driven by replication which begins to question ownership, but, more poignantly, the act of blocking reveals rather than conceals. The window becomes a printer's screen or block on which her secret is inscribed. In this episode it is hard to say which is socially made and which individual space, so deeply ambiguous is the window framing it.

The generically ambiguous window in George Eliot's *Middlemarch* belongs to the boudoir of another privileged woman, Dorothea:

When Dorothea passed from her dressing room to the blue-green boudoir that we know of, she saw the long avenues of limes lifting their trunks from a white earth, and spreading white branches against the dun and motionless sky. The distant flat shrank in uniform whiteness and low-hanging uniformity of cloud. The very furniture in the room seemed to have shrunk since she saw it before: the stag in the tapestry looked more like a ghost in his ghostly blue-green world; the volumes of polite literature in the bookcase looked more like immoveable imitations of books. The bright fire of dry oak-boughs burning on the dogs seemed an incongruous renewal of life and glow. (Harvey 1961: 306)

We know that Dorothea looked through a pretty bow-window, but George Eliot has obliterated the window in this scene. External and internal are in continuum, without the intervention of the third term of the window. This must be because they have the same meaning, as inside and outside have shrunk to an ontological 'white enclosure'. The death of light is a psychic death, projected on to all objects. Yet a surrogate window *does* appear, smuggled into the description through a reference to popular scopic media. 'Each remembered thing in the room was disenchanted, was deadened as an unlit transparency.' This is brilliantly prepared for by the ghostly deadness and diminished size of objects, which look like replications of themselves. Because it requires an artificial light source to come into being a transparency has a mechanical existence at best, but without light it drains objects of significance. The unmentioned window has become like this. The white room returns us to an earlier reference to 'tertiary' scopic media, the trauma of the honeymoon in Rome, which is seen as pictures viewed with a 'magic lantern in a doze'. Rome is indeed offered to us with the discontinuous intensity of a series of jumbled tourist's plates. The glut of images is as sterile as the dearth of images in the white landscape is terrible. In the boudoir the white enclosure has become a magic lantern without plates, a tabula rasa. The white universe is as much a disease of the retina as the red landscape of St Peters seems to be.

George Eliot uses the instruments of high science in the analogies of her novel, but she also refers to the controlling lens and angle of popular visual media, with their *trompe l'oeil* and optical illusions. Do they create a disease of the retina? It might seem so. When Will views in 'passivity' the 'panorama' of his future life without Dorothea, George Eliot would have known of a version of the panorama in London in which audiences viewing panoramic scenes were seated on a rotating platform which was winched round from scene to scene (Altick 1978: 165–6). So this is a reference to literal passivity, and may seem hostile. On the other hand, Dorothea's husband, Casaubon, lives in his 'closet' world without windows, not even inhabiting the camera obscura. 'Most people are shut out from it', Dorothea says to Will of the high art of Rome, as if George Eliot is implying that there are resources and cultural possibilities in popular forms. Images, Eliot remarks in one of her authorial asides, are 'the brood of desire'. They may deceive but without them we cannot feel or think. There are times when she invokes the creativity of popular image-making forms. When she believes she has lost him, the image of Will moves with Dorothea wherever she moves, as in optical games which depend on shadow play. When she and Will come together, George Eliot daringly uses the scenic lighting effects of the public garden, the crash of thunder and lightning, with unashamed melodrama. Certainly, her understanding of the importance of images makes *Middlemarch* a challenge to the common epistemology of realism as representation which assumes a stable relation between subject and object. Changing perspectives, lights and shadows, *images*, organize both experience and art. Images control you if you lose your capacity to interact with them, to light them up.

Perhaps the turn to stained glass from the time of the Pre-Raphaelites on is a move to assuage the strenuousness of tertiary mediation, for the strains of transparency are lessened once one looks not through but on or at a stained-glass window. Perhaps the popularity of stained glass is not a move to the transcendental, or 'pleasing mystery', as one arts and crafts worker put it later in the century, but a giving over of the invisibility of the window to the untroubled mediation of coloured glass. The stained-glass window represents an ideal state of reverie, as it stands between the dark church interior and the light which irradiates it, reminding us of our vulnerability because of the brittle, ephemeral nature of the material with which its representations are fused. It is a gathering of colours which *are* 'the glory of the heavens' and the 'fulness of the earth':

One thinks of mornings and evening . . . of clouds passing over the sun, of the dappled glow and glitter, and of faint flushes cast from the windows on the cathedral pavement; of pearly white, like the lining of a shell; of purple bloom and azure haze, and grass-green and golden spots, like the budding of the spring.[24] (Whall 1905: 198)

CONCLUSION

I have tried to give some indication of the questions thrown up by the first phase of scopic culture, a phase which tends to be subject to amnesia for us now because all its components were in existence before mass production and because we have taken them for granted and naturalized the history of glass consciousness in the nineteenth century. What is the point of reviving this forgotten history? Post-modern thinking does not ask the same questions as this earlier phase of scopic experience, forced as it was to consider mediation as a central question and, arising from this, the ways we do and do not own and control experience as well as things. In this way, the mid nineteenth century flashes up warning images for us, the kind of admonitions and warnings which Walter Benjamin asked of history. In a recent updating of the history of Pilkingtons, the firm which, of course, absorbed Chance, I am struck by the change from one system of production to another, and by the uncanny absence of people. 'Float glass factories are quiet places remotely controlled from monitor screens', the firm's historian wrote in 1994 (Barker 1994: 82). Such automation has eliminated the urgency of nineteenth-century questions. The firm was committed to remove the many environmental eyesores left by the coke, chemical, and glass industries of the previous century. 'Derelict industrial sites were thus freed for new housing, business, development and

---

[24] I am grateful to Chris L. Brooks for this reference.

amenities of various kinds.' This erasing of the nineteenth-century environment should not go on without some memory of the anxieties and questions which it raised. No one would want the sound and fury of nineteenth-century glassmaking back again, but it may be timely to remember the questions it persuades us to ask.

REFERENCES

Altick, Richard D. (1978). *The Shows of London*. Cambridge, MA. and London: Belknap Press of Harvard University Press.

Barbier, Carl Paul and Millan, Charles Gordon (eds) (1983). *Poésies, Oeuvres Complètes* (by Stephane Mallarmé). Paris: Flammarion, 144–5.

Barker, T. C. (1977). *The Glassmakers: Pilkington: The Rise of an International Company 1826–1976*. London: Weidenfeld & Nicolson.

Barker, T. C. (1994). *An Age of Glass*. London: Boxtree.

Benjamin, Walter (1969). 'The work of art in the age of mechanical reproduction', in Hannah Arendt (ed.), *Illuminations: Essays and Reflections*. New York: Schocken, 237.

Bentham, Jeremy (1791). *Panopticon; or, The Inspection-House* (2 vols). Dublin and London: T. Payne.

Berg, Maxine (1979). 'The paper trade and printing', in *Technology and Toil in Nineteenth-Century Britain*. London and New Jersey: CSE Books and Humanities Press, 116–21.

Berg, Maxine (1994). *The Age of Manufactures 1700–1820: Industry, Innovation and Work in Britain* (2nd edn). London and New York: Routledge.

Briggs, Asa [1963] (1990). *Victorian Cities*. Harmondsworth, UK: Penguin.

Brontë, Charlotte, *Jane Eyre* (1985) ed. Q. D. Leavis. Harmondsworth: Penguin. (Originally published 1847).

The Builder (1855). 'Metropolitan communications. Mr. Gye's plans for a glass street', XIII: 603.

Chance, Henry (1883). 'On the manufacture of crown and sheet glass', in Harry James Powell (ed.), *The Principles of Glass Making*. London: George Bell and Sons.

Chance, James Frederick (1919). *A History of the Firm of Chance Brothers & Co., Glass and Alkali Manufacturers*. London (privately printed).

Cook, E. T. and Wedderburn, A. (eds) (1903–1912). *The Works of John Ruskin* (39 vols). London: G. Allen.

de Certeau, Michel (1984). *The Practice of Everyday Life*, trans. by F. Steven Rendall. Stanford: University of California Press.

Dickens, Charles (1970). *Dombey and Son,* ed. *Peter Fairclough*. Harmondsworth: Penguin. (Originally published 1848)

Dickens, Charles (1985). *Bleak House*, eds. Norman Page and J. Hillis Miller. Harmondsworth: Penguin. (Originally published 1852)

Eliot, George (1961). *Middlemarch*, ed. W. J. Harvey. Harmondsworth: Penguin. (Originally published 1872)

Fletcher, George Chadwick (1961). *The Works of Joseph Paxton, 1803–65*. London: Architectural Press.

Gloag, John Edwards (1970). *Mr Loudon's England: The Life and Work of John Claudius Loudon and his Influence on Architecture and Furniture Design*. Newcastle upon Tyne: Oriel Press.

The Illustrated Exhibitor and Magazine of Arts (1852a). 'A visit to Apsley Pellatt's flint glass works', 1: 54–9, 70–4.

The Illustrated Exhibitor and Magazine of Arts (1852). 'On the methods of silvering and ornamenting glass', 1: 258–9.

Kenyon, Frederic George (ed.) (1914). *Casa Guidi Windows* (1851), Vol. II, *The Poetical Works of Elizabeth Barrett Browning* (1897). London: John Murray.

Loudon, John Claudius (1824). *The Green-house Companion*. London: Harding, Triphook, and Lepard, and John Harding.

Loudon, John Claudius (1835). *Encyclopaedia of Agriculture* (3rd edn). London: Longman, Rees, Orme, Green and Longman.

Loudon, John Claudius (1838). *The Suburban Gardener and Villa Companion*. London.

Loudon, John Claudius (1839). *Hortus Britannicus. A Catalogue of All the Plants Indigenous, Cultivated In, or Introduced to Britain*. London: Longman, Orme, Brown, Green, and Longmans.

Meredith, George (1975). *One of Our Conquerors*, Margaret Harris (ed.). Brisbane: University of Queensland Press, St. Lucia. (Original work published 1891)

Reichlin, Bruno (1984). 'The pros and cons of the horizontal window: the Perret–Le Corbusier controversy', *Daidalos: Berlin Architectural Journal*, 13 September, 65–78.

Ruskin, John (1851–3). *The Stones of Venice*, in E. T. Cook and A. Wedderburn (eds), *The Works of John Ruskin*. London: G. Allen.

Scott, Joan Wallach (1974). *The Glassworkers of Carmaux: French Craftsmen and Political Action in a Nineteenth-Century City*. Cambridge, MA: Harvard University Press.

Stafford, Barbara M. (1991). *Body Criticism: Imaging the Unseen in Enlightenment Art and Medicine*. Cambridge, MA. and London: MIT Press.

Taut, Bruno (1972). In *Glass Architecture* by Paul Scheerbart and *Alpine Architektur* by Bruno Taut, ed. Dennis Sharp. New York and Washington: Praeger, 125.

Whall, C. W. (1905). *Stained Glass Work: A Text-Book for Students and Workers in Glass*. London: W. R. Lethaby, 198.

Woodward, H. W. (1978). *'Art, Feat and Mystery': The Story of Thomas Webb & Sons, Glassmakers*. Stourbridge: Mark & Moody Limited.

7

Our Animal Environment
Harriet Ritvo

AT LEAST on the surface, what is perhaps the best known passage from Thomas Carlyle's *Past and Present*, has nothing to do with animals:

A poor Irish Widow, her husband having died in one of the Lanes of Edinburgh, went forth with her three children, bare of all resource, to solicit help from the Charitable Establishments of that City. At this Charitable Establishment and then at that she was refused; referred from one to the other, helped by none;—till she had exhausted them all; till her strength and heart failed her: she sank down in typhus-fever; died, and infected her Lane with fever, so that 'seventeen other persons' died of fever there in consequence. The humane Physician asks thereupon, as with a heart too full for speaking, Would it not have been *economy* to help this poor Widow? She took typhus fever, and killed seventeen of you!— Very curious. The forlorn Irish Widow applies to her fellow-creatures, as if saying, 'Behold, I am sinking, bare of help; ye must help me! I am your sister, bone of your bone; one God made us: ye must help me!' They answer, 'No, impossible; thou art no sister of ours.' But she proves her sisterhood; her typhus fever kills them: they actually were her brothers, though denying it! Had human creature ever to go lower for a proof?[1]

Carlyle borrowed this sad episode from a study of the management of the poor in Scotland—its author, Dr Alison, was the 'humane Physician' referred to in the passage—and the primary moral (or immoral) that he drew from it related to economics. Despite the contrary suggestions of what he condemned as the reigning 'Gospel of Mammonism', he insisted that some rights and duties overrode the acquisition and protection of property. Carlyle ironically sugarcoated this bitter pill by suggesting that charitable giving might not be a total loss even in financial terms; seventeen more valuable lives saved ('seventeen of you') would, after all, have been a good return on a small investment in food and shelter.

While primarily focusing on money, however, this passage also broached another general issue, one that may have been nearly as impor-

---

[1] Thomas Carlyle, *Past and Present* (1843; rpt London: Everyman, 1960), 143.

tant to Carlyle's original audience—and to his later ones. In condemning their complacency and selfishness, their irresponsibility and indifference, Carlyle assumed that the heartless city fathers of Edinburgh had wilfully denied an incontestable connection. They had refused to succour a 'poor Widow' (surely a category with which they were familiar), a 'fellow creature', a 'sister, bone of your bone'. But perhaps Carlyle's disagreement with the Edinburgh establishment was less profound and radical than this language of linkage suggested. Perhaps they differed only about where the obligation to charity ended, not about whether it existed. The principled humanitarianism ('one God made us') apparently endorsed in this passage may have been intended less than universally. After all, if it was clear to Carlyle in 1843 that the rhetoric of sibling relationship connected the Irish to other human inhabitants of the British Isles, he was less generous in his later discussions of West Indian freed slaves. In addition, although Carlyle was not much inclined to hedge his moral bets, the fact that he proposed two bases for connection rather than one may have indicated not superabundant certainty, but a felt need for reinforcement. If the figurative assertion of family membership failed to convince, the physical evidence of shared vulnerability to contagion would be incontrovertible, no matter how 'low'.

Thus, the merely human environment resisted easy demarcation. Even among people who lived in the same place and belonged, at least arguably, to a single society it could be difficult to tell who counted as connected, and what the basis of the connection was. Groups that, from one point of view, seemed separated by an unbridgeable gulf, could seem contiguous from a different angle. And failure to recognize connections could have serious consequences, most obviously for the excluded, but also, as Carlyle pointed out, for those in apparent control of categorization. To put it another way, the construction or non-construction of linkages constituted a self-fulfilling prophecy. People tended to be constrained by the environment they had defined, unable to see or act beyond its limits. The human environment as constituted by experience could be a counterpoint to the human environment as constituted by logic or principle or rhetoric.

The difficulty in understanding the limits of connection among people—in determining the point where likeness became more significant than unlikeness—was both mirrored and exaggerated with regard to animals. Even in Victorian terms, this shift from the human to the animal was not so great a leap as it may have seemed at first glance. On both the physical and the rhetorical levels the relationships between people as a group and other animals were analogous to the relationships among

groups of people—in their indeterminacy and their fluidity, as well as in
other ways. For example, there was no universal consensus about the
content of the dichotomy that separated people from other animals.
Uncertainty ran in both directions. That is, some members of what the
late-twentieth century recognizes as the human species could be relegated
to the category of 'animal', while some members of other species could
be included within the human circle.

Even in Carlyle's exemplum, with its intensely familial rhetoric, the
suggestion that the Irish might be less fully human than the Scots was
implicit in the humiliating public death of the widow's husband (stray
dogs and abused horses and livestock were the likeliest creatures to die
in that way), and nineteenth-century iconography was rich in connection
between the Irish physiognomy and that of the great apes. Further, as
Carlyle's own work, like that of many of his contemporaries, shows, non-
Europeans were still likelier to be the subjects of such taxonomic dis-
paragement. On the other hand, Victorian commentators often compared
well-bred horses and dogs favourably with what they regarded as inferior human types, on grounds of intellect, as well as of disposition and
personal appearance. And, then as now, if people were asked whether
they felt themselves to be closely related to (other) animals, they were
liable to give a different answer (no), than the one that would be suggested by their unselfconscious behaviour (yes).

This profound inconsistency helped to structure the most powerful
figurative representation of relationship—the most explicit and self-
conscious delineation of humankind's animal environment. This was
zoological classification. From its enlightenment beginnings, most formal
taxonomy recognized not only the general correspondence between
people and what were then known as quadrupeds, but also the more particular similarities that human beings shared with apes and monkeys. (It
was the non-functional physical details that proved most compelling: the
shape of the external ear, for example, or the flatness of fingernails and
toenails.) Thus, in 1699 the anatomist Edward Tyson published a treatise
entitled *Orang-Outang, sive Homo Sylvestris. Or the Anatomy of a
Pygmie compared with that of a Monkey, an Ape and a Man.* Tyson stated
in his preface that his purpose was to 'observe *Nature's Gradation* in the
Formation of *Animal* Bodies, and the Transitions made from one to
another', thus implicitly including humanity in the animal series.[2] And
not only did Tyson present people as anatomically continuous with
animals, but his choice of terminology further implied that the categories
of 'human' and 'orang-utan' (by which he meant what is now known as

---

[2] Edward Tyson (London: Thomas Bennet, 1699), 'Preface' n.p.

a chimpanzee) might not be completely distinct. Both of the synonyms for orang-utan mentioned in the title conflated it with people: the translation of 'Homo Sylvestris' is 'wild man of the woods', (figure 7.1) and, conversely, the humanity of the quasi-mythical pygmies had long been the subject of European speculation. Even at the end of the eighteenth century, naturalists could claim that the 'race of men of diminutive stature' or 'supposed nation of pygmies' described by the ancients, was 'nothing more than a species of apes . . . that resemble us but very imperfectly'.[3]

The celebrated eighteenth-century systematizer Carolus Linnaeus also located people firmly within the animal kingdom, constructing the primate order to accommodate humans, apes, monkeys, prosimians, and bats. In what has become the definitive (1758) edition of his *Systema Naturae*, he included two species within the genus *Homo*. One was *Homo sapiens*, subdivided into (mostly) geographical subspecies or races, such as *H. sapiens Americanus* and *H. sapiens Europaeus*, and the other was *Homo troglodytes*, which was also known, Linnaeus pointed out, as *Homo sylvestris Orang Outang*.[4] Thus Linnaeus grouped Tyson's chimpanzee with humanity, rather than including it in the crowded genus *Simia* with the monkeys and the other apes.

And this taxonomic connection was not necessarily confined to the realm of abstraction; through passion or sentiment it might be embodied in living flesh. The birth of hybrid infants has conventionally (although always problematically) been taken to indicate identity of species on the part of the parents. Obviously, such births require at least that individuals of apparently different types recognize each other as possible reproductive partners. For a variety of reasons, cross-breeding has tended to engage both vulgar and learned curiosity, and the possibility of mixed parentage has long been guaranteed to make an infant interesting. In the eighteenth and nineteenth centuries, most reported hybrids involved other kinds of animals—for example, cattle and bison, dogs and wolves, horses and zebras, even such unlikely pairs as sheep and raccoons (figure 7.2).[5] But humans too could be the objects or the originators of passions that transcended or violated the ostensible species barrier, although accounts of such episodes tended to be carefully distanced by scepticism or censure. Indeed, the most common such breaches, those involving

[3] *An Historical Miscellany of the Curiosities and Rarities in Nature and Art . . .* (London: Champante & Whitrow, *c.* 1800), iii, 288–9.

[4] Carolus Linnaeus, *Systema Naturae: Regnum Animale* (1758; rpt London: British Museum (Natural History); 1956), 20–4.

[5] For an extended discussion of 18- and 19-century hybrids and cross-breeds, see Harriet Ritvo, *The Platypus and the Mermaid, and Other Figments of the Classifying Imagination* (Cambridge, MA: Harvard University Press, 1997), ch. 3.

FIGURE 7.1   Edward Tyson's 'wild man of the woods', which appears as a frontispiece to *Orang-Outang* (see note 2).

FIGURE 7.2   A lion–tiger hybrid. From Richard Lydekker (1896). *A Handbook to the Carnivora. Part I. Cats, Civets, and Mungooses*, plate III, p. 44. London: Edward Lloyd.

farmyard animals, were much more likely to figure in a legal than a scientific context.[6]

Zoologists were more interested in courtships that seemed to offer a better chance of offspring. Thus, at the end of the eighteenth century Charles White reported that orang-utans 'have been known to carry off negro-boys, girls and even women . . . as objects of brutal passion'; more than sixty years later the Anthropological Society republished Johann Friedrich Blumenbach's summary of travellers' accounts claiming that 'lascivious male apes attack women'.[7] Still more suggestively, White recorded rumours 'that women have had offspring from such connection' and proposed that 'supposing it to be true, it would be an object of inquiry, whether such offspring would propagate, or prove to be mules'.[8] Blumenbach, more cautious, asserted 'that such a monstrous connection

[6] E. P. Evans, *The Criminal Prosecution and Capital Punishment of Animals: The Lost History of Europe's Animal Trials* (1906; London: Faber & Faber, 1987), 147–53.
[7] Charles White, *An Account of the Regular Gradation in Man, and in Different Animals and Vegetables; and from the Former to the Latter* (London: C. Dilly, 1799), 34; Johann Friedrich Blumenbach, *The Anthropological Treatises . . .* trans. and ed. Thomas Bendyshe (London: Longman, Green, Longman, Roberts & Green/The Anthropological Society, 1865), 73.   [8] White, *Account of the Regular Gradation in Man*, 34.

FIGURE 7.3   The hairy Julia Pastrana. From George M. Gould and Walter L.
Pyle (1896). *Anomalies and Curiosities of Medicine*, p. 229. Philadelphia: W. B.
Saunders.

has any where ever been fruitful there is no well-established instance to
prove'.[9] Along the same lines, in his account of chimpanzee anatomy,
Edward Tyson had gone out of his way to assure his readers that
'notwithstanding our *Pygmie* does so much resemble a *Man* . . . : yet by
no means do I look upon it as the Product of a *mixt* generation'.[10] Outside
the community of experts, claims could be less restrained, or more enthu-
siastic. For example, a Victorian impresario advertised the merely hairy
Julia Pastrana (figure 7.3) as 'a hybrid, wherein the nature of woman pre-
dominates over the ourang-outangs'.[11]

[9] Blumenbach, *Anthropological Treatises*, 80–1.
[10] Tyson, *Orang-Outang*, 2.
[11] Jan Bondeson and A. E. W. Miles (1993). 'Julia Pastrana, the Nondescript: an example
of congenital generalized hypertrichosis terminalis with gingival hyperplasia'. *American
Journal of Medical Genetics*, 47: 199.

And there were other ways of positing concrete connections between people and the non-human animals most nearly allied to them by anatomy. Well into the nineteenth century, physicians explained many kinds of birth defects as the unfortunate consequences of maternal imagination—that is, of the mother's fascination with an external object that had somehow influenced the development of her unborn child. Where the object was animate, it could occasion a kind of mental hybridization—a child whose parentage involved more than one species. Thus, in 1867 the *Lancet* attributed the dense fur that covered an unfortunate girl's back to the fact that her mother had been frightened by an organ grinder's monkey. In addition, the evolutionary theories that were widely accepted in the late Victorian periods assumed the existence of extinct forms that were intermediate between humans and apes, at least in the sense of having given rise to both modern groups. But the rhetoric of evolution could also be deployed to suggest that human–ape mixtures existed at the present time, as well as in the ancestral past. For example, a Laotian girl was exhibited in 1883 as 'Darwin's missing link', not only because she was unusually hairy, but because she allegedly possessed prehensile feet and could pout like a chimpanzee.[12]

This strong sense of anatomically based continuity was reinforced by a tradition of natural history illustration that portrayed apes as particularly human in both appearance and behaviour (figure 7.4). Typically, apes were shown assuming erect posture, using human tools, and approximating human proportions in the trunk and limbs. And this visual tradition was not confined to the page or the canvas. It was also constantly re-enacted in the display of the chimpanzees and orang-utans, who were predictable features of nineteenth-century zoos and menageries (figure 7.5). Show apes ate with table utensils, sipped tea from cups, and slept under blankets. An orang-utan who lived in London's Exeter Change Menagerie amused herself by carefully turning the pages of an illustrated book. At the Regent's Park Zoo a chimpanzee named Jenny regularly appeared in a flannel nightgown and robe. Consul, a young chimpanzee who lived in Manchester's Belle Vue Zoological Gardens at the end of the nineteenth century dressed in a jacket and straw hat, smoked cigarettes, and drank his liquor from a glass.[13] At about the same time, the London zoo routinely dressed a chimp named Mike to impersonate Captain Cuttle, a character from Dickens's *Dombey and Son*. And the

---

[12] *Nature*, 12 May 1882, cited in Martin Howard, *Victorian Grotesque: An Illustrated Excursion into Medical Curiosities, Freaks and Abnormalities—Principally of the Victorian Age* (London: Jupiter Books, 1977), 56–7.

[13] C. V. A. Peel, *The Zoological Gardens of Europe: Their History and Chief Features* (London: F. E. Robinson, 1903), 205–6; 'In Memory of Consul', pamphlet in the Belle Vue collection, Chetham's Library, Manchester.

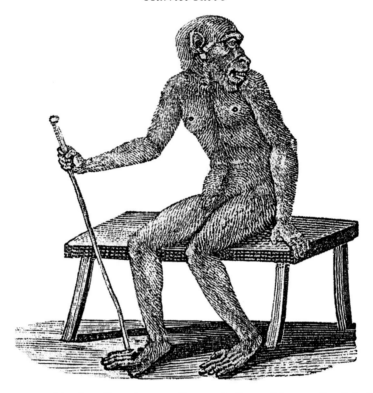

FIGURE 7.4 'An inordinately man-like ape'. From Thomas Bewick (1824).
A General History of Quadrupeds, p. 452. Newcastle: T. Bewick.

behaviour even of apes with no public role to play tended to assimilate
them to people. For example, a chimpanzee acquired by the Earl
Fitzwilliam in 1849 was reported to walk 'perfectly erect' and handle
'everything like a human being'; in addition, his food was 'choice, and
wine a favourite beverage'.[14] (figure 7.5) But not everybody was persuaded by Tyson and Linnaeus, or even by Darwin, Jenny, and Consul.
Commitments that were explicitly or essentially theological made many
naturalists reluctant to embed their own species within the system of
animal connections, whether it was figured in the enlightenment mode
as a chain, or in the Victorian mode as a tree. Despite Linnaeus's iconic

[14] William Bingley, *Animal Biography* (London: R. Phillips, 1803), I, 45–50; Edward
Jesse, *Gleanings in Natural History*, 2nd Series (London: John Murray, 1834), 40; William
Broderip, *Zoological Recreations* (London: Henry Colburn, 1847), 250; 'Importation of
Another Specimen of the Chimpanzee', *Zoologist*, 7 (1849), 2379.

FIGURE 7.5   A zoo ape in human clothing. From Charles Knight (1856–8).
Knight's Pictorial Museum of Animated Nature. London: London Printing and
Publishing Company. (Reproduced by kind permission of the Ernst Mayr
Library, Museum of Comparative Zoology, Harvard.)

status as a systematizer, his inclusive primate order was frequently
rejected. According to the late eighteenth-century naturalist Thomas
Pennant, 'my vanity will not suffer me to rank mankind with *Apes,
Monkies, Maucaucos*, and *Bats*'; a contemporary similarly asserted that
'we may perhaps be pardoned for the repugnance we feel to place the
monkey at the head of the brute creation, and thus to associate him . . .

with man'.[15] Other dissenters simply proposed their own counter-taxonomies, which posited a much wider separation. Thus, early in the nineteenth century the anatomist William Lawrence suggested that 'the principles must be incorrect, which lead to such an approximation' (that is, between humans, apes, and monkeys in the primate order); instead, he argued that 'the peculiar characteristics of man appear to me so very strong, that I not only deem him a distinct species, but also . . . a separate order'.[16] Naturalists who recognized this exclusively human order normally designated it as 'Bimana', which stressed the erect posture and purpose-built feet characteristic of people, in contrast with the four-handed apes and monkeys who were segregated in the order 'Quadrumana'.[17]

As evolutionary theory suggested a more concrete and ineluctable connection, it provoked still more forceful resistance. After *On the Origin of Species* was published in 1859, for example, the geologist Adam Sedgwick, who had been one of Darwin's early scientific mentors at Cambridge, anonymously expressed his 'deep aversion to the theory' on taxonomic grounds. He asserted that 'we cannot speculate on man's position in the actual world of nature, on his destinies, or on *his origin*, while we keep his highest faculties out of our sight. Strip him of these faculties, and he becomes entirely bestial; he may well be (under such a false and narrow view) nothing better than the natural progeny of a beast, which has to live, to beget its likeness, and then die for ever'.[18] As Darwin sadly noted at the end of *The Descent of Man*, written a decade after the appearance of *On the Origin*, 'The main conclusion arrived at in this work, namely that man is descended from some lowly-organised form, will, I regret to think, be highly distasteful to many persons'.[19]

And the scientific resistance to locating people within a specifically primate context also found an echo in visual tradition. One way of denying the human–ape connection—as of denying the connection between human groups—was to posit an alternative alliance. If non-

[15] Thomas Pennant, *History of Quadrupeds* (London: B. & J. White, 1793), iv; William Wood, *Zoography; or the Beauties of Nature Displayed* (London: Cadell & Davies, 1807), xvii.

[16] William Lawrence, *Lectures on Comparative Anatomy, Physiology, Zoology, and the Natural History of Man; delivered at the Royal College of Surgeons in the Years 1816, 1817, and 1818* (London: R. Carlile, 1823), 127, 131.

[17] See e.g. Richard Owen (1855), 'on the Anthropoid Apes and their relations to Man'. *Proceedings of the Royal Institution of Great Britain* 2: 41.

[18] [Adam Sedgwick], 'Objections to Mr. Darwins Theory of the Origin of Species', *Spectator* 14 March, 1860/7 April 1860; rpt in David L. Hull, *Darwin and His Critics: The Reception of Darwin's Theory of Evolution by the Scientific Community* (University of Chicago Press, 1973), 164–5.

[19] Charles Darwin, *The Descent of Man* (1871; rpt New York: Modern Library, 1950), 919.

primate animals resembled humans more closely than apes, then they would necessarily displace apes from their awkward proximity. Such displacement required that a different set of qualities be identified as the most significant for purposes of comparison. Most frequently, evidence from the behavioural or moral sphere replaced the merely anatomical. Thus, throughout the nineteenth century naturalists debated the rival claims of dogs and apes to be top animal, and therefore closest to humankind. In 1881, for example, George J. Romanes, a close friend of Darwin's with a special interest in animal behaviour, celebrated the 'high intelligence' and 'gregarious instincts' of the dog, which gave it a more 'massive as well as more complex' psychology than any member of the monkey family.[20] And since the alternative closeness thus constructed was clearly figurative, the whole animal creation was thereby implicitly removed to a more comfortable distance.

From this perspective, the creatures who approached human beings most closely were likely to be the domesticated pets and livestock who shared their lives, the wild creatures whom they routinely hunted, or, in a more attenuated relationship, the animals, wild or tame, who served as traditional metaphors for human attributes. And although, as a rule, these alternative associations were not embodied in abstract schema, they did reflect persistent conventions in the graphic portrayal of people and animals. The notion that similar appearance indicated similar character, for example, had a long history. As an English translation of the seventeenth-century French artist Charles LeBrun, who himself consolidated and elaborated a much older tradition of linking human attributes with those of beasts, noted, 'the Physiognomists say that if a Man happens to have any part of his Body resembling that of a Brute, we may ... draw Conjectures of his Inclinations'.[21] LeBrun's mechanistic deconstruction of personality traits doubled as a recipe for depicting them. He proposed, for example, that the point of intersection between the line across the upper eyelid and a line drawn from the nose indicated mental power: 'when these two lines meet in the Forehead, it is a sign of Sagacity, as ... in the Elephants, Camels, and Apes: But if the Angle meets upon the Nose, it shews Stupidity and Weakness, as in Asses and Sheep'.[22] Humans could follow the pattern set by any of these creatures.

And although the authority of LeBrun's analyses waned along with the

[20] George J. Romanes, *Animal Intelligence* (New York: D. Appleton, 1896), 439.

[21] Charles Le Brun, *Conference of Monsieur Le Brun, Chief Painter to the French King, Chancellor and Director of the Academy of Painting and Sculpture; upon Expression, General and Particular* (London: John Smith, Edward Cooper & David Mortier, 1701), 40; Jennifer Montagu, *The Expression of the Passions: The Origin and Influence of Charles LeBrun's Conférence sur l'lexpression générale et particulière* (New Haven: Yale University Press, 1994), 20–4.   [22] Le Brun, *Conference*, 46.

FIGURE 7.6 Human–animal affinities. A coloured lithograph by W. Clee, *Matters of taste. No. 1. As regards natural history.* (Reproduced by kind permission of The Wellcome Institute Library, London.)

assumption that the essential nature of each individual and each species was so obvious and so invariant, English editions of his work continued to appear well into the nineteenth century. Images evoking the reciprocal resemblance between humans and members of other species constituted part of the stock visual repertory of both humorous and sentimental social commentary, figuring in genres from ephemeral satire to academic painting. Thus, a mid-Victorian lithograph displayed a crammed panorama of natural history buffs, whose physical appearance unflatteringly reflected the adjacent objects of their fascination (figure 7.6), while *Punch* presented a gentleman with a pendulous belly and a beaky nose gazing with embarrassed recognition at a penguin. So conventional was this mirroring that, as the many anthropomorphic canvases of Edwin Landseer illustrated, its evocation required the presence of only a single member of the pair (usually the non-human one).

These juxtapositions matched people with a wide variety of zoological doubles, implicitly constructing polymorphous, eccentric, and inconsistent patterns of relationship. Such counter-taxonomies could even be based on conventionally scientific evidence. Thus, when the late eighteenth-century painter Sawrey Gilpin claimed that 'The lines, w[hich] form y. countenance of y. lion approach nearer to those of y. human countenance, than y. lines of any animal with w(hich] we are acquainted', he may have been influenced primarily by the animal's traditional role as the 'King of y. beasts' and by analogy in the style of LeBrun, as by any technical analysis,[23] but a few years later, after actually dissecting a lion, the romantic artist Benjamin Haydon agreed that 'the lion was but a modification of the human being'.[24]

One of the final anatomical works undertaken by George Stubbs, for example, was entitled *A Comparative Anatomical Exposition of the Human Body with that of a Tiger and a Common Fowl*. In it, Stubbs too expressed an alternative understanding of the human context in conventional anatomical terms. The mere juxtaposition of these three creatures suggested relationships that were usually unnoticed or nonexistent, and Stubbs's aggressively realistic depictions nevertheless exaggerated the unusual resemblances produced by his selection. The meticulously detailed plates showed primate, carnivore, and gallinaceous bird in identical positions (more or less) and stages of dissection, from the intact body, through the successive removal of skin, muscles, and internal organs, to the naked bones (figure 7.7). Not only did the human model assume quadrupedal postures, but he was portrayed with a skeletal configuration—relatively narrow shoulders and wide hips—that made him resemble the fowl much more closely than might have been expected.[25]

In a similar vein the author of a Victorian anatomy book designed for artists, in which creatures were shown first with their skins and flesh, and then without them, noted that the juxtaposed skeletons of a dancing bear and a human bear warden illustrated that 'the bears (genus Ursidae) have a claim superior to that of apes and monkeys for the nearest proximity to human beings, on account of their plantigrade feet and ... erect attitude'.[26] And in 1891, the director of the British Museum (Natural History) used a drawing of a human skeleton standing next to an equine one, with their corresponding joints anthropomorphically and vernacularly labelled as 'wrist', 'knee', 'ankle', and so forth, as the frontispiece to a monograph entitled *The Horse: A Study in Natural*

[23] Sawrey Gilpin, 'On the character and expression of Animals', 5, 13 (Bodleian Ms. Eng. misc.d.585 [folio 5–21]).
[24] Benjamin R. Haydon, *Lectures on Painting and Design* (London: Longman, Brown, Green, & Longmans, 1844–6), I, 13.
[25] The drawings are reproduced in *George Stubbs 1724–1806* (London: Tate Gallery, 1985), 186–215.
[26] Benjamin Waterhouse Hawkins, *Comparative Anatomy as Applied to the Purposes of the Artist* (London: Winsor & Newton, 1883).

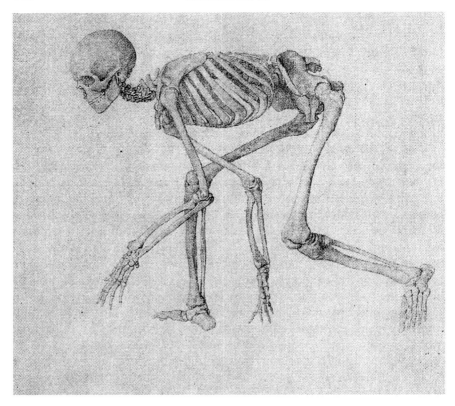

FIGURE 7.7   A human in the guise of a tiger. From a drawing by George
Stubbs. Reproduced in *George Stubbs 1724–1806* (1985). A catalogue published
jointly by the Yale Center for British Art, Tate Gallery, and Salem House.
(Reproduced by kind permission of the Yale Center for British Art.)

History.[27] The exhibit on which it was based, actual skeletons standing
side-by-side, was the first thing encountered by visitors to the museum's
large and (otherwise) elaborately classified collection of equids.[28] The
juxtaposition implicitly presented the social connection between the
thoroughbred horse and his rider or keeper as at least equivalent to
the anatomical or phylogenetic connection between the horse and the
zebras and asses that constituted the rest of the exhibit.

[27] William Henry Flower, *The Horse: A Study in Natural History* (London: Kegan Paul,
Trench, Trübner, 1891), frontispiece.
[28] Richard Lydekker, *Guide to Specimens of the Horse Family (Equidae) exhibited in
the Department of Zoology, British Museum (Natural History)*; (London: British Museum
(Natural History), 1907), 4.

It is clear—and it has been frequently remarked—that the construction of our animal environment in this taxonomic sense both represents and determines the way we understand human character, and even human responsibility and human destiny. It is equally clear—although not as frequently noted—that it also, reciprocally, represents and determines our notions about the character and destiny of various other creatures. The consequences for them are more concrete and less metaphysical. These consequences are also far from predictable: we (however 'we' may be defined) have disagreed strongly, and continue to disagree strongly, about which of these understandings and notions to endorse. But even when they are inconsistent with each other, the totalizing power of our patterns makes them share another kind of effect. After all, whatever their bases, they are evidently imposed by us. They convert animals from physical presences into counters in an intellectual game, under the unquestioned control of the classifier. And this abstract vulnerability to human arrangement mirrors the physical vulnerability of most animals (at least most of those who figure prominently in our taxonomic environment, however it is constituted) to human necessity or caprice. We can categorize them at will, just as we can buy and cherish them at will, dispossess and transport them at will, or kill and eat them at will.

Even those animals most concretely present in ordinary life have frequently been sublimated into rhetoric. During the eighteenth and nineteenth centuries, for example, livestock animals figured regularly in the experience of city dwellers, who saw them driven through the streets to market or to slaughter. Of course, they occupied a still more prominent position in the experience of country people, as was endlessly recorded by professional and amateur painters of the agricultural landscape. Indeed, without a substantial delegation of cattle or sheep, no such painting was complete. Manuals produced to guide amateur painters emphasized the need to include portraits of what they referred to, for example, as 'the various species of cattle, calculated to heighten and give sublimity to picturesque effect' or 'the various domestic animals that embellish rural scenery'.[29] To this end, they offered sample animals for copying, in case the actual scene had unaccountably lacked them. But the function of cattle and sheep in the paintings did not precisely mirror their function on the farm. These creatures were, as the title of one manual put it, *Landscape Animals*, thoroughly reconstituted by the aesthetic terms of their representation, serving primarily to mark the genre of the painting.[30]

[29] John Hassell, *Hassell's Drawing Magazine, of Rural. Scenery, or the Self Taught Artist* (London: Thomas Tegg, n.d. [1809]), n. pag.

[30] W. M. Craig, *Landscape Animals. No. 1 in a Series of Progressive Studies* (London, n. pub.: 1811).

Of course, this is not to suggest that this was the only function that the animals served, in the eyes of the artists or of anyone else. And, in addition to producing meat, milk, and wool, livestock could at least as plausibly be claimed to create their setting, as merely to adorn it. From a political or economic perspective, the decision to reallocate land to grazing from arable or waste—a decision that was a frequent prerequisite to the creation of the placid landscapes depicted by artists—often occasioned major re-engineering of the physical countryside and traumatic dislocations among its human inhabitants. From an ecological perspective, cattle and sheep had an enormous impact on the other species that populated their rustic settings. As Darwin pointed out in the *Origin of Species*—in the chapter where he attempted to demonstrate the interconnectedness of all life—a much greater number of plant species thrived in fields that were closely browsed by sheep, than in similar fields where the vegetation grew unmolested; and cattle could completely halt the spread of a tree species like the Scotch fir.[31] The massive environmental impact of domestic ungulates has continued to the present time; it has made headlines in, for example, the dedication of large tracts of Africa and Central America to manufacturing the raw material for McDonald's, and the rumoured contribution of the global cattle herd to the increase of greenhouse gases. Nevertheless all this agency, as well as the suffering experienced by farm animals as they fulfilled their industrial functions, can be implicitly denied, or at least glossed over, by a label like 'landscape animals'.

Such categorizations simultaneously distance animals from their industrial functions and from ourselves. But like Carlyle's Irish widow, they have ways of claiming kin. Indeed, her strategy has provided some of the most compelling alternative answers to the question, 'Where do we belong?' To repeat Carlyle's words, she 'infected her Lane with fever, so that "seventeen other persons" died of fever there in consequence'. In a sense this calamity resulted from the collision of inconsistent categories. The widow's victims failed to recognize her sisterhood because they understood their relation to her in terms of a different system, which emphasized hierarchy and social distance rather than identity embedded in flesh and blood. The classificatory principles to which they subscribed thus made their deaths not only tragic, but also degrading and incomprehensible.

In our own time, if anything, infectious disease has become more taxonomically troubling, even within the human sphere. Its persistence

---

[31] Charles Darwin, *On the Origin of Species* (1859; Cambridge MA: Harvard University Press, 1964), 67–8, 71–2.

(or re-emergence) elides categories that express some of our most basic cultural assumptions—about the distinctions between disparate social groups or, on a larger scale, about the distinction between modern societies, self-defined at least in part by their ability to control nature through science, and earlier or less fortunate societies. Thus, excitable reportage about the appearance of drug-resistant strains of tuberculosis often reductively describes the down-and-out sufferers who fail to take their medicine properly as ambulatory disease incubators, spewing infection at the innocent and hygienic citizens who share public conveyances. The dichotomies invoked by this imagery are not only sick *vs.* healthy, contaminated *vs.* clean, and disreputable *vs.* upstanding, but also atavistic *vs.* advanced (or even highly evolved). Obviously, tuberculosis is a very serious illness, and exposure to it can be a terrible misfortune. But what is notable in such responses is not the sense of distress provoked by this levelling vulnerability, but the sense of surprise, violation, and outrage.

And if infectious diseases transmitted by fellow humans produce upsetting taxonomic problems, zoonoses—diseases that are transmitted to humans by other animals—are still more troublesome. Not only do they close any remaining gap between these groups, but they reverse the conventional relationship between them, substituting victimization for custodianship or conquest. The resulting uneasiness conditions many discussions of infectious diseases—after all, it is likely that most of them had a zoonotic origin. It appears in suggestions that our annual influenza visitations originate in rural southeast Asia, where viruses from people, pigs, ducks, and even fish may swap genetic material to produce constantly changing epidemics. It lurks in speculation that the human AIDS virus is a cross-specific transfer from African monkeys. (Of course, both these examples also raise issues of purely human taxonomy.)

But perhaps the most unsettling zoonoses are those that complicate associations based on social or moral categories—that is, associations that privilege figurative over physical resemblances. And when animals whose special closeness has been understood in affectionate, almost totemic terms become the vectors of terrible disease, shift in the basis of connection can be particularly alarming. This may help explain the inordinate emotional charge that rabies has traditionally carried in Britain, where kindness to animals is a cherished component of the national character, and where John Bull is conventionally caricatured as a canine. Rabies, after all, has never been much of a threat to British people. Even in the nineteenth century, when there were frequent outbreaks among wild animals and domestic dogs and cats, the intensity of concern it provoked was grossly disproportionate to the likelihood of actually contracting the

disease. In only one year did as many as seventy-nine people die, and that
figure was more than twice the next-highest annual toll of thirty-five,
which was itself unusually high—numbers that faded into insignificance
in comparison with the human mortality attributed to many more
common infectious and non-infectious causes.

But the terms in which the offending dogs were routinely discussed
suggested that their major transgression had been categorical: not
only had they shifted from man's best friend to his worst enemy, but
the source of their affinity had become newly physical. Thus, responses
to the public health problems posed by rabid dogs were primarily concerned with categorization. In general, they attempted to segregate good
dogs, who were not liable to expose their owners to rabies, from bad dogs
who were. In a final turn of the taxonomic wheel, these dangerous
bad dogs were most easily identified by their association with human
groups of which the classifier disapproved, which ranged from rich ladies,
who drove their dogs to rabies through excessive gratification of their
appetites, to violent members of the working classes, such as poachers or
butchers, whose dogs shared their aggressive propensities, to foreigners,
whose alien dog breeds were feared to have excessively excitable and
therefore susceptible nervous systems.[32] Nearly a century has passed
since rabies was eliminated in Britain, but its ability to provoke heated
responses has scarcely diminished. Indeed, since rabies can now be
viewed solely in terms of foreign invasion, its emotional charge may
even have increased. In any case, it seems likely that current quarantine
policy is partly based on traditional taxonomic (or counter-taxonomic)
concerns.

And before John Bull was a canine he was a bovine. The 'roast beef of
Old England' and the animals who provided it have for centuries been
valued as much more than an efficient source of nourishment. In the same
way that 'Carnivorous Animals have more Courage, Muscular Strength
and Activity', so a meat-heavy diet was believed to contribute to British
'energy . . . sense of fitness . . . [and] craving for work. . . . The beef of
the British soldier has always been regarded as a factor in his valour'.[33]
Beef-eating was viewed by observers within the British polity and outside
it as an essential component of the national character. Further, as the

---

[32] For a fuller discussion of rabies in the Victorian period, see Harriet Ritvo, *The Animal
Estate: The English and Other Creatures in the Victorian Age* (Cambridge, MA: Harvard
University Press, 1987), ch. 4.

[33] John Arbuthnot, *An Essay Concerning the Nature of Aliments, and the Choice of
Them, According-to the Different Constitutions of Human Bodies* (London: J. Tonson,
1732), 225; J. Milner Fothergill, *The Food We Eat: Why We Eat It and Whence It Comes*
(London: Griffith & Farran, 1882), 53–4.

Quarterly Journal of Agriculture complacently noted in 1830, 'our domestic cattle . . . have long yielded us . . . good beef (of which the very name is almost identified with the character and propensities of the nation)'.[34] According to *Household Words*, 'beef is a great connecting link and bond of better feeling between the great classes of the common-wealth', inspiring respect second only to 'the Habeas Corpus and the Freedom of the Press'.[35]

Naturalists and agricultural experts, chefs and gourmets agreed that Britain was pre-eminent for the quality of the meat it produced, as well as the quantity it consumed, claiming, for example, that British cattle were 'preferable to the cattle of any other country in the world'; that 'the cattle and sheep of this country we may justly regard . . . as unequalled in any other territory'; and that 'no country produces finer sheep than Great Britain'.[36] Even a cookbook whose irreverent author disparaged the finished products of British cuisine acknowledged that its raw mater-ials were unrivalled: 'In this country we have the best of all descriptions of butcher's meat in the world, and, with a few exceptions, the worst cooks. If the poor, half-fed meats of France, were dressed as our cooks, for the most part, dress our well-fed excellent meats, they would be absolutely uneatable'.[37] In any country, the possible condemnation of the national cattle herd would be viewed as an impending disaster, both eco-nomic and epidemiological. But because of this deeply ingrained tradi-tion of metonymic identification, the crisis triggered in Britain by the spread of BSE or mad cow disease has been especially difficult and threat-ening. The reluctance to recognize the problem, the inclination of government (and even, to some extent, of consumers) to stand behind the industry, the initial lack of sympathy with foreign import bans, and the reciprocal foreign eagerness to impose them—all these responses have been conditioned by historic associations to a larger extent than might have been expected of public policy with such potentially serious implications for public finance and public health. So, too much identifi-cation can have the same effect as too little. Reluctance to see a closely

---

[34] 'On the Origin and Natural History of the Domestic Ox, and its Allied Species', *Quarterly Journal of Agriculture* (1830) 2: 196–7.

[35] Quoted in Peter Lund Simmonds, *The Curiosities of Food; or the Dainties and Del-icacies of Different Nations Obtained from the Animal Kingdom* (London: R. Bentley, 1859), 2–3.

[36] William Bingley, *Useful Knowledge; or a Familiar Account of the Various Productions of Nature, Mineral, Vegetable, and Animal, which are Chiefly Employed for the Use of Man* (London: Baldwin & Craddock, 1831), III, 94; D. G. F. MacDonald, *Cattle, Sheep, and Deer* (London: Steele & Jones, 1872), 8; Duncan McDonald, *The New London Family Cook; or, Town and Country Housekeeper's Guide* (London: Albion Press, 1808), 25.

[37] *The Guide to Service: The Cook* (London: Charles Knight, 1842), 12–13.

associated category as threatening can be as problematic as reluctance to see a threatening category as close. In the end, moral affinity may not be so very different from anatomical affinity after all. Our animal environment is not as much a matter of construction as we might like to think.

8

Environment as Heritage

David Lowenthal

THE WORD 'environment' generally refers to our material surroundings, above all to those we regard as natural. Its derivative 'environmentalism' connotes the current crusade to amend our relations with nature. But this gloss on environment is quite new. Its lexical looseness might have vexed Thomas Linacre, a classical translator praised as intellectually fastidious by his pupil Erasmus.

Classically, environment meant 'surroundings' of every sort. It embraced all around us, ideas and feelings along with nature, artefacts, and other people—John Gower wrote of 'Lucrece all environed with women'. Early usage implied that we ourselves do the environing, in circumnavigating our own beings. So Thomas Traherne spoke of 'the holy soul of a quiet man invironed with its own repose'.[1] Environing in this all-embracing sense still endures—the headline 'Rome Plans Cleanup of Pantheon's Image' refers to cobblestoning the square in front of it and banning loiterers nearby.[2] But only in the nineteenth century did environment come to stress *external* determinants. And not till this century did these specifically denote the circumstances of nature, as distinct from, or even opposed to, those of culture.

Environmentalism underwent a further and more drastic shift in meaning. Echoing Hippocrates, nineteenth- and early twentieth-century savants supposed that environment—landforms, climate, soils, vegetation—formed national culture and personal traits. Friedrich Ratzel, Ellen Semple, Ellsworth Huntington, Griffith Taylor, and their numerous devotees held physical geography to be the key to history and human destiny.[3] But environmentalism today means something radically different: a campaign to restore environment. What a contrast! Previously

---

[1] For these usages, the *Oxford English Dictionary* cites John Gower, *Confessio Amantis* (1390), and Thomas Traherne, *Christian Ethics* (1675). Rolston (1996: 10–15) posits a similarly inclusive use of 'environment'.

[2] The Pantheon news item is from *International Herald Tribune*, 17 July 1996, 8.

[3] These and other sources are summarized in Spate 1968.

nature's passive pawns, we now see ourselves as prime agents in its historic destruction and, we hope, its future regeneration.

The term 'heritage', as I use it here, refers to all that we receive and value (or dread) from the past: artefacts and heirlooms, homilies and memories. Heritage is encapsulated in legends about origins and ancestors that lend us identity and continuity and that armour us in patriotic stewardship. Such legends are mandatory; allegiance compels us to believe in them, however shaky the evidence. Heritage is faith passionately upheld rather than objective demonstrable truth.[4]

ENVIRONMENT AS HERITAGE

Like the legacies of culture, those of environment are keenly cherished—and bitterly contested by rival claimants. Our own environments, individual, local, and national, are seen as uniquely precious, as *unlike* all others.

Each people treasures physical features felt to be distinctively their own. Landscapes are compelling symbols of national identity. Patriotic feeling builds on talismans of space and place: hills and rivers and woods become ideological sites of shrines, battles, birthplaces. Every national anthem praises special scenic splendours and natural bounties. Rugged mountains, dense forests, deep lakes, storm-scarred coasts and cliffs equip myriad chauvinisms. Thus, the Swiss ascribe their sturdy freedom to frugal, communitarian mountain life and pure Alpine air. In contrast, the English vaunt humanized rural scenes as schools of decorum. Environment is everywhere an emblem of national identity.[5]

Environmental concerns are also intensely parochial. In enhancing surroundings and in warding off risks, the general good normally takes a back seat to the local, to what is most deeply our own. The NIMBY syndrome—put that obnoxious waste somewhere else, 'not in my back yard'—is a universal and, in most circumstances, rational response to threats of impact. In Edelstein's (1988) summary: 'Pollution will occur, victims will suffer. The challenge is to avoid being one of those victims'. Hence global and even national concerns ever founder on parochial rocks.

Yet the global reach of environmental heritage is today beyond dispute. Unlike most of our precursors, we now view the living globe as a common legacy requiring communal custody. Fresh water and fossil

---

[4] These concepts of heritage are adumbrated in Lowenthal 1997.
[5] I discuss landscape as identity in Lowenthal 1994 and 1996.

fuels, rain forests and gene pools are recognized as legacies common to all—and needing all our care.

Environmental legacies overspill all bounds; they are the heritage of the whole world, as in UNESCO's World Heritage sites. More than cultural monuments, natural and scenic realms inspire collaborative protection. International treaties prohibit development in Antarctica, global mandates protect Tasmania's wilderness, international skills and resources are enlisted to combat marine pollution and space debris.

Awareness of global interdependence is newly potent. Only since Rachel Carson's *Silent Spring* appeared in 1962 has realization of environmental hazard become pervasive. Millions today express alarm about nuclear decay, global warming, ozone depletion, species loss, ecodiversity—the end of nature as we know and cherish it.

ENVIRONMENTALISM AS REACTION TO THREATS OF CRISIS

So great is contemporary concern about environmental impact that many suppose consciousness of it is unique to our era. But they are mistaken; the acceleration of environmental transformations blinds us to their antiquity. Mankind has been altering the earth since before the dawn of history, albeit more slowly and less visibly in earlier times than now. Yet even long ago, appalled by some adverse effects, many blamed themselves or others for fancied environmental degradation.[6]

Those who think modern awareness of impact unprecedented wrongly suppose our predecessors as little aware of their environmental powers as of their environmental perils. 'The idea that humans can change nature' is quite recent, supposed Ehrenfeld (1986: 168), but the opposite was in fact the case; many pre-moderns attributed environmental change more readily to human agency than to nature, god, or chance.

The roots of modern concern are mainly traceable to eighteenth-century observations and nineteenth-century ecological insights. Yet analogous environmental fears had engaged previous epochs, when men were likewise seen as major agents of terrestrial change—notably for the worse. Such alterations were commonly ascribed to divine punishment for mortal misdeeds, as with Biblical accounts of the Flood. The view that human evil engendered nature's decay permeated late sixteenth- and early seventeenth-century European thought. In Luther's sacred history, Adam had initiated not only the Fall of man but the decay of nature, and

---

[6] These paragraphs are condensed from Lowenthal 1990: 121.

subsequent sins induced further deterioration; some theologians thought global dissolution imminent. 'Man drew the curse upon the world, and crack'd the whole frame with his fall', wrote Vaughan (1666: 440). Decay thus predicated was confirmed by every fallen leaf—and by geographical exploration, the telescope, and the microscope.[7]

Were those who found man responsible for nature's decay preternaturally perceptive about human impact? Not at all: they fantasized change, used spurious data to forecast degradation, and 'explained' natural events as divinely ordained. Wanting to believe that sin caused decay, they massively misread the environmental evidence to limn a reprehensible and admonitory chronicle.

Many today remain pre-scientific catastrophists. Because the notion of a nature unresponsive to man's desires seems to them impious, intolerable, or incomprehensible, modern doomsters retain anti-scientific millenarian apprehensions. We inherit outworn environmental attitudes along with often worn-out environments.

Today's environmental concerns seem paramount. Yet even our scientific forebears thought they faced no less dire problems. Consider the portent in George Perkins Marsh's pioneering *Man and Nature* (1864: 42–3):

[In] parts of Asia Minor, of Northern Africa, of Greece, and even of Alpine Europe . . . the operation of causes set in action by man has brought the face of the earth to a desolation almost as complete as that of the moon. . . . The earth is fast becoming an unfit home for its noblest inhabitant, and another era of equal human crime and human improvidence . . . would reduce it to such a condition of impoverished productiveness, of shattered surface, of climatic excess, as to threaten the depravation, barbarism, and perhaps even extinction of the species.

That tirade was penned 135 years ago. What environmental impacts then menaced? Deforestation, overgrazing, erosion, flooding, and dessication. These still haunt us; but they are not now our prime concerns. New environmental threats recurrently overshadow old ones. In the 1960s they were pollution and chemical poisons and The Bomb. Today they are acid rain, stratospheric ozone depletion, global warming, nuclear waste. Except for the last, none of the key issues raised at the global environmental conference held in Rio in 1992 had seemed worth stressing at Stockholm just two decades before.[8]

Today's perils differ neither in imminence nor in apocalyptic immedi-

---

[7] For 17th-century environmental views, see Davies 1969; Harris 1949; Lowenthal 1985: 87–8, 136–7; Nicolson 1959: 100–4.

[8] This shift is noted in Gilbert White's 'Emerging issues in environmental policy', *Ambio* (Feb. 1996).

acy; past like present Jeremiahs enjoined instant reform against impending doom. What is new is menaces that cannot be seen: threats invisible to everyday view. The effects of soil erosion, even of DDT, were patent to any observant eye. But today's risks are clear only to arcane experts themselves deeply at odds over how much they see: the 1995 Madrid working group on climatic change barely agreed to call human influence on global climate 'discernable' instead of 'appreciable', 'notable', 'measurable', or 'detectable'.[9]

Those afflicted by toxins that cannot be tasted, touched, smelled, or seen, like the victims of Bhopal or Three Mile Island, feel petrified by deadly poisons that 'slink in without warning', in Erikson's (1994: 150–1) phrase, 'and then begin their deadly work from within—the very embodiment of stealth and treachery'. Deprived of confidence in a fruitful and manageable environment, victims lose faith in the good will as well as the good sense of public officials and scientific experts who prove equally baffled and impotent.

Lengthening time lapses between cause and effect make it ever more difficult to ensure precautions, assign liability, or provide compensation. In Beck's (1996: 31) telling illustration, 'the injured of Chernobyl, years after the catastrophe, are not even all *born* yet.' At Yucca Mountain, Nevada, the American government plans to bury nuclear waste in containers designed to be leak-proof for ten thousand years. But even assuming a civil stability without precedence, this span of time would be far too brief. For radioactive carbon-14 remains lethal in air or groundwater for up to a million years.[10]

Science is feared and resented both as remote and authoritarian and because its unintended consequences seem ever more ominous. Once-radiant innovations now cast the darkest shadows. Nuclear power was but yesterday a glittering technological panacea. Today, economic, health, and safety fears all but throttle the nuclear industry in many lands.[11]

Popular confidence that science can or government will mount effective controls erodes year by year for other reasons as well. Scientific enterprise is seen to be ever more costly, and the public, accustomed to progress, now largely discounts its miracles in advance. The social effects of this double disillusionment—that technological progress brings happiness; that saving miracles will continue to unfold—are as depressing as

[9] Intergovernmental Panel on Climate Change, Working Group I, 'Summary for Policy Makers', reported in Kathy Sawyer, 'Panel: humans affect climate', *International Herald Tribune*, 2–3 Dec. 1995; see Houghton *et al.* 1996.
[10] On Yucca Mountain see Erikson 1994: 203–25, and Fri 1995 (summarizing US National Research Council, *Technical Bases for Yucca Mountain Standards*, Washington, DC, 1995). [11] See Pasqualetti and Pijawka 1996: 57.

the physical anxieties they foreshadow. The failure of inflated expectations and of Utopian reform and the loss of faith in progress induce
despondency, impotence, and *après nous le déluge* escapism.[12]

FROM THE CONQUEST OF NATURE TO THE
COLLAPSE OF NATURE

The shift in public sentiment can be simply stated. In the past, the forces
of nature seemed vastly to exceed those of man. Whatever humans did
could not seriously harm the natural fundament. Technology would
remain a minor geological force: the gravest man-made disasters were
only small and temporary setbacks in progressive mastery of an infinitely
resourceful earth. Eighteenth- and nineteenth-century observers detailed
impacts of forest loss, intensive farming, and wildlife extermination. But
these untoward effects were noted in scattered and abstruse sources that
were rarely heeded. Meanwhile the faith of environmental determinism
left ultimate power safely sheltered in nature's might. And cornucopian
progressivists went on assuming that science could safely enlarge its
power over malign nature.

For nature *was* malign: ruthless, cruel, savage, wasteful, and selfish,
Huxley and Spencer termed it. Nature had to be subdued to ensure
civilized virtue. 'Visible nature is all plasticity and indifference', wrote
William James (1896: 43); 'to such a harlot we owe no allegiance'. Marsh
(1860: 34, 56, 60–1) inveighed against *mis*use, not *any* use; do not stop
conquering, do it *better*, for 'wherever man fails to master nature, he can
but be her slave'.

As late as 1929, Freud (1946: 53–4) extolled the conquest of nature in
terms of imperious hubris:

A country has attained a high state of civilization when . . . everything in it [is
used] in exploiting the earth for man's benefit and in protecting him against
nature . . . the course of rivers . . . regulated . . . the soil industriously cultivated
. . . mineral wealth brought up assiduously from the depths . . . wild and
dangerous animals . . . exterminated.

Many, maybe most, still think technology's impacts largely benign. But
how much less sanguine we now are! Two generations on, Freud's
accolade to progress seems naïvely anthropocentric. Such blithe neglect
of technology's malign effects flouts today's conventional piety, if not
wisdom. Almost two out of three Americans identify themselves as en-

---

[12] Declining faith in science is explained in Rescher 1980 and Cohen 1996.

vironmentalists, valuing environment over economic growth.[13] (That few behave in accordance with such intent is another tale.)

UNDERLYING MYSTIQUES

Environmentalists characteristically embrace certain creeds about nature, people, and culture. Like other heritage givens, these creeds defy evidence or reason; some are demonstrably false. But they are taken as true because deeply desired. I look at three such faiths: that supreme virtue lies in nature unspoiled by culture; that environmental wisdom is inherent among primitive indigenes; that environmental impacts must be reversible.

The Legacy of Natural Purity

Environmentalists polarize nature and culture as implacable opposites. In their eyes, human manipulation spoils natural purity and degrades the environment.

The notion of nature as sacred has classical, Christian, and romantic roots. Its modern version owes more, perhaps, to nineteenth-century Americans who deified New World scenery to make up for absent history. They set primordial nature above degenerate human annals. They decried 'temples built by roman robbers' and 'towers of feudal oppression' so as to extol their own 'deep forests which the eye of God has alone pervaded. What is the echo of roofs that a few centuries since rung with barbaric revels . . . to the silence which has reigned in these dim groves since the first Creation?'[14]

But forest worship was long more literary than literal. The actual wilderness was a mortal menace—a howling waste to be extirpated for farms and towns and factories, scenes of civilized progress. Only with the closing of the frontier did more than a handful of Thoreauvians find comfort in the wild—and even Thoreau famously baulked at the bleak rawness of truly savage Mount Katahdin in Maine.

Wilderness worship today owes much to remorse for its felt disappearance. The cult of the wild ranges from rural nostalgia to radical rejection of all trace of culture; humanity itself is seen as a terrestrial cancer. Some invest nature with a plan, a purpose, an order it achieves when

[13] 1995 Gallup Poll figures in Jane Fritsch, 'Ecologists spy facade: do pillagers hide behind cute names?' *International Herald Tribune*, 26 March 1996.
[14] Charles Fenno Hoffman and other 1830s observers quoted in Lowenthal 1976: 101–4.

David Lowenthal

undisturbed. Others posit innate human affinity with nature, a 'biophilia' that needs eco-diversity for its own well-being.[15] Still others damn only *previous* impacts, arguing that when we repair environmental damage we are working *with* nature.

Environmentalism comprises several related credos, often unconsciously held. In brief: existence is profoundly dualistic; nature and culture are separate and incompatible essences; untouched nature is materially and morally superior to any human impress; wilderness is health, civilization a disease. Imagining nature as an escape, a place to be born again, a paradise where work is unneeded, environmentalists reserve wild lands for sport or spiritual contemplation.[16]

The ideal of untouched nature gained a scientific imprimatur in Frederic Clements's equilibrium model of ecology in the 1920s. This model held nature most fruitful when least altered. If left undisturbed, flora and fauna in time attained maximum diversity and stability. Extractive despoliation thwarted or abridged this beneficent climax; technology did not improve nature, it degraded nature.[17] This ecological mystique, which seemed consonant with mounting environmental disasters, became sacrosanct.

Enthroning stability and passive non-interference mirrored determinist views about human nature, too. Ecological Utopia became the supreme moral order. To 'replace the chaos of a world torn by human greed and voraciousness with a well-ordered moral universe', reformers continue to adjure us to curtail our numbers, technology, and consumption.[18]

This reversed eighteenth-century views of nature as an unfinished fabric to be perfected by human ingenuity, and commending its conquest. Enlightenment savants and Social Darwinists had envisioned artifice ever improving environment. Twentieth-century reformers thought to restore environmental well-being by curtailing human impact. By the 1950s 'ecology' had become a token of correct thinking even in government agencies.[19]

To be sure, ecologists had by then disowned the Clementsian paradigm. It was mainly *non*-ecologists who extolled equilibrium, eco-diversity, and non-interference. And today's environmentalists still deploy these views as 'ecological'. Aldo Leopold's famous 'Land Ethic'

[15] Exemplified in Kellert 1995, these views of nature are savaged by Budiansky 1995.
[16] On the range of environmentalist postures, see Ellis 1995.
[17] For such views see Murray 1954; Rolston 1979; Sears 1935; Worster 1977: 209–42. Barbour (1995: 252) adds a critique of Clements.
[18] The quote is from Taylor 1986: 258; see also Birch and Cobb 1981: 273–4, 282–3; Evernden 1985: 15–16, 18, 22.
[19] On the canonization of ecology, see Hays 1987: 27, 347; Barbour 1995.

(1949)—'A thing is right when it tends to preserve the integrity, stability, and beauty of the biotic community. It is wrong when it tends otherwise'—remains gospel. Nature is cast as normative good, technology as aberrant evil.[20]

Manipulative greed is held to subvert most environments and to threaten the few remaining pristine locales. Though divine, nature can no longer mend itself; voiceless nature is 'an oppressed and silent class, in need of spokespersons'.[21] Such spokespersons, typically animal rightists more caring of other creatures than of people, are now legion. In 1994 a young woman jogging in California's Sierra Nevada foothills was stalked and pulled from the trail by a female mountain lion and then mauled to death. The lioness was hunted down and shot, lest she kill again. The woman left behind two small children; the lion, a seven-week-old cub. Public appeals on behalf of these young orphans yielded $9,000 for the two children—and $21,000 for the lion cub.[22]

Images of wild nature as exemplary, culture as toxic, suffuse environmental discourse. Even those whose *raison d'être* is to exploit resources feel forced to don Thoreauvian masks as 'greenscammers' with environmentally friendly names. As people become 'more and more environmentally sensitive, it's more difficult to be burdened with a name that speaks the truth about your intentions'. Lauding their own recycling of plastic as reducing landfill waste, Phillips Petroleum boasts of thereby having 'left another little corner of the world all alone'.[23]

Leaving nature alone is a dogma that shapes global agency land reform in defiance of local realities. 'Wherever there are some trees, a presumption is made that there was [and hence] ought to be continuous forest cover'. Thus, the World Wide Fund for Nature, alarmed over forest loss in West Africa, assumes almost by definition that human presence degrades landscape; so 'we' must stop 'them' destroying the forests. But some patches of forest exist only because local farmers planted them; other areas are only temporarily deforested by swidden cultivation. Similarly, protecting the Amazon rainforest from 'developers' is an environmentalist article of faith. But Amazonia, long altered by human impact, might be enhanced rather than exhausted by appropriate development.[24]

[20] On these environmentalist trends, see Cowan 1966: 56; F. F. Darling 1956: 407–8; Frank Egler 1956: 447, 940–1; Flader 1978: 34–5, 270–1; Oldfield 1983. Typical of such avowals are McKibben 1990 and Sagoff 1990.

[21] John Tallmadge (*Orion*, 9:3 [1990], 64) quoted approvingly by Buell 1995: 20–1.

[22] This cautionary tale from the *New York Times* (29 May 1994) appears in Cronon 1995a: 48.

[23] Wilderness Society spokesman Bennett Beach quoted in Jane Fritsch, 'Ecologists spy facade: do pillagers hide behind cute names?' *International Herald Tribune*, 26 March 1996; Phillips Petroleum advert., *New York Review of Books*, 19 Sept. 1996, 7.

[24] For Africa and Amazonia, see *New Scientist*, 27 April 1996, 36–9, and 21 Sept. 1996, 27–8; also Fairhead and Leach 1996.

Even a 1995 UNESCO volume explicitly aimed at promoting *cultural*
landscapes reiterates the conventional wisdom that 'every natural region
of the world loses much of its intrinsic value under human influence.'[25]
One lone contributor attests that 'in many parts of the world human
intervention has created and maintained environments . . . arguably
richer and more diverse . . . than the natural forest and other ecosystems
they have replaced.'[26] The other essayists mainly disagree, one citing
'harmony with nature' as a prime criterion for placing cultural landscapes
on the World Heritage list.[27]

National Parks' policy in America long reified imaginary wildness. To
restore nature by erasing traces of occupancy was gospel from Yellowstone on. Anything suggestive of progress or advancement was taboo.
These sacred Edens were emptied of people to be preserved as pure
wilderness. Parks could contain no permanent settlers; those already
there were uprooted.

But the illusion of supposedly untouched nature required massive
intervention. Park managers exterminated wolves, cougars, and coyotes
lest they eat the deer. They introduced exotic fish and European grasses.
They suppressed fire, as evil as the carnivores. As a result, elk prolifer-
ated and ate up the more palatable trees; and undergrowth accumulated
over a half-century of fire prevention fuelled huge conflagrations.[28]

Now wolves are brought back and Smokey the Bear has shed his incen-
diary warning. But it is hard to persuade a public brought up to loathe
fire that keeping nature 'natural' means letting fires burn unchecked,
even deliberately setting them. Only now are people becoming aware, as
parks' spokesmen put it, that 'the human presence has always been part
of the wilderness experience'; even Yellowstone is celebrated as a 'cultural landscape'.[29]

In the Virgin Islands, Laurance Rockefeller envisioned St. Johns
National Park as tropical wilderness. To 'restore' a pre-Columbian
paradise he bought out and expelled the island's slave descendants, then
expunged traces of two and half centuries of shifting cultivation. As
Olwig (1980; 1985: 162–73) relates, this zeal for wilderness mystified the
native islanders; and no wonder. For what emerged was no primeval
forest but a thorny tangle of alien plants imported to keep slaves far away
from plantation mansions. In this bush roamed not jungle beasts but feral

---

[25] Plachter and Rössler 1995: 16.   [26] Green 1995: 405.
[27] Phillips 1995: 390. For cultural imprints on natural sites, see Thorsell 1995.
[28] On U.S. National Parks policy, see Chase 1986; Young forthcoming; on unintended
consequences, Rackham 1996: 55.
[29] US Department of the Interior, *Archeology in the Wilderness* (1993), quoted in Layton
and Titchen 1995: 179–80; on public perception of fire, see Kurt Kleiner, 'Fanning the
wildfires', *New Scientist*, 19 Oct. 1996: 14–15.

jackasses, mongooses originally brought in to control snakes in cane-fields, and voracious mosquitoes.

The Legacy of Indigenous Virtue

Some today would leave the natives on their lands. They see environmental evil emanating only from Western culture. Blameless are primitive indigenes whose 'nurturant tribal ways, integrative communitarian values, and rich interplay with nature' respect its balance (Sale 1990: 368–9). Heeding tribal wisdom might repair the damage and restore environments fit to live in and to hand down.

For nature's sake we ourselves must revert to the wild. 'Before agriculture was midwifed', holds an Earth First! guru, 'humans were in the wilderness and *we were a part of it*. But with irrigation ditches, crop surpluses, and permanent villages, we became *apart from* the natural world . . . Between the wilderness that created us and the civilization that we created grew an ever-widening rift'.[30] But the ecological nous lost by technocrats estranged from nature still survives among indigenes. Backwardness becomes a bona fide of stewardship. American Indians once loathed as uncouth savages now surface as ecological saviours, their innate tribal wisdom undimmed over the millennia. Respect for all nature is held a 'particularly Indian' legacy (Laxson 1991: 374–5; see also Maybury-Lewis 1992).

Current pieties get read back as tribal heritage. The nonpareil anachronism is Chief Seattle, whose 1854 plea to President Franklin Pierce, 'Brother Eagle, Sister Sky', is endlessly intoned at Earth Day pow-wows:

> The earth is our mother. I have seen a thousand rotting buffaloes on the prairies left by the white man who shot them from a passing train. What will happen when the buffalo are all slaughtered? The wild horses tamed? . . . when the secret corners of the forest are heavy with the scent of many men and the view of the ripe hills is blotted by talking wires?

Yet no buffalo had roamed within six hundred miles of Chief Seattle's Puget Sound; the railroad crossed the Plains only in 1869, three years after his death; the horrific buffalo slaughter came a decade later. In fact, the letter that lent the Chief eco-fame was penned only in 1971 by Texan scriptwriter Ted Perry. 'The environmental awareness was based on my own feelings', Perry later confessed; he hadn't 'the slightest knowledge of Indian views on the environment'.

---

[30] Earth First! founder Dave Foreman, *Confessions of an Eco-Warrior* (New York: Harmony Books, 1991), 69, quoted in Cronon 1995b: 83.

But for Susan Jeffers, whose children's book of the speech sold 250,000 copies, Chief Seattle incarnates a creed that made sacred 'every creature and part of the earth . . . Basically, I don't know what he said—but I do know that the Native American people lived this philosophy, and that's what is important.'[31] She 'knows' this because modern rhetoric has made it a heritage virtue. In the same fashion, the ecological maxims of Amazon rainforest defenders gain an Amerindian imprimatur.

Tribal others soon learn eco-speak themselves. Maoris and Ghanaians, Inuits and Aborigines refer in identical terms to respect for nature, to ancestral instincts for conserving, to tribal taboos against degradation, and so forth. Minorities emulate tribal virtue. The First National People of Color Environmental Leadership Summit conference of 1991 not only 'reaffirmed traditional . . . support for the natural world'; they boasted of being *identical* with nature.[32] But the rhetoric like the sentiment is that of the Western mainstream.

Some who damn high-tech farming as environmental sin would replace it with low-tech virtue. The nature writer Wendell Berry relies on animal power and urges others to do likewise. His advice is best taken by literary farmers. Only his writing enables Berry to farm with horses. Such work resembles gardening, a favoured model these days for getting reconciled with nature. It yields lovely florid insights; but it does not yield a living.

Modern romantics hold that those who live in and depend on a place will not harm it. Yet Berry 'restores' land that others, just as fully of that place, had 'destroyed' through their use. Both destruction and construction bring a knowledge of nature. Sometimes work is destructive and constructive at the same time, as when a meadow is cut or burned to prevent forest encroachment (White 1995).

The notion of indigenous rapport with nature is not wholly invented; it stems in part from two evident contrasts. Primitive economies past and present do impact environments more slowly and less intensively than modern agriculture and engineering. And tribal folk do live closer to 'nature', as usually defined, than do urbanized and industrialized folk. These differences matter; in Ray Dasmann's (1975) comparison, 'eco-sphere people' confined to their local milieu impact resources more lightly than do 'biosphere people' who draw indiscriminately on the whole world.[33]

---

[31] Chief Seattle's 'letter' is in Jeffers 1991 (not paged); Ted Perry is quoted by John Lichfield in *Independent on Sunday*, 26 April 1992, 13; Susan Jeffers is quoted in Timothy Egan, 'Mother Earth? From the film, not the Indian', *International Herald Tribune*, 22 April 1992, 2.
[32] People of Color delegates quoted in Di Chiro 1995: 305–6.
[33] On this distinction, see also McNeely and Keeton 1995: 31–2.

But this does not make tribal indigenes necessarily wiser, more caring, or less destructive in the long run. Indigenous ignorance or short-sightedness induced the extinction of moas in New Zealand, soil exhaustion in central Mexico, salinization in the Tigris/Euphrates, and wholesale ecocide among Arizona Anazasi and Guatemala Mayans. Tribal Papuans, to whose rituals anthropologists assigned ecological functions, knew nothing about 'carrying capacity' and expressed no moral concern for nature.[34] But like the unicorn, the ecologically noble savage is a mythical creature too useful to disavow. And tribal indigenes, from the sacred groves of Ghana to the Pequot gambling casinos of Connecticut, now disguise themselves as environmentalists in Western garb.

The Myth of Reversible Harmony

Reversibility is a third shibboleth. Environmentalists posit two sorts of change: irrevocable events, like the extinction of species, that can never be retrieved; and lesser changes that can be halted before some point of no return, allowing reversion to an original or previous state. Untouched nature is presumed stable, undergoing only seasonal and other cyclic oscillations—Mircea Eliade's (1959) myth of the eternal return. In contrast, most human alterations are deemed irreversible, subverting the natural order, at length fatal to life itself. In this view, only restoring and husbanding a stable equilibrium can avert catastrophe.

Such fears are not confined to the realm of nature. Since Ruskin and Morris, would-be restorers of art and architecture have been accused of irreversible damage to fabric and quality—as in the National Gallery cleaning controversy forty years ago, provoked by displays of newly restored paintings whose bright colours and flat tones shocked viewers accustomed to dark old varnish; and in current alarm over the radical restoration of the Sistine Chapel. Connoisseurs exhort conservators that 'every method must be reversible; do nothing which cannot be undone'.[35] But more than any artistic canvas, it is the irrevocable fabric of nature that arouses the gravest anxiety, as in Marsh's portent cited above.

To distinguish reversible from irreversible effects was until lately supposed a simple empirical exercise. But it is neither simple nor wholly empirical. Whether a process is irreversible may be unknown at the start and often still in doubt when prevention seems needed. Many

[34] Denevan 1992; Krech 1999; McNeely and Keeton 1995: 28; Roy Rappaport on the Papua New Guinea Tsembaga, cited in Szerszynski 1996: 128.
[35] Caroline Keck, letter, *New York Review of Books*, 24 June 1983, 4; on the National Gallery controversy, see Lowenthal 1985: 161.

environmental impacts are subtle, multiple, and long-delayed. Hence, the safeguards needed for reversibility tend to be grossly underestimated.[36]

Predictive doubts augment environmentalists' fears. Faced by myriad unknowns, they incline to embargo any action unless sure it can be reversed. But in real life such a stance is wholly quixotic. Art historians rightly term irreversibility a myth used by conservators to justify their own interventions (Talley 1996: 169). Ageing and accretions of memory and history implacably alter every object, as they do each sentient being. Most acts, individual and collective, are fundamentally irreversible (Cramer 1994). Whether heroic or horrific, few deeds can be undone. W. W. Jacobs's 'The Monkey's Paw' (1902) limns the futility of yearning, like Shakespeare's Richard II, to 'call back yesterday, bid time return'.

We are mostly resigned to seeing life as a one-way stream. But we somehow persuade ourselves that the environment, like incorruptible relics, should be exempt from time's arrow. Environmentalists idealize a fictitious nature unchanged by history, a sacred entity in eternal equilibrium.

CONCLUSION

These and no doubt other mystiques suffuse environmental concern. And media hype elevates that concern to catastrophe. Urgency is assumed. 'We must make the rescue of the environment the central organizing principle for civilization', said American vice-president Albert Gore (1992: 269). A Harvard professor of literature found Gore's mission so self-evident that 'I hardly need', he begins his own book (Buell 1995: 2), 'to spend many pages defending the reasonableness of the claim'. Ardent environmentalists need no proof to feel sure their cause is supreme.

To be sure, cornucopians who find the environment in fine fettle equally deploy invective unbacked by evidence or logic. Indeed, it is hard to find environmental texts that eschew partisan extremism based on wishful thinking. The environmental historian William Cronon is execrated for writing about nature as a cultural construct. Such 'ecofascist relativism' is held to give comfort to the enemy—what entrepreneur or politico need take reform seriously when a noted scholar says environment is all in the mind![37]

---

[36] On the economics and psychology of reversibility, see Arrow and Fisher 1974: 318–19; Bishop 1978; Meadows *et al.* 1972: 72; Randall 1986; SCEP 1970: 125–6.

[37] Review of Cronon 1995a by David Rothenberg, *Amicus Journal* (Summer 1996), 41–4. In the same genre is Alexander Cockburn, 'Roush xed', *Nation*, 8 April 1996,

Like nature, like wilderness, environment *is* a construct, not an essence; its existence predicates our own. The idea of preserving 'virgin' nature is 'entirely a creation of the culture that holds it dear, a product of the very history it seeks to deny'. The home of a God who remains unchanged by time's arrow, the wilderness vision leaves the human outside the natural. If nature must be wild to be truly nature, then our very presence implies its fall (Cronon 1995b: 79–81). It has no place for humans, save as a museum of relics or a retreat for contemplative sojourners. To actual environmental problems, such environmentalism offers only passive despair, not practical solutions.

Our environmental heritage is embedded in both time and culture. How can we learn to cheer rather than to scorn these inescapable links, to view our own environmental habits not just as burdens but as benefits? I close with four thoughts:

1. *Inheritors and stewards.* We inherit our environment from myriad forebears. That legacy includes all their transformations, unwitting and otherwise. As temporary denizens we make the best of that environment according to our own lights. As stewards we pass it on to future generations, never knowing how they will view or what they will do with their legacy. We know only that our heirs will revise, even though they cannot entirely reverse, whatever we do.

2. *Sovereignty of the present.* The environment is never merely conserved or protected; it is bound to be altered—both enhanced and degraded—by each new generation. To be valuable enough to care for, we must make the environment feel truly our own. Like our forebears and our heirs, we do this by adding to it our own stamp, now creative, now corrosive, but always in some degree indelible.

3. *Intergenerational equity.* We face often agonizing choices between extraction and stewardship. 'We have to cut down trees to feed our families', a Mexican farmer puts it; 'we're living in the present so that our children can have enough to eat and go to school'—and perhaps become environmentally concerned. 'The tragedy', comment his interlocutors (Arizpe *et al.* 1996: 66) 'is that to feed his children today, he has to destroy that which would give them sustenance tomorrow'. Envisioning more efficient and less destructive future modes of retrieval, some would leave fossil fuels untapped, prehistoric sites unexcavated. But such selfless stewardship is uncommonly rare.

---

10. See also Ehrlich and Ehrlich 1996; Rolston 1996. Far from terming wilderness *just* a state of mind, Cronon critiques environmentalist pieties from a belief that nature is shaped by human intervention but is 'not *entirely* our own invention' (Cronon 1994: 40).

4. *Ancestral possession.* We are possessed by the past as well as possessing it. So might have said Linacre's seventeenth-century Oxonian successor Sir Thomas Browne, like Linacre a medical *philosophe.* Just as our environment embraces material and mental relics of countless forebears, so it also remains these ancestors' property, and not merely their resting place. We continue to be obligated to progenitors who gave us not just life but earthly legacies reshaped by themselves. Every atom of our being contains some particle of Plato and Phidias; we neglect to our own diminution the awareness of being environed by manifold Parthenons and *Republics.*

REFERENCES

Arizpe, Lourdes, Paz, Fernanda, and Velásquez, Margarita (1996). *Culture and Global Change: Social Perceptions of Deforestation in the Lacandona Rain Forest in Mexico.* Ann Arbor: University of Michigan Press.

Arrow, K. J. and Fisher, A. C. (1974). 'Environmental preservation, uncertainty and irreversibility', *Quarterly Journal of Economics,* 88: 312–19.

Barbour, Michael G. (1995). 'Ecological fragmentation in the fifties', in William Cronon (ed.), *Uncommon Ground.* New York: W. W. Norton, 233–55.

Beck, Ulrich (1996). 'Risk society and the provident state', in Scott Lash, Bronislaw Szerszynski, and Brian Wynne (eds), *Risk, Environment and Modernity: Towards a New Ecology.* London: Sage, 27–43.

Birch, Charles and Cobb, Jr., J. E. (1981). *The Liberation of Life.* Cambridge: Cambridge University Press.

Bishop, R. C. (1978). 'Endangered species and uncertainty: the economics of a safe minimum standard', *American Journal of Agricultural Economics,* 60: 10–18.

Budiansky, Stephen (1995). *Nature's Keepers: The New Science of Nature Management.* London: Weidenfeld & Nicolson.

Buell, Lawrence (1995). *The Environmental Imagination: Thoreau, Nature Writing, and the Formation of American Culture.* Cambridge, MA: Harvard University Press.

Carson, Rachel [1962] (1982). *Silent Spring.* Harmondsworth, UK: Penguin.

Chase, Alston (1986). *Playing God in Yellowstone: The Destruction of America's First National Park.* Boston: Atlantic Monthly Press.

Cohen, Maurie J. (1996). *Risk Society, Modernization, and Declining Public Confidence in Science.* Environmental Risk Management Working Paper ERC. Edmonton: University of Alberta, 96–7.

Cowan, I. M. (1966). 'Management, response, and variety', in F. F. Darling and J. P. Milton (eds), *Future Environments of North America: Transformation of a Continent.* Garden City, NY: The Natural History Press, 55–65.

Cramer, Friedrich (1994). 'Durability and change: a biochemist's view', in Wolfgang E. Krumbein *et al.* (eds), *Durability and Change: The Science, Responsibility, and Cost of Sustaining Cultural Heritage.* Chichester, UK: John Wiley, 19–25.

Cronon, William (1994). 'Cutting loose or running aground?', *Journal of Historical Geography*, 20: 38–43.

Cronon, William (1995a). 'Introduction: in search of nature', in William Cronon (ed.), *Uncommon Ground: Toward Reinventing Nature.* New York: W. W. Norton, 23–56.

Cronon, William (1995b). 'The trouble with wilderness; or, getting back to the wrong nature', in William Cronon (ed.), *Uncommon Ground.* New York: W. W. Norton, 69–90.

Darling, F. Fraser (1956). 'Discussion: man's tenure of the earth', in W. L. Thomas, Jun. (ed.), *Man's Role in Changing the Face of the Earth.* Chicago: University of Chicago Press, 401–9.

Dasmann, Ray (1975). 'National parks, nature conservation, and "future primitives"', *Ecologist*, 65: 164–7.

Davies, G. L. (1969). *The Earth in Decay: A History of British Geomorphology 1578–1878.* London: Macdonald.

Denevan, William M. (1992). 'The pristine myth: the landscape of the Americas in 1492', *Annals of the Association of American Geographers*, 82: 369–85.

Di Chiro, Giovanna (1995). 'Nature as community: the convergence of environmental and social justice', in William Cronon (ed.), *Uncommon Ground.* New York: W. W. Norton, 198–320.

Droste, Bernd von, Plachter, Harald, and Rössler, Mechtild (eds) (1995). *Cultural Landscapes of Universal Value.* Jena: Gustav Fischer.

Edelstein, Michael R. (1988). *Contaminated Communities: The Social and Psychological Impacts of Residential Toxic Exposure.* Boulder, CO: Westview, 171–96.

Egler, Frank (1956). 'Comments', in W. L. Thomas, Jun. (ed.), *Man's Role in Changing the Face of the Earth.* Chicago: University of Chicago Press.

Ehrenfeld, D. (1986). 'Life in the next millennium: who will be left in the earth's community?' in L. Kaufman and K. Mallory (eds), *The Last Extinction.* Cambridge, MA: MIT Press, 167–86.

Ehrlich, Paul R. and Ehrlich, Anne H. (1996). *Betrayal of Science and Reason: How Anti-Environmental Rhetoric Threatens Our Future.* Covelo, CA: Island Press.

Eliade, Mircea (1959). *Cosmos and History: The Myth of the Eternal Return,* trans. by W. R. Trask. New York: Harper.

Ellis, Jeffrey C. 1995. 'On the search for a root cause: essentialist tendencies in environmental discourse', in William Cronon (ed.), *Uncommon Ground.* Chicago: University of Chicago Press, 256–97.

Erikson, Kai (1994). *A New Species of Trouble: Explorations in Disaster, Trauma, and Community.* New York: W. W. Norton.

Evernden, Neil (1985). 'Constructing the natural: the darker side of the environmental movement', *North American Review*, 270: 15–19.

Fairhead, James and Leach, Melissa (1996). *Misreading the African Landscape: Society and Ecology in Forest–Savanna Mosaic*. Cambridge: Cambridge University Press.

Flader, Susan L. (1978). *Thinking Like a Mountain: Aldo Leopold and the Evolution of an Ecological Attitude toward Deer, Wolves, and Forests*. Lincoln: University of Nebraska Press, Bison Books.

Freud, Sigmund [1929] (1946). *Civilization and its Discontents*, trans. by J. Rivière. London: Hogarth Press and the Institute of Psycho-analysis.

Fri, Robert W. (1995). 'Using science soundly: the Yucca Mountain standard', *RFF* [Resources for the Future] *Review*, (summer): 15–18.

Gore, Albert (1992). *Earth in Balance: Ecology and the Human Spirit*. Boston: Houghton Mifflin.

Green, Bryn H. (1995). 'Principles for protecting endangered landscapes: the work of the IUCN-CESP working group on landscape conservation', in Bernd von Droste *et al.* (eds), *Cultural Landscapes of Universal Value*. Jena: Gustav Fischer, 405–11.

Harris, Victor (1949). *All Coherence Gone*. Chicago: University of Chicago Press.

Hays, Samuel P. (1987). *Beauty, Health, and Permanence: Environmental Politics in the United States, 1955–1985*. Cambridge, MA: Harvard University Press.

Houghton, J. T., Meiro Filho, L. G., Callender, B. A., Kaltenburg, A., and Maskell, K. (eds) (1996). *Climate Change 1995: The Science of Climate Change*. Cambridge: Cambridge University Press.

Jacobs, W. W. [1902] (1994). 'The monkey's paw'. In W. W. Jacobs, *The Monkey's Paw and Other Stories*. London: Robin Clarke, 139–53.

James, William (1896). *The Will to Believe*. New York: Longmans, Green.

Jeffers, Susan (1991). *Brother Eagle, Sister Sky: A Message from Chief Seattle*. New York: Dial Books.

Kellert, Stephen (1995). *The Value of Life: Biological Diversity and Human Society*. Covelo, CA: Island Press.

Krech, Shepard, III (1999). *The Ecological Indian: Myth and History*. New York: W. W. Norton.

Laxson, Joan D. (1991). 'How "we" see "them": tourism and Native Americans', *Annals of Tourism Research*, 18: 365–91.

Layton, Robert and Titchen, Sarah (1995). 'Uluru: an outstanding Australian Aboriginal cultural landscape', in Bernd von Droste *et al.* (eds), *Cultural Landscapes of Universal Value*. Jena: Gustav Fischer, 174–81.

Leopold, Aldo (1949). 'The land ethic', in Aldo Leopold, *A Sand County Almanac and Sketches Here and There*. New York: Oxford University Press, 201–26.

Lowenthal, David (1976). 'The place of the past in the American landscape', in David Lowenthal and Martyn J. Bowden (eds), *Geographies of the Mind*. New York: Oxford University Press, 89–117.

Lowenthal, David (1985). *The Past is a Foreign Country*. Cambridge: Cambridge University Press.

Lowenthal, David (1990). 'Awareness of human impacts: changing attitudes and emphases', in B. L. Turner II et al. (eds), *The Earth as Transformed by Human Action*. New York: Cambridge University Press, 121–35.

Lowenthal, David (1994). 'European and English landscapes as national symbols', in David Hooson (ed.), *Geography and National Identity*. Oxford: Blackwell, 15–38.

Lowenthal, David (1996). 'Paysages et identités nationales', in Marcel Jollivet and Nicole Eisner (eds), *L'Europe et ses campagnes*. Paris: Presses de la Fondation Nationale des Sciences Politiques, 245–71.

Lowenthal, David (1997). *The Heritage Crusade and the Spoils of History*. London: Viking.

Marsh, George Perkins (1860). 'The study of nature', *Christian Examiner*, 58: 33–62.

Marsh, George Perkins [1864] (1965). *Man and Nature; or, Physical Geography as Modified by Human Action*, David Lowenthal (ed.). Cambridge, MA: Harvard University Press.

Maybury-Lewis, David (1992). *Millennium: Tribal Wisdom and the Modern World*. New York: Penguin Viking.

McKibben, Bill (1990). *The End of Nature*. Harmondsworth, UK: Penguin.

McNeely, Jeffrey A. and Keeton, William S. (1995). 'The interaction between biological and cultural diversity', in Bernd von Droste et al. (eds), *Cultural Landscapes of Universal Value*. Jena: Gustav Fischer, 25–37.

Meadows, D. H., Meadows, D. L., Randers, J., and Behrens, W. W. (1972). *The Limits to Growth: A Report for the Club of Rome's Project on the Predicament of Mankind*. New York: Universal Books.

Murray, E. G. D. (1954). 'The place of nature in man's world', *American Scientist*, 42: 130–5, 142.

Nicolson, Marjorie H. (1959). *Mountain Gloom and Mountain Glory: The Development of the Aesthetics of the Infinite*. Ithaca, NY: Cornell University Press.

Oldfield, Frank (1983). 'Man's impact on the environment: some recent perspectives', *Geography*, 68: 245–56.

Olwig, Karen Fog (1980). 'National parks, tourism, and local development: a West Indian case', *Human Organization*, 39: 22–31.

Olwig, Karen Fog (1985). *Cultural Adaptation and Resistance on St. John: Three Centuries of Afro-Caribbean Life*. Gainesville: University of Florida Press.

Pasqualetti, Martin J. and Pijawka, K. David (1996). 'Unsiting nuclear power plants: decommissioning risks and their land use context', *Professional Geographer*, 48: 57–69.

Phillips, Adrian (1995). 'Cultural landscapes: an IUCN perspective', in Bernd von Droste et al. (eds), *Cultural Landscapes of Universal Value*. Jena: Gustav Fischer, 380–92.

Plachter, Harald and Rössler, Mechtild (1995). 'Cultural landscapes: reconnecting culture and nature', in Bernd von Droste *et al.* (eds), *Cultural Landscapes of Universal Value.* Jena: Gustav Fischer, 15–18.

Rackham, Oliver (1996). 'Hatfield Forest', in David Morgan Evans *et al.* (eds), *'The Remains of Distant Times': Archaeology and the National Trust.* Society of Antiquaries of London, Occasional Paper 19. London: Boydell Press, 47–58.

Randall, Alan (1986). 'Human preferences, economics, and the preservation of species', in B. G. Norton (ed.), *The Preservation of Species: The Value of Biological Diversity.* Princeton, NJ: Princeton University Press, 79–109.

Rescher, Nicholas (1980). *Unpopular Essays on Scientific Progress.* Pittsburgh: University of Pittsburgh Press.

Rolston, Holmes, III (1979). 'Can and ought we to follow nature?' *Environmental Ethics*, 1: 7–30.

Rolston, Holmes, III (1996). *Nature for Real: Is Nature a Social Construct?* Man and Nature Working Paper 78. Odense, Denmark: Odense University, Humanities Research Center.

Sagoff, Mark (1990). *The Economy of the Earth: Philosophy, Law, and the Environment.* Cambridge: Cambridge University Press.

Sale, Kirkpatrick (1990). *The Conquest of Paradise: Christopher Columbus and the Columbian Legacy.* New York: Knopf.

SCEP (Study of Critical Environmental Problems) (1970). *Man's Impact on the Global Environment.* Cambridge, MA: MIT Press.

Sears, Paul B. (1935). *Deserts on the March.* Norman: University of Oklahoma Press.

Spate, O. H. K. (1968). 'Environmentalism', *International Encyclopedia of the Social Sciences*, 5. New York: Macmillan, 93–7.

Szerszynski, Bronislaw (1996). 'On knowing what to do: environmentalism and the modern problematic', in Scott Lash, Bronislaw Szerszynski, and Brian Wynne (eds), *Risk, Environment and Modernity: Towards a New Ecology.* London: Sage, 104–37.

Talley, M. Kirby, Jr. (1996). 'The original intent of the artist', in Nicholas Stanley Price, M. Kirby Talley Jr., and Alessandra Melucco Vaccaro (eds), *Historical and Philosophical Issues in the Conservation of Cultural Heritage: Readings in Conservation.* Los Angeles: Getty Conservation Institute, 162–75.

Taylor, Paul W. (1986). *Respect for Nature: A Theory of Environmental Ethics.* Princeton, NJ: Princeton University Press.

Thorsell, Jim (1995). 'How natural are World Heritage natural sites?' *World Heritage Newsletter*, No. 9 (Dec.): 8–11.

Vaughan, H. [1666] (1957). 'Corruption'. in *Works.* Oxford: Clarendon Press, 387–545.

White, Richard (1995). '"Are you an environmentalist or do you work for a living?": work and nature', in William Cronon (ed.), *Uncommon Ground.* New York: W. W. Norton, 171–85.

Worster, D. (1977). *Nature's Economy: A History of Ecological Ideas.* Cambridge: Cambridge University Press.

Young, Terence (forthcoming). 'Virtue and irony at Cades Cove', in Terence Young and Robert Riley (eds), *The Landscape of Theme Parks.* Washington, DC: Dumbarton Oaks.

INDEX